search for Nirvana
Robin Maugham

W. H. Allen · London
A division of Howard & Wyndham Ltd
1975

© Robin Maugham, 1975

This book or parts thereof may not be
reproduced without permission in
writing.

Printed in Great Britain by
Fletcher & Son Ltd, Norwich,
for the Publishers, W. H. Allen & Co. Ltd,
44 Hill Street, London W1X 8LB

Bound by Richard Clay (The Chaucer Press), Ltd,
Bungay, Suffolk

Designed by Kathleen Thorpe

ISBN 0 491 01704 9

I would like to dedicate this book to the companions on my various quests for nirvana, especially to William who accompanied me on my most recent voyage.

I would also like to write a separate word of thanks to Peter Burton who has been responsible for helping me with the text, for compiling the index, and for assisting me with the arrangement of the whole book.

Acknowledgements

I would like to express my gratitude to those who have helped me with
this book and to those who have allowed me to quote from their work
or make use of material from my own published writings – particularly,
in this last instance, Chapman and Hall (*Journey to Siwa*), and the
Editor of *The People*.

For permission to quote from the work of others I am especially
indebted to William Heinemann Ltd and the estate of W. Somerset
Maugham (*A Writer's Note-Book, The Razor's Edge*, and *The Summing Up*),
Commander de Mauny (Count de Mauny; *The Garden of Taprobane*),
Pamela Sherek and William Heinemann Ltd (Henry Sherek; *Not in
Front of the Children*), Victor Gollancz Ltd and the estate of Humbert
Wolfe (*This Blind Rose*), Aubrey Menen and Hamish Hamilton Ltd (*The
Space Within the Heart*), Paul Bowles and *Holiday Magazine* (*How to Live
on a Part-time Island*), Robert Lane Fox and Allen Lane Ltd (*Alexander
the Great*), Peter Burton and *Gay News* (*Robin Maugham: The Man and
the Author*), and to Chatto and Windus and the estate of Aldous Huxley
(*Drugs That Shape Men's Minds*) and Peter Giddy for his encouragement.

And I gratefully acknowledge the editorial, research and secretarial
work of Karen de Groot, Timothy d'Arch Smith, Ruth Dziuna de
Groot, Clive Moyse of the Press and Television Section of Imperial
Tobacco Ltd, the editorial staff of *Who Was Who*, the library staff at the
British Film Institute, Harold Rosenthal, editor of *Opera*, M. C. Blair
of the Lord Chancellor's Office, the staff of the British Newspaper
Library, Mrs Ursula d'Arch Smith, Billy Gaff for allowing Peter
Burton time to work with me on this book, William Lawrence for his
help on Buddhism and Hinduism, Keith Monk and Ralph de Saram
for helping to keep life running smoothly during the writing of the
book, Jeanne Francis for her advice and typing, Nancy Hosegood,
Mary Healey and Michael Davidson for editorial advice, Dr Ian
Dunbar, and the Venerable Sindhamma Bodhimalu Vinhara of Lindula.

Robin Maugham

Photographic Acknowledgements

I am extremely grateful to the photographers who have helped me with this book. In particular I would like to thank:

Don Bachardy, for permission to reproduce his portrait of me.
Robin Constable, for his photographs of Bevis Bawa and of Taprobane and of tea estates in Ceylon.
Terence Daum, for his photograph of me.
Fayer, for permission to reproduce the portrait of me taken in 1936.
Nihal Fernando, for his pictures of Brief.
The Hong Kong Government Information Service.
William Lawrence, for his photograph on board the *M.S. Tiber*, and of Taprobane, and of photographs of up-country Ceylon.
Miguel Sanchez Marco, for his photographs of Essouira.
Dmitri Papadimos, for all the photographs of the Oasis of Siwa.

search for Nirvana

I am sitting aft on a coil of rope on the deck of a cargo boat, watching the wake of the ship. On the upper deck, sitting at a small table, my assistant William Lawrence is typing out the chapter of my novel *The Sign* which I dictated to him this morning. The ship is moving south; we are leaving Europe for at least a year. We are travelling to Ceylon.

I have left Casa Cala Pada, my villa in Ibiza – perhaps for good; for if I were offered a good price I would sell it, for I can no longer afford the expense of it. Certainly I would regret my writing-room with its view over the garden which runs down to the sea. I would miss having old and new friends to stay. I would regret not having the comfort and security which the married Spanish couple who look after me provide. I would miss lunch parties on the terrace and coffee in the garden afterwards. I would miss drives away from the tourist-ridden coast which is dominated by vast hideous concrete hotels – drives in my little car over bumpy cart-tracks into the centre of the island which is still so unspoilt and uninhabited that one can get lost along the narrow tracks. Certainly, I would miss my friends on the island. Why, therefore, am I leaving? I am told I will never find a more beautiful and comfortable place to live. But there comes a moment when beauty and comfort can be stagnating. And I have become once again curiously restless. I feel that somewhere in the world there *must* lie some place in which I can find a kind of liberation of spirit and tranquillity – some form of nirvana,* in fact.

I looked up the word 'nirvana' in the *Oxford English Dictionary* and discovered that it comes from a Sanskrit word meaning 'blowing out, extinction, disappearance, etc.'. That is not at all what I am seeking. But the *O.E.D.* goes on to define the word.

(Following pages) A view of the gardens of Casa Cala Pada, my villa on Ibiza.

---

*Nirvana is spelt with a capital 'N' when it is used in its strictly Buddhist sense meaning release from the wheel or birth and rebirth. But when in this book I have used the word in its popular and secular form I spell it with a small 'n'.

'In Buddhist theology', it means 'the extinction of individual existence and absorption into the supreme spirit'. I fear I am still far from reaching that state of enlightenment which would enable me to be thus absorbed. However, the *O.E.D.* concludes 'or the extinction of all desires and passions and the attainment of perfect beatitude'. Well, if nirvana can extinguish *my* passions there must be a lot to say for it.

I then consulted *Roget's Thesaurus*. I looked up nirvana in the index at the back. 'Paradise', I read. 'Eden' – I do hope it doesn't mean the politician, I never did like the man. 'Abode of the blessed' – not very attractive, I would say. 'Bower of bliss' – more promising. 'Seventh heaven' – certainly. 'Resuscitation' – perhaps useful after a night out. 'Deification' – *that* I will leave to the critics. 'Supernal' – I cannot imagine what it can mean. 'Para-

Casa Cala Pada, my villa on Ibiza.

disical, beatific, arcadian' – splendid.

So I am once more on my way to discover nirvana. I am using the word 'nirvana' in its fullest sense and in its colloquial sense, meaning not only – as the Buddhists think of it – an extension of individuality and absorption into the supreme spirit – but a place of contentment in which one intends to live until one dies. Nirvana, in fact, is the perfect abode which might be on the top of a mountain in Greece or in a bed-sitter in the Fulham Road.

I'm making this journey of uncertain duration – as I have done on various occasions in the past – to find the perfect place to live in or to find nirvana in some form or other. From this journey, I hope to write a book.

Whenever I set out on my travels, I doubt – as I doubt before each book that I write. I doubt whether what I provide will attract the reader. But I am consoled by Freya Stark's* words in her review in *The Observer* of my third travel book *Journey To Siwa*.† *Robin Maugham is one of the young writers whose travels in Africa and Arabia we hail with pleasure because of the pleasure with which he himself has undertaken them: his books have that primary quality in books of travel – the atmosphere of a journey that would have been undertaken if it were never to have been written about at all.*

I will return to the rest of Freya Stark's review of my book *Journey To Siwa* at a later moment because it has a distinct bearing on what I want to say.

During my life I have made other attempts to reach some form of nirvana. Perhaps I shall live to make yet further attempts.

As a fairly successful writer, I may appear to live in some kind of splendid isolation. However, this is not completely true. Less than fifteen years ago, I drove a Land-Rover into the Sahara and bought a slave from his Tuareg master to prove to the world that slavery still exists today. Only a few years ago, I was the first writer to stand before the B.B.C. television audiences and proclaim that throughout my life I had loved boys more than girls, and still do. Only a year ago the film based on my Maiden Speech on slavery in the House of Lords was shown on *Les Dossiers de L'Ecran* – a major television programme in Paris – and afterwards, still on television, the question of slavery today was debated by a panel of experts. I was forced to defend my position for over an hour – and in French. I mention these facts only to make it clear to my readers who, quite possibly, have never heard of my name,

---

*Now Dame Freya Stark.
†Robin Maugham: *Journey to Siwa*: Chapman & Hall, London: 1950.

that my life has not been led in complete seclusion from the social troubles of this world.

But how many people in this world can claim that they have indeed found nirvana in the wider sense of the word in which I have defined it? For I am aware that nirvana of any kind is difficult to discover. Moreover, worse, how many people, alas, can afford to change their lives in any way? Horribly few! And here the sense of guilt I think I have known all my life enters in.

Since the days when I left home at the age of eighteen to study music in Vienna, and witnessed the poverty there and its result, I have hated inequality. This is the reason why I joined the Socialist Party when I went to Cambridge. Perhaps I have become disillusioned in late middle-age, but it seems to me that there exists no country in the world in which a serious attempt by the government to abolish inequality has not produced a vicious police-state.

I try to salve my perhaps unreasonable guilt over the inequality in the world by my efforts to combat slavery in Africa and Arabia and to change the conditions of near-slavery in which I find several people whom I know. But the days are over when I was sufficiently optimistic and vain to believe I could change if not the world, then at least a portion of it – the days when I worked frantically to achieve a partition of Palestine before the first war between the Arabs and the Israelis broke out. However, the letters I receive from far and wide encourage me to believe that my personal crusade to win tolerance for homosexuality has, to some extent, been successful.

Perhaps everyone has his place – not in 'Society', God knows! – but in doing what he can. I now know some of my limitations. No longer do I see myself swaying the House of Lords to adopt a new policy in the Middle East – nor, on a smaller scale, to reduce the age of consenting homosexuals to sixteen which is the age that applies to girls and boys in heterosexual affairs. But I can and still do make a vigorous effort to speak on television upon subjects about which I feel strongly.

The world's major religions have always been in doubt as to whether a person's main responsibility is to himself or to society. I have come to suspect that his responsibility may very possibly be primarily to himself – for surely the incomplete man will be less able to be of use to society than a person who has resolved his or her approach to life and become totally whole, and thus become more properly equipped to be of value to mankind.

During these last ten years which have been disrupted by my various ailments and illnesses and disturbed by personal anxieties, I have come to the decision that the time is appropriate, since I am almost sixty, for me to try and put my confused mind in order and to come to terms with my own spirit.

So here I am sitting aft on the deck of a cargo boat, perched on a coil of rope, watching the wake of the ship . . .

But as I re-read that line, I laugh to myself, for I remember that I once began a book with those words, and I can still remember the result of them. Soon after the book, *The Slaves of Timbuktu*, was published, my uncle Willie Somerset Maugham invited me to stay with him at the Villa Mauresque.

'I enjoyed your book about slaves,' he told me suddenly one evening on the terrace. 'It is fascinating to realise one can buy a young black man for thirty pounds. . . . But in the book you talk too much about yourself.'

'Some of the critics said I didn't talk *enough* about myself,' I answered in protest.

'Well,' my uncle said to me, adapting his stammer to its best advantage as usual, 'I can ger-give you a perfect example. You say, "I am writing these words per-perched on a coil of rope". But who cares a fer-fuck *where* you are sitting? The reader is only interested in what you have to say about slavery.'

But I still must disagree with that eccentric old man. An author's attitude towards – let us say – prostitution will presumably differ slightly according to his physical position – if he is lying in bed in a hospital recovering from a severe operation, for instance, or if he is in superb health and entering a bordello. In any case, in this book I need not be afraid of writing too much about myself, for it is the story of my own search for happiness – my search not only at present on this journey but my search in the past. In this respect, I realise, it will in a way be a sequel to my autobiography *Escape From the Shadows*.* Also, the book in some ways is bound to resemble the autobiography in shape, because I cannot explain the reasons for my sporadic journeys to seek nirvana without sketching a little of my background. However, I promise I will not repeat myself; I will not retell any story or episode – though for the sake of continuity I may be forced to refer to one. And, before I continue further on this journey south from Lisbon on board the cargo boat the *M.S. Tiber* of the Wilhelmsen Line, on which William and I are the only passengers, each with his own cabin and bathroom, it is essential that I look back for a while into the past, because it is owing to my past that I am now making this journey.

Suddenly I find myself wondering if my Uncle Willie ever set out on a journey in search for nirvana. Then I remember. Of course he did. From the moment he had divorced his wife and settled abroad,

*Robin Maugham: *Escape From the Shadows*: Hodder & Stoughton, London: 1972.

each journey he made with his beloved Gerald Haxton was a new pursuit of nirvana. And when the blaze of his passion for Gerald cooled in later years until its embers were almost cold he set out on several religious quests. His attitude towards nirvana and religions in general is admirably explained in his partly autobiographical book *The Summing Up*.* Willie wrote: 'Evils are there, omnipresent; pain and disease, the death of those we love, poverty, crime, sin, frustrated hope: the list is interminable. What explanations have the philosophers to offer? Some say that evil is logically necessary so that we may know good; some say that by the nature of the world there is an opposition between good and evil and that each is metaphysically necessary to the other. What explanations have the theologians to offer? Some say that God has placed evils here for our training; some say that he has sent them upon men to punish them for their sins. But *I* have seen a child die of meningitis. I have only found one explanation that appealed equally to my sensibility and to my imagination. This is the doctrine of the transmigration of souls. As everyone knows, it assumes that life does not begin at birth or end at death, but is a link in an indefinite series of lives each one of which is determined by the acts done in previous existences. Good deeds may exalt a man to the heights of heaven and evil deeds degrade him to the depths of hell. All lives come to an end, even the lives of the gods, and happiness is to be sought in release from the round of births and repose in the changeless state called Nirvana. It would be less difficult to bear the evils of one's own life if one could think that they were but the necessary outcome of one's errors in a previous existence, and the effort to do better would be less difficult too when there was the hope that in another existence a greater

*W. Somerset Maugham: *The Summing Up*: William Heinemann, London: 1938.

happiness would reward one. . . . I can only regret that I find the doctrine impossible to believe.'

Willie also made extensive use of his visit to a holy man in India in his novel *The Razor's Edge*.* But though the character of Elliott Templeton, the snobbish queen, is fascinating, his hero Larry Darrell remains dull and unreal. The truth is that although Willie toiled up mountains to visit gurus and plodded his way conscientiously through dozens of holy works, he remained a materialist to the end. And it is when he writes unashamedly as a materialist as in *Cakes and Ale* that his genius is displayed at its best.

W. Somerset
Maugham.

*W. Somerset Maugham: *The Razor's Edge*: William Heinemann, London: 1944.

The Razor's Edge, however, is particularly fascinating to me because when Willie's character Larry gains some kind of religious power, he practises methods of healing which Willie himself had learned from a most unusual hypnotist who was then alive and practising in London. His name was Dr Leahy.

Dr Leahy had lost a leg in the First Great War. During his period of intense suffering in various military hospitals he had learned a method of self-hypnosis which enabled him – as he would tell his patients – to put a screen between himself and his pain and thus to reduce its intensity. He had then found out that this method which he had practised successfully on himself could be used on other soldiers in the same hospital who were in agony. When the war ended he set up his practice in Harley Street. Willie went to him for help to master his stammer. By that time Dr Leahy was a large, heavy, broad-shouldered, scarlet-faced, jovial man of about sixty. He was also slightly deaf.

Willie advised me to visit this Dr Leahy because one side of Willie's nature always retained the conventional morality of his upbringing, and he was determined that I should not be a bisexual but a complete heterosexual and marry an heiress whom he and Emerald Cunard had selected for me. I made an appointment to see Dr Leahy.

Four or five people were sitting in the waiting-room. The *Tatler* or *Punch* was held rigidly between their hands. But I soon noticed that not a page was being turned. After I had been sitting down for a while, I realised the reason why the patients awaiting their turn were so intent and motionless. The wall between the waiting-room and Dr Leahy's consulting-room was thin, and I remembered that Dr Leahy was a little deaf. From next door we could all hear the female patient whom he was trying to help saying to him in a faltering voice, 'Dr Leahy, my trouble is that I am in love with my footman.'

'Ah, me dear lady,' Dr Leahy would reply in his loud Irish brogue, 'you have come here to relax, so please make yourself at home. But if you don't mind, me dear, please could you repeat what you just said – because to tell you the truth I'm a bit hard of hearing.'

'I'm in love with my footman,' the poor lady would shriek.

And in the waiting-room next door the magazines would remain motionless.

Dr Leahy's method of hypnotism was to make one hold a matchbox between the thumb and the middle fingers. He would then tell one that gradually a tingling sensation would be felt in one's shoulder which would spread down to the arm and wrist until it reached one's hand. Presently, the thumb and finger holding the matchbox would open without conscious effort on one's part, and the matchbox would then drop out of one's grasp as if of its own volition.

'And just as the matchbox drops from your hand,' Dr Leahy would continue firmly, 'so will your desire disappear.' Thus desire for one's footman, alcohol, cigarettes, or boys – whatever one's particular craving was – would vanish.

'I will now slowly begin to count up to ten,' Dr Leahy would announce. 'And by the time I reach ten, the matchbox will have dropped to the carpet.'

This is how Willie describes this method in *The Razor's Edge*, when his hero Larry is trying to cure the chronic and acute headache of his friend Gray:

W. Somerset Maugham (*second from the left*) with Barbara Back, Raymond Mortimer and Gerald Haxton (*far right*).

' "Close your fingers on it tightly and hold your hand palm downwards. Don't fight against me. Make no effort, but hold the coin in your clenched fist. Before I count twenty your hand will open and the coin will drop out of it."

'Gray did as he was told. Larry seated himself at the writing-table and began to count. . . . One, two, three, four. Till he had got up to fifteen there was no movement in Gray's hand, then it seemed to tremble a little and I had the impression, I can hardly say I saw, that the clenched fingers were loosening. The thumb moved away from the fist. I distinctly saw the fingers quiver.

24

When Larry reached nineteen the coin fell out of Gray's hand and rolled to my feet.

. . . ' "Are you quite comfortable in that chair?" asked Larry.

' "As comfortable as I can be when my head's giving me hell."

' "Well, let yourself go quite slack. Take it easy. Do nothing. Don't resist. Before I count twenty your right arm will rise from the arm of the chair until your hand is above your head. One, two, three, four."

'He spoke the numbers slowly in the silver-toned, melodious voice of his, and when he had reached nine we saw Gray's hand rise, only just perceptibly, from the leather surface on which it rested until it was perhaps an inch above it. It stopped for a second.

' "Ten, eleven, twelve."

'There was a little jerk and then slowly the whole arm began to move upwards. It wasn't resting on the chair any more. . . . It was a curious effect. It had no likeness to voluntary movement. I've never seen a man walking in his sleep, but I can imagine that he would move in just the same strange way . . .

'Larry glanced at his watch. "It's thirteen minutes past eight. In sixty seconds your eyelids will grow so heavy that you'll be obliged to close them and then you'll sleep. You'll sleep for six minutes. At eight twenty you'll wake and you'll have no more pain." '

So far as I was concerned Dr Leahy's treatment was over-efficacious. The matchbox positively shot out of my hand.

'Now I am going to put an idea into your mind,' Dr Leahy told me. 'But first I must know what you're doing tonight.'

I explained that I was going to a cocktail party given by Moura Budberg and that I was then dining with an author who though unknown to Dr Leahy was one of the most famous authors alive.

'Well,' said Dr Leahy, 'this is the idea I am going to put into your mind. During the course of the evening you will meet a beautiful young girl, and you will fall wildly in love with her – so you will – and you'll both go off and spend a happy evening together.'

With those words I left him, and hurried past the waiting-room.

At Moura's party there was no young girl to be seen, but I spent a happy time talking to Michael Redgrave about a film called *Time Without Pity* in which he was acting. Joseph Losey, who was directing, had asked me to help on the script.

I then arrived happy and tipsy at the author's house in Hampstead. And there – to my delight – was a most beautiful girl of about nineteen. She was as intelligent as she was attractive and sat next to me at dinner, where wine after wine flowed generously. The girl and I got on better and better. When we eventually reached the drawing-room, we sat down together on the sofa. I nestled against her in a contented way, and put an arm around her. At that moment a series of furious blows descended on my forehead. It was the author. I scrambled from the sofa and stood up. I was knocked down again. Once more I tried to stand up and was promptly knocked back. At last, I escaped from the room.

The next morning when I awoke with a headache a large bouquet of roses appeared with a sincere and charming letter of apology. The telephone rang. A friend who had also been at the dinner-party was on the line. From her I learned that the girl to whom I had been so attracted was soon to become engaged to the author. I now decided that I was the one who should write a letter of apology. And I did so. When I appeared in Dr Leahy's room that morning, I had two very large black eyes, and I was limping badly because the famous author had thrown me down the staircase. Dr Leahy was intently examining his notes.

'And now, my dear boy,' Dr Leahy began, 'tell me how my suggestion worked for you last night.'

'Extremely well,' I replied.

But his hypnotism for the following evening and the next had no effect whatsoever. So I have remained bisexual and predominately homosexual ever since.

Looking back now on the past, I wonder why I was so desperately disturbed by the homosexual side of my nature. I think the answer was that my parents were older than most when I was born – my father was fifty – and they were both of them extremely conventional.

My mother was a Romer. Her father had been a Lord Justice, her brother was a Lord Justice, and another brother was General Sir Cecil Romer. My mother never openly discussed any homosexual matter with me until I was sixteen and I had been at Eton for three years – by which time it was too late. When I was sixteen she told me that my uncle Cecil Romer, the General, had told her that he had been asked by an important official in the Home Office to warn my Uncle Willie that his homosexual activities in England must stop or he would be put into prison. My mother was extremely shocked and all the more upset because she was fond of Willie.

As I have said in another book, the Romers were as extrovert as the Maughams were introspective. To use the words of my darling sister Kate, the Romers tended to be, 'friendly, affectionate, rumbustious, boisterous, demonstrative'.* There is a pleasant

*Towards the end of her life my sister Kate Mary Bruce wrote the first draft of a short book mainly about the Romers and the Bruces, which she intended to revise. The provisional title was *Family Group*.

A pleasant picture
of the Romer family
which was exhibited
at the Royal
Academy in 1837.

picture of the Romer family which was exhibited in the Royal Academy in 1837 which shows the nine children of John Romer and his wife Sarah Cooper. Sarah was a gypsy and it was murmured that John had met her at a boxing booth. Emma, one of the girls, in a white dress, is sitting at the piano. She was a professional singer, and for several seasons she was Prima Donna at the English Opera House. Her sister Helen, who resembled her in face, in form, and in height, stands behind her in the painting and is wearing a dark dress.

Helen was 'a pretty, gentle girl', wrote my grandmother, 'with a lovely voice, but she never sang in public, except on one occasion when in consequence of the sudden indisposition of her sister Emma, she represented her for one week at the opera and no one noticed the change. She had always accompanied her sister to rehearsals, so she was word-perfect and note-perfect, but it was nervous work for a novice, as her first entrance was up a "trap" and her first note A natural. The opera was *The Magic Dove* and she was only eighteen at the time.'

Such was my grandmother's story. But my mother's account of it was slightly different, for she was endowed with a lively imagination.

In my mother's version, an hour before the curtain rose on *The Magic Dove* the impresario who was well aware that Emma, the Prima Donna, was over-fond of drink, went to her dressing-room to make certain that she had arrived and had begun to make herself up and to change into her elaborate costume. There was no sign of Emma. He called out her name in vain. Then he looked behind a screen in the room – and there was Emma, drunk and insensate. The house was filling up, and everyone had come to hear Emma sing.

'What is to be done?' he asked the stage manager in desperation.

It was then that the stage manager told him about Emma's devoted sister Helen, who was married to a banker and lived in Kensington Square. She admired her sister so much, he explained, that she rehearsed all her rôles. There was only one hope. If the sister could be persuaded to appear, no one in the audience would notice the difference.

'Right,' said the impresario, 'send my carriage for her.'

'Now,' my mother would continue, '*as* it so happened, the banker was out at a City dinner which would last late into the night, and Helen was seated at the piano – when suddenly a carriage drove up to the door. The stage manager sprang out, was admitted to the house and rapidly explained the desperate situation to her. Without hesitation, Helen wrapped a shawl around her shoulders and entered the carriage. By the time they reached the Opera House, there were only a few minutes before the curtain was due to rise.

'Imagine Helen struggling into Emma's dove costume,' my mother would continue, 'dabbing her face with the hare's foot, trying to subdue her fluttering heart. Imagine her awful moment in the wings, waiting for her cue to "pop up through the trap" and that crucial moment of hitting that A natural.'

But Helen – and for once only a cliché is apt – rose to the occasion. She received cheers after her first aria, and at the finale she was given a standing ovation.

'But there was no time to linger, listening to the applause,' my mother continued. 'Helen was bundled into the carriage after changing back into her own clothes and rushed home to Kensington Square. She was lying peacefully in bed, when her husband returned slightly drunk from his City dinner. But the shouts of applause still echoed in her ears.

'What was the effect on Helen?' my mother would enquire. 'We do not know for certain because she only confessed the matter to one of her sons on her deathbed. But did she return without regret to her respectable existence, her dark marino dress, her visits to Mudie's Library and her walks in Kensington Gardens? I wonder,' my mother would conclude.

What an ideal B-picture!

But either my mother was telling the story to entertain me or my memory is at fault. For, in fact, Helen was not married to a banker; she married Mark Lemon, the part-founder and editor of *Punch* and the founder of *The Field*. Lemon was a friend of Dickens and Longfellow and had a passion for amateur theatricals. He was my great-grandfather. My grandfather, Robert Romer, who became a distinguished lawyer, married his first cousin, Betty Lemon, Mark Lemon's daughter. They had five sons and two daughters. My sister Kate enjoyed a most happy relationship with her grandmother. My grandmother, it seems, was a profoundly religious woman, and she obeyed her own high principles.

'She lived under a Victorian bell-glass,' wrote Kate. 'Nothing disagreeable or sordid ever touched her. She chose deliberately to spend her time among the dignified, gracious things of the century in which she lived; music, travel, flowers, pleasant homes, the society of cultivated people, the laughter of children.'

By the time my mother had grown up the gypsy, Bohemian side of the Romers had either disappeared or gone underground. My mother would proclaim that she enjoyed only the company of 'clean decent people'. However, in appearance there was still a trace of the gypsy Romers in my mother. For she was 'darkskinned, small-boned, with expressive grey eyes, and a mass of brown curly hair which remained brown to the day she died'.

As Kate says, my mother was a stoic. She taught us self-control at an early age. We were never allowed to cry. If we made a scene, she said we were overwrought and put us to bed until we recovered. She taught us to be ashamed of illness and to bear with pain – as she herself did.

She was an essentially happy person, finding delight in her friends, her family, the countryside and animals. Though beautifully dressed in London, she refused to wear anything but old clothes in the country. So old were her clothes, and such was her love of animals – tame and wild – that in the district of Hartfield where we lived she came to be known as 'the old woman who lives in the big house on the hill and who loves animals so much that she lets the mice eat her clothes' – or so my mother would tell us.

My mother disapproved of blood-sports. On one occasion, hounds ran a fox to earth in the wood at the end of the garden of our house – Tye House, near Hartfield. My mother, who enjoyed sitting for hours watching the fox-cubs playing, stood over the earth and defied the Hunt. The Master of Fox-Hounds was patient and courteous – I rather think that he supposed my mother was mad. After a brief exchange of views he called off the pack. The disgruntled huntsmen rode away.

As I grew up, I began to realise that my mother was a strange mixture of prudishness and mischievousness. A generation of 'clean decent people' had made her strictly conventional. But beneath her horror of any form of immorality or what she would call 'scruffiness' there still flowed the Romer gypsy blood. She was an excellent mimic and would impersonate her children to themselves if she thought that one of us was behaving stupidly. She attended church regularly and had hilarious paraphrases of all the hymns which bored her. Such was her interest in the local church that once in the country she was invited to a tea-party at which by mistake she was the only lady present among fifty clergymen. After tea they all settled down to play a game called 'The Flowers' Wedding'. My mother, who was an expert horticulturalist, found the whole game ridiculous.

'After they had been married a year, what did the Bride call the Bridegroom?' was one of the questions. The answer was, of course, 'Sweet William'.

'Balearic Sandwort', wrote my mother on her pad.

But her sense of humour did not extend to any transgression of the Commandments. If she had known the force of my inclinations towards homosexuality, she would have been appalled and disgusted.

My mother's sense of humour was seldom appreciated by my father who appeared in our home to be a stern, cold and solemn character. I have written about him at length in my autobiography,

so here I will only say that as one of the greatest lawyers of his day who eventually became Lord Chancellor of England my father would not have welcomed the knowledge that his son was predominantly homosexual. Indeed, a scandal might well have damaged his career.

But my father *did* have a dry humour all of his own. As I have said elsewhere, my father had the conviction that if a man had a first-class brain he could master any task or science to which he applied himself. I have told of the episode when he bought a new car in London, watched the salesman drive it for an hour, dropped the salesman at a station and then steered an erratic course to our country house and drove straight into the front-porch. But when the car had been recovered and during the years that followed my father still insisted on having a car which he could drive himself. The house where we now lived overlooking Ashdown Forest had a drive which wound its way down to a road that led to London. Some two miles away, this road crossed another which led from Tunbridge Wells to Holtye. There was no notice to show which was the major road, and there was no 'Stop' sign. Those who lived in Hartfield considered that any road leading to London must be the main road. Those, however, who lived in Tunbridge Wells were convinced that since Tunbridge Wells was ten times the size of Hartfield, the road from Tunbridge Wells to Holtye should take precedence over the lesser one leading from Hartfield to London. The result of these conflicting beliefs was a series of accidents which led to the cross-road being known as 'Break-neck Crossroad'. So frequent were these accidents that a cottage on one side of the crossroad had been converted into a First Aid Post, and a garage to mend the broken cars had been erected on the other, whilst on the far corner had started up a sweet-shop which sold humbugs, peppermints, lollipops and gob-stoppers to the surviving children of the afflicted.

One afternoon my father was driving himself along the road from Hartfield to London. He had recently been extremely perturbed by the number of accidents on the roads of England. He had publicly advocated that the speed limit should be reduced to thirty miles an hour throughout the land, and he himself in order to set an example drove his car at a steady thirty uphill, and, indeed, down dale – with the handbrake on. Unfortunately, on this particular afternoon as he approached 'Break-neck Crossroad' so did another car coming from Tunbridge Wells. Still driving at thirty miles an hour, my father drove straight into it. My father was uninjured. The driver of the other car who was the only occupant suffered a sprained ankle and was promptly treated at the crossroad hospital. My father gave an accurate account of what had happened; his insurance company paid up for the cost of a new car for the other driver and also considerable

34

damages for his sprained ankle. A few months later my father received a letter from the driver in which he said that his ankle was still hurting him: he suggested that my father should pay him a thousand pounds extra in compensation.

'I am sorry to hear that your ankle still afflicts you,' my father wrote back. 'But I am glad that at least you have not *lost your nerve.*'

Another conviction held by my father was that should he choose to demean himself by practising the profession of a writer he would undoubtedly produce better works than his brother Willie. My father wrote short stories under a pseudonym for *The Bystander*; he certainly had a remarkable talent. At dinner one night at the Mauresque, for example, my uncle told us of an incident someone had related to him with the suggestion that he should write a story from it. But Willie had given it up because he could not find a suitable end. Here is the incident as told by Willie:*

'Two young fellows were working on a tea plantation in the hills and the mail had to be fetched from a good way off so that they only got it at rather long intervals. One of the young fellows, let us call him A, used to get a lot of letters by every mail, ten or twelve and sometimes more, but the other, B, never got one. He used to watch A enviously as he took his bundle and started to read. He hankered to have a letter, just one letter, and one day, when they were expecting the mail, he said to A: "Look here, you always have a packet of letters and I never get any. I'll give you five pounds if you'll let me have one of yours." "Right-ho," said A and when the mail came in he handed B his letters and said to him: "Take whichever you like." B gave him a five-pound note, looked over the letters, chose one and returned the rest. In the evening, when they were having a whisky and soda after dinner, A asked casually: "By the way, what was that letter about?" "I'm not going to tell you," said B. A, somewhat taken aback, said: "Well, who was it from?" "That's my business," answered B. They had a bit of an argument, but B stood on his rights and refused to say anything about the letter that he had bought. A began to fret, and as the weeks went by he did all he could to persuade B to let him see the letter. B continued to refuse. At length A, anxious, worried, curious, felt he couldn't bear it any longer, so he went to B and said: "Look here, here's your five pounds, let me have my letter back again." "Not on your life," said B. "I bought and paid for it, it's my letter and I'm not going to give it up."'

The first night at dinner, after we had returned from the Mauresque, my father stared round the table with his usual mournful gaze. 'I cannot imagine why my poor brother Willie

*W. Somerset Maugham: *A Writer's Note-Book*: William Heinemann, London: 1949.

35

has so little power of invention that he cannot find an ending to
that interesting tale he told us,' my father said. 'I myself could
find an end without the slightest effort.'

'What?' we asked.

My father fixed his monocle in his left eye with a quivering
hand. (He drank only two glasses of wine a day, but he had the
tremor of an alcoholic.)

'Well,' my father began – and at this point I must make it
clear that I cannot remember precisely the words that he, or any
other character in this book, used; I can only reconstruct from
memory and from their habit of speech – 'you will remember that
B has bought and chosen the letter and has refused to tell his
friend A what are its contents or whom it is from. Meanwhile A
goes to his room in that remote bungalow and reads through the
rest of his mail. Now for some months past A has been very

worried by the nervous and strange behaviour of B. Accordingly, he had written to a friend of his in London who was a doctor, explaining the symptoms in detail and asking for advice. In his mail A finds a letter from the doctor which reads as follows: "I must tell you that the symptoms of B which you have described alarm me considerably. They suggest an extremely disturbed mind and a paranoia which might well develop into a violent form of lunacy. I am no expert on this subject, but I have taken the liberty of sending your letter to my colleague Dr Kindersley who is an alienist. You should be hearing from him in the same post as this letter."

'So there is A, living in this bungalow in the wild hills, a day's ride away from the nearest white neighbour sharing a bungalow with a man who may be a dangerous lunatic. Worse, a man who may know the truth about himself, for the letter which B purchased could well have been the letter from the alienist.'

My father let the monocle drop from his eye.

'And on that note,' he concluded, 'I would end the story.'

My father was also determined that he could bring his intelligence to bear on the world of finance. Through a broker whom he had met at some banquet he bought a whole rubber plantation in Malaya. The kindly broker supplied me with an almost endless stock of rubber balls. Never can any child have been given such an expensive present, for when the rubber market 'crashed' it was reckoned that each bounce of each rubber ball must have cost the family a hundred pounds.

However, my father persisted in his conviction that he could apply his first-class brain to the business world. And then came the disaster. At some respectable club in London, my father met a gentleman called Dr Brynar Owen.

The family first met Dr Owen when he appeared, to our surprise, at breakfast which we all ate at nine o'clock in the dining-room of our London house at 73 Cadogan Square. I was thirteen at the time, but I can distinctly remember that Dr Owen looked exactly like the villain in one of Edgar Wallace's thrillers. He wore a Prince of Wales double-breasted check suit, very tightly fitting, a heavy gold monocle, and shining black and white patent leather shoes. A large carnation trembled in his button-hole. He was the most obvious crook I have ever seen.

'That man,' said my mother to my father after he had gone, 'is an obvious charlatan.'

My father put his monocle into his eye and regarded my mother mournfully. 'My dear Nellie,' he said, 'I have spent my life and made my fortune from my knowledge of human beings in the law courts, so kindly allow me to know better than you do about a man as distinguished as Dr Owen.'

Perhaps in order to remove the poor impression that he might have given us, Dr Brynar Owen then began to display his generosity. My father in particular, and the family in general, were sent presents by him once a week. The gift which gave me most pleasure was a wireless set which was so enormous that it arrived in a removal van and it took three powerful men to carry it into the living-room of our country house.

In each of the twelve sections of which the set was comprised there glowed a large valve each with its own tuning control and rheostat. Beneath each section was a large car battery, for the set's voltage unfortunately was not that of our generator at the end of the garden which supplied the house with electric light. Above this magnificent assemblage stood a huge loudspeaker which seemed to crane its vast horn anxiously into the living-room as if longing to be heard. But tuning the set to the wavelength of Daventry was a difficult matter. For each of the twelve valves had to be tuned separately. However, finally, I would be rewarded and the loudspeaker, shivering with excitement, would gain the power of speech. 'Hello, hello,' it would crackle excitedly. '2LO calling.'

A few weeks later the wireless was banned from the living-room because the acid from the batteries leaked all over the parquet flooring. However, I took it to pieces, segment by segment, and reassembled it in the attic where the loudspeaker could regain the power of speech and talk for hours at a time.

But Dr Brynar Owen's eclipse was soon to come. He sold my father a hundred farm tractors which existed only in his own imagination. It was then discovered that Dr Owen had been selling farm tractors by the score. He was arrested, tried, and sent to prison.

However, my father's faith, though slightly disturbed at the time, soon rallied.

'Consider advertising,' said my father one evening a few months later at dinner. 'Take, for instance, Three Nuns Tobacco which I always smoke. You must have observed that on each tin of tobacco is printed their slogan, "None nicer!" Now, the company's advertising for its product is rather good – I grant you that. But were I in charge of their advertising department, I would devise a poster which would seize the imagination of the whole public.'

'What?' we dutifully asked once again.

'Well,' my father began. '*My* poster would have the slogan "None nicer, None finer, None purer", and would be painted in bold vivid colours. In the background you would see the walls of a beautiful convent. In the foreground there would run a limpid stream. And in the middle-ground would be standing gazing down at the stream three very beautiful and gracious young ladies, attired decorously but charmingly in their nun's habits. Beneath each nun you would observe a large scroll. Written on the scroll beneath the first nun would be the words "Nun Nicer". Beneath the second nun the scroll would read "Nun Finer", and beneath the third nun "Nun Purer".'

My father let his monocle fall from his eye and gazed round at his family.

'I will give you that idea,' he announced. 'Any one of you who so wishes can take out a paint-box, execute the poster and send it to the tobacco company with a covering letter.'

However, not one of my three elder sisters was interested, but I was fascinated by the idea. The holidays were ending. On the first Sunday at school I got out my paint-box and a large sheet of cartridge paper, and I did my best. Now, at Eton, boys wrote their letters on paper headed with their housemaster's name, putting their own name above. Accordingly, the address I gave was

> Robin Maugham, Esq.,
> c/o J. C. Butterwick, Esq.,
> Eton College,
> Windsor,
> Berks.

And I sent off the letter and the poster in a large envelope.

Days and weeks passed by without any acknowledgement from Three Nuns Tobacco. In the misery of my life at school, mingled as it was with strange moments of ecstasy, I forgot all about the poster. But one day, after a wonderful afternoon of unrestrained passion with a friend on a little island in the Thames, when I was feeling particularly guilty for my transgression, I was summoned to the study of M'Tutor, as we called him.

'I've always suspected you of infamy, Maugham,' he growled. 'I now have the proof of it.'

I gazed at him in terror.

'You have been trying to smuggle tobacco into the house,' he announced.

'I promise you, sir, I haven't,' I blurted out.

Dramatically he raised his hand and pointed to a package in a corner of the room.

'Then how do you explain that parcel, which is addressed to you?' he demanded.

Nervously I approached the package and saw that it was full of tins of Three Nuns Tobacco. At that moment an explanation dawned on me. For I could see that on top of the tins lay an envelope addressed to me.

'May I please open the envelope, sir?' I asked.

'Certainly.'

Hastily I ripped open the envelope. It was evident from the tone of the letter that the tobacco company had not realised I was only a schoolboy. It had been supposed I was a master at the college, for the letter ran roughly as follows:

Dear Sir,

We are writing to thank you for the poster which you kindly sent us as a suggested advertisement for our tobacco.

The originality of the idea has been much appreciated. Unfortunately, we have been obliged to reject the idea for fear it would give offence on religious grounds.

However, we are very much impressed by the originality you have displayed. We enclose some tins of our tobacco as a token of our appreciation.

We trust that you will send us any further suggestions for advertisements which occur to you.

In silence, I handed the letter to M'Tutor. He read it and began to smile. When I told him the full details of the story he began to laugh.

After the success of the advertising venture, my father assumed the responsibilities of a Law Lord and later of Lord Chancellor of England without any hesitation. One of his new duties was to supervise the appointment of clergymen in various dioceses. Now, apart from official ceremonies, my father had not attended church for at least half a century. In fact, he had never even entered the village church at Hartfield because he would always play golf on Sunday mornings. But now that he was Lord Chancellor and the 'livings' were in his power we noticed that my father began to assume a slightly proprietorial attitude towards churches in general and the church in Hartfield in particular. One morning my sister Kate, who had managed to reach the driving seat of the car before my father could get there, was driving us to the golf-links. As we passed through Hartfield my father suddenly pointed to the church.

'Behold that edifice,' he said. 'It stands, as it should, dominating the whole village. To that place of worship each man and woman and each child who has reached the age of discretion wend their way to make their simple prayers. Within those walls they are christened. Before that altar they are married. In that churchyard they are buried. It is, in fact, the very centre of their lives.'

Kate turned and gave me a wink.

At lunch after golf my father turned to my mother and to her amazement informed her that he intended to attend divine service with her the following Sunday. So the next Sunday my father drove my mother to the Hartfield church. Unfortunately, his knowledge of the procedure of an ordinary service was strictly limited. His obstinacy was such that when he stood and the rest of the congregation knelt, despite the prodding from my mother, he would remain standing. So indignant was he that the rest of the congregation did not follow his example by standing when he stood and kneeling when he did that he never attended the village church again.

By the time I was seventeen I had come to adore my mother, but I was still afraid of my father, and I resented the austerity and coldness with which he treated me. By this time, my sisters were married. During the holidays I now lived alone with my parents in a cold, grey world of loneliness.

As I grew older I found a kind of nirvana while staying with my Uncle Willie at the Villa Mauresque. In previous books I have written critically about his behaviour, but in those early days he was sometimes wonderfully kind to me. He would take me for walks around Cap Ferrat, and he would make me *see* the umbrella pines, the inlets and the enchanting landscapes in a way which at that time I could not envisage for myself. Moreover, he would tell me stories that were in his mind and which he had never written in full – though he had made notes of them.

Garden of the Villa Mauresque.

One story has remained clearly in my memory – perhaps because of the strange conditions under which Willie first told it. When the war broke out and it was obvious that France would be invaded, Willie decided to return to England to search for a war job. He left France in July 1940. He sailed from Marseilles on an over-crowded collier. On Willie's arrival in London I got leave from my regiment which was soon to go to the Western Desert in order to dine with him at the Savoy. That evening he talked about his journey from Marseilles to London.

'Der-do you know that the most amazing thing happened to me on board the boat,' Willie told me. 'The Captain of the ship came up to me and said he wanted to see me in his cabin. Naturally, I wondered what it was all about. At my advanced age I didn't think he'd taken a fancy to me. But I will confess that I was surprised by what he said after he'd given me a whisky and soda.

' "Mr Maugham," he began, "I'm addressing you not as the Captain of this ship, but as a deputy for the passengers."

' "Yes?" I replied, wondering what in heaven's name he was going to say.

' "As you know," he continued, "with this strict blackout we are forced to have, the nights seem very long." He gave a short laugh. "Particularly when a torpedo from a submarine may blow us up at any moment. Not that I give your fellow passengers *that* piece of information," he added. "But for all of them, the long evenings are a bit of a strain."

' "Precisely," I agreed. "But what can I do to help?"

' "To come to the point," the Captain continued, "some of the passengers thought it might make the time pass by more quickly if you told them a few stories."

' "But I couldn't do that!" I exclaimed.

' "Why not?" the Captain asked.

' "I wouldn't know where to begin," I told him.

'The Captain smiled at me. "If I may say so, Mr Maugham," he said, "you've been writing to my certain knowledge for forty years, so surely by now you can tell a story!" '

Willie took a sip of his wine.

'Under the circumstances I could hardly refuse,' Willie continued. 'But I cer-can't tell you what a strange experience it was to sit on that open deck surrounded by passengers sprawling all around me, with the stars clear in the sky above. Each time I'd pause for a moment in the tale I was telling them, we could hear the throb of the ship's engine and the wash of the waves.'

'What stories *did* you tell them?' I asked.

'Any that came into my head,' Willie answered. 'And the strange thing was that though the passengers were an odd mixture – retired colonels and their ladies, oily-faced stokers, women of fashion and schoolgirls – they were a far better audience than any

I've ever addressed when giving lectures. They listened intently to every word I said. For instance, I told them my story about Australia. I'm sure I must have told it to you dozens of times, though I've never written it.'

'No,' I replied truthfully. 'I don't think you've ever told it me.'

Willie put down his glass of wine.

'Well,' he began, 'it is a curious tale I heard when I was in the Antipodes some years ago. A salesman for a dried goods firm whom I will call Stoner, aged about thirty, handsome, fit and healthy, was driving alone across a desolate stretch of desert in Southern Australia towards Perth. He was enjoying the long drive but hoped to reach the township where he had business to carry out before midnight. However – to his dismay – at about six o'clock his car broke down. He got out and opened up the bonnet. But though he knew a little about mechanics, nothing he could do would get the car to start. By now darkness was falling. No other car had passed by. He was beginning to resign himself to sleeping the night in the back of his car. And as you may know, it gets der-damned cold in the desert at night. Suddenly he noticed that far away on the horizon there was a light. It did not move. It obviously belonged to a homestead. So he decided to make for it in the hopes that at least he might find shelter there for the night.

'Stoner began to walk towards the light, but as he walked he saw the headlights of a car approaching him along the road from the region of the homestead. As the car drew up beside him he saw that it was a Rolls driven by a chauffeur in uniform.

' "Mr Bryant, my employer, saw that you were in difficulties, so he sent me to find out if there was anything I could do to help," the man said.

'Briefly, Stoner explained his predicament.

' "Mr Bryant had a notion that might be the case. I didn't much fancy trying to repair your car in darkness, so Mr Bryant wondered if you'd care to stay the night with him."

' "That would be fine," said Stoner; and climbed into the Rolls beside the chauffeur.

'As they neared the lights of the house, now gleaming close to them, Stoner saw to his surprise that the house resembled a castle more than a mansion. It was large and impressive, with two turrets and a battlement. The car stopped inside an imposing portico. The chauffeur ushered Stoner into a high-ceilinged hall. His host stood in front of a vast chimney-piece, beneath which a log fire was burning.

'Bryant was a man of around fifty, tall and lean, with iron-grey hair and a distinguished-looking face. The two men introduced themselves. Stoner was offered a drink.'

By now we had finished our meal. Willie lit a cigarette and

ordered two brandies.

'The two men sat on either side of the fire,' Willie continued. 'Bryant asked his guest polite questions about his background and his reasons for driving along so remote a road. Stoner was perfectly happy to answer his host's questions, but he noticed that Bryant was strangely reticent about himself. Stoner could not help wondering what a man so obviously rich and cultured could be doing in a castle in the middle of the Australian desert. He was about to put this question to Bryant when his host looked at his watch and rose from his chair.

' "We'll be dining at eight thirty," Bryant said. "We always change for dinner. You and I are about the same height, so I think my spare dinner-jacket will fit you. My chauffeur will show you to your room." '

Willie watched the waiter pour brandy into two *ballons*.

'In the room to which he was led,' Willie continued, 'Stoner found a dinner-jacket, a shirt, and a tie, carefully laid out on the bed. In the marble bathroom which was *en suite* with his bedroom there were soaps and bath essences, perfumes and shaving tackle. As Stoner relaxed in his bath he wondered why his host had used the word "We" when he had said "We'll dine." Was his host married? He was soon to discover.

'When Stoner descended to the hall, he saw that facing his host and standing against the chimney-piece was the most ber-beautiful girl he had ever seen. She was no more than eighteen, with wheat-coloured hair, a lovely figure, and an adorable face.

' "This is my daughter," Bryant said by way of introduction. "My wife died some years ago, so Susan keeps house for me."

'As Stoner and Susan shook hands, their eyes met. At that moment Stoner's heart gave a lurch of excitement, for he had immediately sensed that the girl was attracted to him. Indeed, throughout the excellent dinner served in a white-and-gilt dining-room by an elderly butler, Bryant at the head of the table continued to make pleasant and urbane conversation. Meanwhile Stoner could see that the girl was looking at him covertly, and once when yet again their eyes met she gave him a smile of sweetness mixed with utter complicity.

'Stoner was tired. Two different wines were served, and by the time they moved back into the hall for coffee and liqueurs his head was swirling. But he was still sober enough to observe that the girl was no longer looking at him surreptitiously. As her father turned his back to pour the liqueurs, she gazed at Stoner with open admiration. He could almost feel the desire emanating from her.

'By now Stoner was so excited that he could hardly pay attention to his host's conversation. However, he managed to make reasonable replies – while all the time he could feel his heart beating in his breast. For the girl was not only of an extreme beauty, but she was per-possessed of an odd animal quality.

'Suddenly his host glanced again at his watch.

' "We go to bed early here," Bryant announced, rising from his chair. "I'm sure you've had a long day, so you won't mind retiring early."

'Stoner glanced sharply at his host. Had Bryant guessed that he was wildly attracted by Susan and had he observed the looks which had been passing between them all evening? But his host was smiling at him benignly. There was no trace of suspicion on his face.

'At the head of the stairs, Susan said goodnight to Stoner and her father and disappeared along a corridor. Bryant escorted Stoner to the door of his room.

' "I think you'll find everything you need," he said. "Breakfast will be at nine. By the time you're ready to leave, I'm sure that my chauffeur will have repaired your car. He is an expert mechanic. Goodnight to you."

'Slowly, Stoner undressed and climbed into bed. He lay there in an anguish of desire. Ber-but what could he do? In that enormous castle, he would never know in which room Susan slept. Feverishly he stared up at the ceiling. But the day had been tiring, and presently he turned out his bedside lamp.

'He awoke from a doze and sat up in bed with a start. He sensed that there was someone standing outside the door. Slowly the door opened. He had not fully drawn his curtains, and by the moonlight which filtered into the room he saw the slim figure of the girl. She was naked except for a thin *chemise*. Quickly she put a finger to her lips, commanding silence. Then she slipped out of her *chemise*, climbed into the bed and wrapped her arms around him.

'They made passionate love. And in the intervals between their love-making, she would lie pressed against him like a child. Towards dawn, in complete silence, she left his room.

'In the morning, when Stoner came downstairs, he found his host waiting in the hall.

' "I hope you slept well," Bryant said, and there was no trace of irony in his voice. "Breakfast is ready."

'Together they walked into the white-and-gilt room. The butler served a large breakfast. But Stoner had little appetite. For his mind was in a turmoil. He longed to see Susan and discover what she really felt about him. But he had no chance to do so. For as they were finishing breakfast, the chauffeur came in and announced that he had repaired Stoner's car. It was waiting for him outside.

' "Thank you," said Bryant. Then he turned, and as Stoner blurted out some words of thanks, he led him to the door.

' "It is I who should be grateful to you," Bryant told him as they stood in the portico beside Stoner's car. "You see, living as we do in this remote part of the world, we seldom, if ever, have any visitors."

'Then Bryant paused and gazed at Stoner in silence for a moment.

' "I have a notion," said Bryant at length, "that you must be wondering why a man of my means should choose to live in such remote circumstances. The truth is this. Susan is not my only daughter. I have another daughter, a year older than Susan. But she can never appear outside the walls of her apartment. You see, she is a leper."

'Bryant opened the door of the car. Stoner clambered in silence into the driver's seat.

' "Goodbye to you," Bryant said. "I've enjoyed our meeting." '

Willie put down his glass of brandy. 'Of course there are several ways of giving the story a fashionable modern twist,' he told me. 'As it *is*, when Stoner was driving himself away he must have been tortured by the doubt as to which sister it was who had come into his bed. But a twist one could give to the story is that Bryant, the host who, after all, was no fool, *saw* that Stoner was attracted by his daughter and was trying to ger-get off with her, found out that Susan had visited Stoner's room during the night, and in his sardonic way had determined to teach the young man a lesson.

'But I see you have found it an interesting story,' Willie concluded, smiling at me sarcastically, 'ber-because I observed that for once you listened to every word I said.'

The society into which I was introduced by Willie seemed to me magical. The friends and celebrities whom I met on the Riviera did indeed belong to a completely different world from that I knew in England, and I soon noticed some of them inhabited, intermittently, a nirvana all of their own which was created by their zest and intelligence – and maintained by alcohol.

Willie, Gerald Haxton and I were invited to a lunch-party in Antibes. Apart from Willie, two other celebrities of the day had been invited – Elsa Maxwell and Dorothy Parker. We arrived late and found that our hostess was afraid her chef would be annoyed because lunch might be spoiled. Elsa Maxwell had already appeared and was as raucous and vulgar as Willie had described her. Miss Parker had not turned up. We drank our cocktails hastily and started to move along a corridor towards the dining-room. But since I was easily the person of least consequence and the youngest present, I had an excuse for going last through the door.

I had seen that a tall glass shaker of daiquiri cocktails, looking most tempting, had been placed on a table behind a screen. I thought I would have one drink to give me courage before I went in to lunch. Therefore, I moved stealthily round the screen and stretched my hand for the shaker. At that instant, from the other side of the screen, a small bony hand appeared and seized the shaker firmly.

'Mine, first, I think,' said an enchanting American voice as the hand lifted the shaker. I peered further round the screen.

I saw a very small, slim lady of middle-age with her hair close on her head and drawn forward in a fringe over her brow. It was Miss Parker. We looked at each other and burst out laughing.

'Let's finish the whole shaker,' Miss Parker suggested.

I was so insignificant that with any luck no one at the lunch-party would notice my absence, and Miss Parker's eccentricities were well known.

'Let's,' I said enthusiastically.

Thus began my friendship with Dottie Parker, a friendship which, as I have said elsewhere, lasted until the day she died.

Ten minutes later, slightly tipsy, we walked arm-in-arm into the dining-room. We were placed next to one another at the long table. Elsa Maxwell was holding forth. She was as gross and bulky as Dottie was slim and small. She proceeded to tell a series of extremely unfunny anti-Jewish stories.

I remained silent, but my face must have registered my distaste, for Elsa Maxwell leaned her bulk on the table and addressed me.

'You don't seem to appreciate my stories, young man,' she said aggressively.

'I don't,' I heard my voice saying to my consternation. 'I don't appreciate anti-Semitism.'

As I spoke, a small hand clasped mine. It was Dottie. I did not then know that she was a Jewess. Perhaps Elsa's stories had been directed against her. Around the table people waited for Dottie to make a counter-attack. But she remained silent. Presently someone mentioned the name of Augustus John.

'Augustus John is one of my very dearest and most intimate friends,' Elsa trumpeted.

At that moment Dottie spoke. 'Indeed yes,' she murmured. 'Elsa knows Augustus John so intimately that she calls him Augustus *Jack*.'

Elsa glared at her. Dottie gave me a wink.

We stayed for a long time at table. Presently Willie and Gerald disappeared – probably so that Willie could have his afternoon siesta. And I must confess that the rest of the day remains slightly confused in my mind. Somehow I left the party with Dottie; somewhere we met Pamela Frankau and Humbert Wolfe. Both of them were already old friends of mine because I had met them through my sister Kate. They were a marvellous couple. Pamela was endowed with fantastic gifts: she was a successful novelist, extremely attractive, and she glowed with an infectious happiness and vitality, and an irrepressible sense of humour. Humbert was a delightful poet and an extraordinarily efficient civil servant. (He was the Permanent Under-Secretary to the Ministry of Labour.)

Though they can still be found in anthologies of the period, I am surprised that some of Humbert's lighter verse is not better known – or if it is ever quoted should so often be mis-attributed. Thus it was Humbert who wrote:

> You cannot hope to bribe or twist
> The honest British journalist.
> But when you think what he will do, unbribed,
> There's no occasion to.*

And it was Humbert who wrote:

> As this blind rose, no more than a whim of the dust,
> Achieved her excellence without intent,
> So man the casual sport of time and lust,
> Plans wealth and war, and loves by accident.†

Once the four of us had met, we went on a bar crawl along the Riviera. I seem to remember that we did not part for forty-eight hours, though I suppose at some stage we must have changed our clothes. At seven o'clock on the morning of the second day we were sitting sodden but undaunted at a little table outside a café in the old town of Nice, drinking coffee laced with cognac – except for Dottie who was drinking brandy neat. By this time I had noticed various quirks that appeared in Dottie's behaviour when the alcohol level in her blood became too high. Her first aberration was to claim that every young girl we saw with a man in a bar or a nightclub was about to be seduced, drugged, abducted and sold to the white slave traffic.

A few hours earlier, in a nightclub in Monte Carlo, she had wrested a young girl from the arms of a millionaire and deposited her with a week's rent in a pension in Nice. I met the girl later, and she told me the evening had been a great disappointment to her since she had been scheming for weeks to meet the millionaire who she had hoped would install her in a large apartment in Cannes. However, Dottie had been intransigent.

'Look at the man,' Dottie had said. 'He's got white slave-dealer written all over him. For what purpose do you imagine he's got

---

*Reproduced from a MS copy of the verse now in the possession of Mrs Ursula d'Arch Smith, sister of Pamela Frankau.
†Humbert Wolfe: *This Blind Rose*: Victor Gollancz, London: 1928.

that great yacht in the harbour he keeps talking about? To transport poor young girls to his dens of vice in Beirut and Cairo. And where do you think all that money he's splashing around comes from?'

'From baby-food,' we told her.

'Nonsense,' Dottie snorted. 'You've told me that before. So I went up and asked him outright, "Does your money come from baby-food?" I asked him. And he blushed scarlet. I know guilt when I see it.'

Her second quirk was to suppose that every horse she saw was vilely ill-treated. Now, as we sipped our coffee, I noticed that Dottie's gaze was fixed upon a horse attached to a cart which was delivering milk to a café on the other side of the little square. To protect the horse's head from the heat of noon or from the flies or as a result of some caprice of its master the animal was wearing a large straw hat through which its fluffy ears protruded. The horse's coat was glossy and its harness gleamed in the early morning sunshine. It was busy chewing hay from a nosebag. If ever I had seen a contented cart-horse, there it was. Unfortunately, in Dottie's eyes, it appeared very differently.

'Just look at that poor creature,' she cried. 'Standing there, wilting in the hot sun.'

'I wish the sun *were* hot,' said Humbert. 'I'm feeling chilly. I only wish I'd brought an overcoat.'

'Let's have some more café-cognacs,' Pamela suggested. 'They'll warm us all up.'

More drinks were ordered.

'To my certain knowledge, that horse has been standing outside that café without moving for half an hour,' said Dottie. 'Already it's sweating with fatigue.'

'That's not sweat,' I pointed out gently.

'But it's shining all over,' Dottie protested.

'It's coat is sleek because it's been very well groomed,' I replied.

But nothing that any of us could do or say had any effect on Dottie.

'Think of that poor horse,' she cried, 'having to stand for an hour in the blazing sunshine outside every café in the town.'

'Each time you mention the sunshine, I feel colder,' said Humbert.

But Dottie was no longer listening to us. In her eyes was the rapt expression of one who is going to perform an act of supreme goodness. 'We must buy that horse and set it free,' she announced with determination. Then she took a swig of brandy and turned to me. 'Robin,' she said. 'You seem to speak French like a native. Take my handbag. There's plenty of money in it. Go and buy that horse, however much it costs.'

'But what shall we do with the horse when we've bought it?'
I asked.

Dorothy finished her brandy and beckoned to the waiter for
another. 'In a big town like Nice there must be a home for retired
cart-horses,' said Dottie – who, I now realised, was getting a little
out of hand. 'If there's not a home, we'll start one.'

Feeling a complete idiot and trying to conceal Dorothy's
handbag as best I could, I crossed the square towards the plump
and contented-looking horse. As I neared it, I observed that it was
a mare. At that moment the mare's owner, the milkman, came out
of the café and gave her an affectionate slap on the rump. The
mare whinnied coyly. It was then that an idea came to me.

'Look,' I said to the milkman, 'I have a proposition to make to
you. It will take you less than half an hour, and it will gain you a bit
of money.'

As I spoke, the milkman's amiable face darkened in suspicion.
'What?' he asked fiercely.

'There's a very kind lady sitting at the café across the square,' I
began in explanation. 'She wants to buy your horse.'

'Buy my Fifi!' the man exclaimed indignantly. 'Not on your life.'

'Precisely,' I said soothingly. I then plunged my hand into
Dottie's handbag and produced several large banknotes which she
had won earlier at the Casino when she had put a *plaque* on number
eighteen *en plein* mistaking it for number twenty-eight. The
milkman eyed the notes with interest.

'Shall we go into this café for a quick drink?' I suggested, and
he nodded.

Five minutes later the deal was arranged. The milkman and I
went out and unharnessed Fifi from the milk-cart and led her,
still wearing her floppy straw hat, across the square to the waiting
Dottie.

'I have bought the horse,' I announced. And gave Dottie
back her handbag.

Dottie sprang to her feet in triumph. She embraced me. She
embraced Fifi. She embraced the milkman. Fifi was given lots of
sugar lumps which we unwrapped hastily from their paper
wrappings. Dottie ordered a bottle of champagne to celebrate.

'There's an excellent home for old cart-horses in Nice,' I
explained. 'It's a little way off, but the milkman has promised to
lead Fifi there.'

'You're sure he won't take her back into captivity?' Dottie
asked nervously.

'I'm certain,' I answered. And, in a way, I wasn't lying. For I was
sure that Fifi could in no way be described as being in servitude.

We finished the champagne. All four of us shook hands with
Fifi's 'former owner'. I suggested that we should take a taxi to
Villefranche and have a last drink before retiring to bed. I found

(*Opposite page*)
In 1936.

a taxi. Dottie gave Fifi a farewell kiss on her glossy neck. And as we drove off in the taxi, I could see Fifi being led happily back to her milk-cart. All five of us were contented – and so, I believe, was Fifi.

But the number of days I could spend with people who could for a while find nirvana through their vitality and intelligence – with the aid of a bottle in their pocket – was limited. In England I had met a young girl with whom I was in love, and I was wonderfully happy when we were together. I was also contented during my first two years at Cambridge where my parents allowed me to take the English Tripos before reading Law in my third year.

With my bisexual nature it was inevitable that at Cambridge I should be attracted to young men of my own age. But I never had an affair with an undergraduate of my choice either because of my stupid diffidence in England or because of his normality. I was very much aware that I was missing chances of nirvana that I might never find again. Only abroad, it seemed, could I hope to satisfy the wild yearning of my homosexual self. Only abroad could I find any hope of nirvana.

'When I see a withdrawn look on your face,' William said to me this afternoon as our cargo boat rolled gently along the west coast of Africa, 'I know you're living in the past.'

'I'm thinking of other searches for nirvana I've made in my life, and I'm trying to work out what went wrong with them.'

In the summer vacation from Cambridge, in 1936, soon after my twentieth birthday, I went to Salzburg with my sister Honor whom I adored – and still do. Though we both had little money we managed to see *Don Giovanni*, *Orpheo* and *Tristan and Isolde*. Then Willie Maugham's companion, Gerald Haxton, appeared in a Voisin coupé, and our existence changed abruptly. In his early forties, well-dressed, attractive and slim, very European though he was an American by nationality, Gerald exuded vitality and charm and money. Two years earlier he had tried to seduce me in Vienna; he now tried – without the slightest success – to persuade Honor to sleep with him. Unabashed, Gerald took us both to *The Meistersingers*. Wagner and schnapps went to his head. After supper, he insisted he had left his camera in Honor's bedroom and made one last ineffectual attempt to get her to bed. Then he said

goodnight to her affectionately, and swept me off to a *Bier-Stube*.

The beer hall seemed packed with fat middle-aged men in ample *Lederhosen* and boys in scanty ones. Gerald spoke to a waiter who evidently knew him. We were shown to one of the wooden tables and given mugs of lager.

'You look surprised, duckie,' Gerald said. 'Don't tell me you've been here a fortnight and haven't visited *this* place?'

'But it's true,' I replied.

'Gaze around, and just see what you've been missing,' Gerald proclaimed with a drunken wave of his hand, as if he were a magician who had produced the whole scene for my benefit. 'Let *that* teach you to travel with an elder sister.'

'But she understands,' I protested.

'She understands only too well,' Gerald laughed. 'But I also rather fancy she still disapproves.'

I was silent. I loved my three sisters. Indeed, we were an unusually united family. But I was aware that my sisters hoped that what they considered to be only a slight homosexual streak in my nature would disappear as I grew older. I tried to find something to say; I need not have bothered. Gerald's eyes were now staring at a boy who was leaning against the bar. I turned to look at the boy. At first glance, he did not appear to be very different from the others who were posed attractively at the bar-counter, waiting to be picked up. He was blonde with pale, corn-coloured hair which flopped over his gentle, slightly fleshy face.

'That's Dieter,' Gerald told me. 'He's a Viennese. He must be nearly seventeen by now. He's a good romp – if you're firm enough with him.'

Gerald raised his hand as he caught Dieter's attention. He beckoned to him. Obediently, Dieter left the bar, came over to our table, and gave Gerald a curt little bow of his head.

'*Servus,*' he said, smiling.

'Sit down,' Gerald told him. 'Sit down and have a drink with us.' Then he turned to me. 'Robin,' he said, 'this is Dieter. Dieter – this is Robin.'

It was when I shook hands with Dieter that I noticed his expression. Though he was smiling pleasantly, his eyes did not link with his appearance. His face showed subservience and a keen look of anticipation; his eyes, which were dark yet blue, proclaimed – or so it seemed to me – mistrust and a doubt that amounted almost to fear, yet in their expression there appeared an odd look which I tried to understand: it was the look of someone lost, someone who was yearning. Or had I transferred my own feelings to his gentle, soft, blonde features? Dieter sat down next to Gerald.

'How long have you been here, Dieter?' Gerald asked him, as the waiter produced a tankard of lager for him.

'*Zwei Wochen,*' Dieter answered. 'Two weeks.'

'I only arrived in Salzburg yesterday,' Gerald explained. 'Or I'd have been down here sooner.'

As Gerald spoke, he moved his chair close to Dieter. Then he slid his hand under the table. Dieter did not move. He was still smiling. Suddenly he winced.

'Not here,' he said to Gerald. '*Später vielleicht.*'

'I just wanted to make sure it was as good as ever,' Gerald laughed. 'And it *will* be later – don't you worry!'

Dieter gave a slight nod of his head. Gerald glanced at me, then turned back to Dieter and spoke in German – which he spoke badly, yet better than I did.

'My friend Robin is all of twenty years old,' he told Dieter. 'But he's shocked because he's pathetically romantic. He still can't understand what our lives are all about.'

Suddenly Dieter looked at me. This time I could not mistake the expression. It was one of complete sympathy. Then, abruptly, he turned towards Gerald. But Gerald had seen the look between us. Laughingly he waved his unsteady hand in my face, and leaned close towards me with his back to Dieter.

'Surely you've learned by now,' he said. 'Am I mistaken? Or do I not remember a previous episode of this kind? When, oh when, will you learn? A boy like Dieter doesn't want your love or your sympathy or your adoration. All he wants is to be thoroughly fucked and given the sum of money he's used to – or more, if he's been particularly amenable – and then to be sent home with the cash for his poor, starving mother. For never doubt it. Dieter has got a starving mother. They all have.'

Gerald swung away from me and faced Dieter.

'Have you got a starving mother?' he asked.

Dieter stared at him. For an instant his face trembled. Then he smiled as pleasantly as usual.

'Yes,' Dieter answered.

'You see!' Gerald cried in triumph. Then, as if to exclude me deliberately from their conversation, he began to talk to Dieter about well-known queers in Vienna. But although Dieter spoke brightly with his delightful smile, I could see that he was growing bored as Gerald's slurred words began to grow more confused. Gerald turned more frequently towards the bar.

'When are you going back to Vienna?' he asked Dieter.

'Soon,' the boy answered, pushing the floppy blonde hair back from his forehead. 'My holiday is finished. I must go back to my work.'

'With a good sum of money for your poor mother,' Gerald said as he lurched round towards me. 'Dieter works in a factory,' Gerald explained. 'But what he earns for the whole year is less than he makes during his holidays. Isn't that true, Dieter?'

'*Jawohl*,' Dieter answered. 'What Gerald says is true.'

'Then why don't you find yourself some rich protector?' Gerald enquired. 'There must be plenty of them about.'

'Not now,' Dieter answered. 'Since they killed Dollfuss there is no one rich except the Fascists.'

'Fascists in bed can't be any worse than Communists,' said Gerald.

'Yes,' Dieter replied. '*Das ist wahr*. But if I go with a Fascist, I can be made to work for the Fascists. And in Austria that can be dangerous for me.'

'See?' Gerald said to me. 'Dieter is a realist.'

Dieter stared at him with solemn eyes, while the waiter brought more drinks.

'My mother is *ein wenig krank* – a little ill. She can only do light laundry to make money,' Dieter said. 'My father has left us. I am the only one who can bring in the bread for us to eat.'

'So there you are!' Gerald exclaimed to me. 'Just like all the rest of them, he's playing for an extra tip. What's more, he'll get it – if he's good enough to deserve it. And I can tell you from experience – he knows the whole bag of tricks. The trouble is . . .'

But at that moment Gerald stopped. He had raised his head. He was staring at a young boy who had just come in and was standing at the bar. The boy was very young, perhaps fourteen, and he was less obviously dressed as 'rent' or 'trade' than Dieter. Probably to disguise his age he wore long trousers rather than the short *Lederhosen* of the other boys at the bar which could reveal as much of their sexual charm as they cared to show. But this boy's black gaberdine trousers were elegantly cut and contrasted with a fawn silk shirt. He was slender, with a pert little face and large brown eyes.

'Well, I never,' Gerald murmured to Dieter. 'That's little Felix. His old friend Rombach would never let him come out to a bar like this. Felix must have done something really naughty and been turned out.'

Gerald gulped down his schnapps and beckoned to the amiable waiter. 'Tell Felix to come over to our table and join us for a drink,' he said, pointing out Felix to the waiter. 'And bring us four beers and four more schnapps.'

'*Jawohl*,' said the waiter with a sly look and crossed the crowded room towards Felix.

I watched little Felix as the waiter spoke to him. At first he looked glum. Then as the waiter pointed to our table he recognised Gerald, and as if he had put on a different mask, his face was suddenly transformed: he became an eager yet innocent schoolboy, smiling in acquiescence at the master who was about to punish him. Immediately he moved with light steps towards us, and as he walked the gaberdine trousers displayed his trained, sinuous control of his muscles as well as did a stallion's coat in the *Spanische Reitschule*.

Gerald rose from the table and kissed him.

'*Mein Schatz*,' Gerald muttered. '*Mein lieber Felix*. Are you free? Are you free for me tonight?'

Felix smiled. His teeth were uneven but very white. He took a quick look round the room. Customers were beginning to leave the *Bier-Stube*.

'*Aber natürlich*,' he said. 'As you know, I am always free for my *Onkel Gerald*.'

Gerald finished the schnapps which the waiter had brought him. 'Now?' he asked. It might have been a command.

Little Felix glanced at me and then at Dieter. He gave a smirk. 'Do you want to leave such good company?' Felix asked coyly.

Gerald stood up. He was drunk. 'Why not?' he demanded.

Then he threw a bundle of banknotes towards me.

'Enjoy yourselves, children,' he said. 'Pay the bill, Robin. This party has been on me.' Gerald paused, and his bleary eyes looked for an instant at Dieter whose face was once again stiff and solemn. 'And one more thing, Robin,' he added. 'Give your new boy-friend what he's accustomed to – financially, I mean. He'll tell you his tariff. The rest I leave to you.'

Unsteadily Gerald moved towards the door. But I noticed that he turned to make sure that little Felix was following him. He need not have worried. Felix, with his trousers now seemingly plastered to his body, was following him, just as Gerald wanted, with a smile on his face and a look of utter subservience.

I was left alone with Dieter.

For a while we drank our lager in silence. Gerald's remark about paying Dieter his usual tariff had managed to subdue my sexual excitement. For it saddened and revolted me to think that if I were the grossly obese Austrian with warts on his flabby face who was sitting at the next table to us, I could still lie with Dieter's slender body clasped against mine – provided I paid 'the tariff'. I realised that I was perhaps stupidly romantic and prudish. But I was twenty years old; I had formed my own ideals, and I wanted to try to follow them.

'You look *traurig*,' Dieter said. 'Why are you sad?'

I smiled. 'I'm not sad,' I said. 'But this place is terribly hot and smoky.'

'Shall we go?'

'Let's have one more drink. I'm not feeling tired. Are you?'

Dieter stared at me. He was frowning with concentration as if he were trying to solve a complicated problem. Then the wrinkles vanished from his forehead and he smiled.

'Listen to me,' he said. 'I have an idea. We cannot go to my room for a last drink, because I share it with two friends, and the

Wirtin will not let me bring back friends. *Ausserdem*, we cannot go to your hotel because they will not let you take me in at this time of night. But I know a path that leads up the hillside. If we buy a bottle of *Kirschwasser* when we pay the bill, we can take the bottle with us and drink it and talk and stay there until the dawn breaks if we want to.'

Though I did not want to sleep with Dieter, I was already fond of him. I wanted to find out more about him and more about the life he led. I also liked Kirsch, the liqueur made from wild cherries.

'Right,' I said and beckoned to the waiter.

We paid the bill with the money Gerald had given me, bought the Kirsch and left the tavern. The night was pleasantly warm. There were no clouds in the sky; there was a full moon. Dieter found the path and led the way up the hillside. He was silent, but now and then he would turn round and give me a smile. The sadness I had felt in the tavern had gone. I was glad to be young and strong; I was happy to be with such an attractive companion.

Presently the path led to a gate beyond which lay a field with a hut in the lower corner of it. Dieter opened the gate. 'They use that hut to put the sheep in during winter,' he explained. Then Dieter pointed to a flat stretch of grass. 'If you like, we can sit there,' he said. 'We should be able to get a good view of the city at sunrise.'

Together we sat down. Dieter opened the bottle of Kirsch and handed it to me. Not only his well-made limbs, but his personality and soft smile attracted me.

'You drink first,' he said.

I took a swig. I could feel the liquid burning its way to my stomach. '*Wunderschön*,' I gasped. 'It's delicious. *Wunderbar*.'

Dieter grinned as I handed him the bottle.

'*Prost*,' he murmured and drank. Then he put a hand on my shoulder. 'Promise you won't leave till we have finished the bottle,' he said.

'I promise,' I answered solemnly.

'Where did you learn your German?' Dieter asked.

'I didn't,' I replied. 'As you can hear, it's *sehr schlecht*. Rotten. *Ich kann garnicht Deutsch*.'

'But you speak with the accent of Wien!' Dieter exclaimed.

'That's because I was staying in Vienna when I learned the little German I know,' I told him.

'When were you in Vienna?'

'Just over two years ago.'

'Think of it!' Dieter cried. 'We might have met. In fact, you may have seen me without knowing it. My two beats were the Kärtner Strasse and the main Bahnhof – railway stations are always a good place to get picked up.'

I stared at him. 'How old are you, Dieter?' I asked.

'Seventeen.'

'And you were getting picked up at the age of fifteen?'

'*Sicher*,' he answered. '*Warum nicht?* I was only thirteen when I was first broken in.'

'How did that happen?'

'It just came about,' Dieter answered. 'Perhaps I was lucky. Perhaps I was unlucky. It's too late to worry about it now.'

'But *how* did it happen?'

'Why do you want to know?'

'Because I like you,' I replied. 'Because I'm interested in you.'

Dieter gazed at me for an instant in silence. With a quick movement he pushed the blonde hair back from his forehead.

'When you've only known me for a few hours?' he murmured.

'Yes.'

Dieter nodded his head as if in agreement. He took a gulp from the bottle and handed it to me.

'*Na also*. If you want the truth, here it is,' he said. 'Very well. During the school holidays I used to make pocket-money by working as a ball-boy at some tennis courts in the town. I realise now that I was paid very little – but then to me it was a fortune. Almost every afternoon towards five there was an Englishman, perhaps forty years old, who used to come and play tennis with an Austrian of his own age. At that time, all I knew about the Englishman was what I had overheard at the tennis club. I knew that he was unmarried and a businessman. But though the Austrian sometimes gave me a smile, this Englishman never even glanced at me. It was always the Austrian who threw me a tip at the end of the game.'

All the time he was talking, Dieter was watching me.

'One afternoon at five o'clock,' Dieter continued, 'I was waiting on the court as usual for the two of them. Soon the Englishman appeared, but not the Austrian. "Have you seen Herr Dirksen?" he called out to me. He spoke almost perfect German. "No," I answered. At that moment a servant came out from the club-house to announce that Herr Dirksen had telephoned to say he had been delayed at a meeting and regretted that he could not come. "Right," said the Englishman and began to walk away. Suddenly he stopped and turned round towards me.

' "Come here," he said. I moved quickly towards him.

' "You'd better have your tip as usual," he said. He put his hand in his pocket and then tossed me a coin.

'Well, I was so surprised he should even think of me – let alone give me a tip – that I missed the catch. The coin fell on the ground. I stooped down to pick it up. When I stood up again, I saw the tip was the largest I'd ever been given.

' "Thank you, sir," I said to him. And I really meant it. Then, for the first time – for the very first time, the Englishman really looked at me. He looked at me from my untidy hair down to my broken gym shoes.

' "What's your name?" he asked in a cold voice.

' "Dieter," I told him.

' "How old are you?"

' "Thirteen," I answered.

'When I spoke he scowled as if I'd said something to annoy him. ' "You can't be only thirteen," he exclaimed.

' "*Aber wirklich*," I said. "Honestly, sir. I'm thirteen."

' "Then you're tall for your age," he said.

'I was silent. He was staring at me with such anger in his face that for a moment I was afraid he would strike me. Then I noticed that his gaze was no longer fixed on my face. The shorts I was wearing were too small for me. I had begged for a new pair, but my mother had said that there was no money. She couldn't afford such useless purchases, she said. It was summer. My skin is very fair, but it goes quite brown in the sun. The Englishman was staring at my thighs which were completely exposed by my small shorts. He turned away, and I thought he was leaving. But his gaze stayed fixed. He couldn't control his eyes. His expression was now so strained that I was afraid of him. I wanted to run away. I had a feeling that something terrible was about to happen. I longed to go, but I couldn't move. His hands had begun to tremble. By now I was really frightened. Suddenly he took in a long, deep breath and then let it out. Then he spoke. His voice was very hoarse.

' "Dieter," he said. "Would you like a present of money? A present twenty times as much as the tip I gave you?"

'I did not reply. I remained silent, for I had suddenly understood what it was all about. I had overheard boys talking about it at school, but I didn't quite know what happened.

' "Answer me," the Englishman said. "Think of it. Twenty times the amount of the tip I gave you. At least twenty times. You understand what I mean? I can see from your face that you do. So answer me, Dieter. I promise I won't hurt you."

'At that moment I realised that he was more frightened than I was. And it was this fact – in addition to the sum of money he was offering – which made up my mind for me.

' "Yes," I muttered.

'The Englishman sighed. His hands were now trembling horribly.

' "And you'll never tell anyone?" he said hoarsely.

' "No," I muttered.

' "You swear it?"

' "I swear it."

'He turned his head nervously to make sure that no one was observing our conversation. But there was no one about.

' "I don't want anyone to see us leaving in my car. *Verstehst Du?* So you'll have to make your own way to my flat. Do you think you can do that?"

' "*Natürlich*," I said. "Of course I can."

'Then he repeated his address several times, and made me repeat it back to him. It wasn't far away from the tennis club. "My flat's on the top floor," he explained to me. "So you ring the top bell outside the front door. I'll come down to let you in. Do you understand? The top bell. I'll be waiting for you. There's no concierge to worry about."

' "I understand," I answered.

' "Then I'll see you in about half an hour's time," he said and walked quickly away from me.

'I found my way to the address easily,' Dieter continued. 'I pressed the top bell as instructed, and a few moments later the man opened the door and let me in. Hurriedly he closed the door behind me. He said no word of greeting. In silence he led me up the stairs and showed me into his flat – or, as we'd call it, *Wohnung*. Carefully he bolted the door behind us. We crossed a small hall and entered a large living-room. Immediately I noticed that the curtains were half-drawn. The room was comfortably furnished with some *fabelhaft* paintings on the walls and a thick carpet on the floor. He pointed to a sofa. "Sit down," he said – and those were the first words he had spoken to me since I entered the building. "The maid who looks after me always leaves at five in the afternoon, so we've got the place to ourselves. We shan't be disturbed. By the way, would you care for a glass of lemonade?"

' "Please, sir," I said.

'He went to the sideboard and poured me a glass, brought it to me, and sat down on the sofa, close beside me. "When we're alone together, you don't have to call me 'sir'," he muttered.

'I could see that his hands were now shaking with nerves, and while he'd been waiting for me he must have had several drinks from the decanter on the sideboard because his breath reeked of liquor. He stared at me in silence while I drank my lemonade.

' "Do you live with your parents?" he asked me after a while.

' "Yes," I told him.

' "Do you get on with them?"

' "I get on with my mother," I answered truthfully. "But not with my father."

' "Why not?"

' "Because when he drinks he becomes *ein Teufel*. A devil."

' "Does he beat you?"

' "Sometimes."

' "Have you any brothers or sisters?"

' "No. I'm the only child."

'The man was silent. He was breathing heavily. I'd finished my drink, but I was still thirsty. "Some more lemonade?" he asked. I nodded my head. His nervousness had infected me. I found it hard not to shiver. The man leaned across me and put my glass on a side-table. Then he began to stroke my head. I didn't move. "You've got a fine mop of hair and it's a glorious colour," he mumbled. His trembling hand now touched my cheek and pressed against it. "And very soft skin," he said, speaking almost to himself. He drew away from me. "Dieter," he said in his hoarse voice, "you're sure you're not going to mind this? Because we can stop at any moment you like, and I'll still give you a present. Would you like to leave?" I shook my head. Suddenly he gave a long sigh and bent down and kissed my forehead. "Oh Dieter," he whispered. "You're wonderfully sweet, and I'm mad for you." Then he began to kiss my mouth and my neck. As he kissed me, his hand had begun to stroke my thigh nearest him, running his fingers up and down my skin, then clenching my thigh so hard I winced. "I'm sorry," he muttered. "I must remember how soft your skin is." Presently, he began to undo the buttons of my shorts. I did not move. Nor did I try to stop him when his hand slid between my legs. Presently he led me to his bedroom and stripped me naked. Then he took off his own clothes.'

Until that moment Dieter had been gazing at me constantly, as if to assess the effect that his story was having on me. But now he turned away and began to pluck at the blades of grass beside him.

'For a man so strong, he was very gentle,' Dieter continued, staring down at the grass. 'He tried not to hurt me. And eventually he managed to get me excited too. When it was all over he held me in his arms. Soon he went to sleep, and so did I. When I awoke, I saw from the clock on his bedside table that it was after eight o'clock. I would get scolded for missing supper. I turned to awake the Englishman, but he was already awake. And for the first time he smiled. "When I awoke I couldn't imagine for a moment what beautiful person could be lying in my arms. Then I remembered." He leaned forward and kissed me. "Oh Dieter," he said, "you've given me such happiness. Promise me you'll come here again." He looked at me so earnestly that I didn't like to disappoint him. "All right," I replied. "I promise." Again he smiled, and his face now looked quite different. He seemed far younger. "Dieter," he said, "what about some cold food? There's masses laid out for me."

' "I must go home," I told him. "I'll get scolded for being so late as it is."

' "I tell you what," he said, "in addition to your present, I'll give you some extra money for a taxi. You can take the taxi to a few streets away from where you live. That will save you time.

Please stay and have some food with me."

'So I stayed a while longer with him,' Dieter continued. 'And over supper – strangely enough, considering the difference of age between us – we became friends. He was no longer at all nervous. Nor was I. And I began to like him – perhaps because he never talked down to me. He treated me as an equal. For instance, he insisted that when we were alone together I should call him by his Christian name – Tony. He told me stories about his life in England, where he'd worked for a big insurance company. He made me eat far more than I'd ever done. He gave me double the money I'd expected, together with careful instructions for hiding it from my parents. His instructions were so expert that I smiled.

' "What are you smiling at, young Dieter?" he enquired.

' "I'm smiling because your instructions for hiding cash are so expert that I realise I'm not the first boy you've taken to bed with you."

'Suddenly he looked sad. "No. You're not," he answered. "But there has only been one other."

' "Here in Wien?"

' "No. In England," he replied. "But he was several years older than you are. He was seventeen when I first met him. He had red hair, and his name was Alec."

' "Where is he now?"

' "I don't know," Tony answered. "He left me to get married. Alec and his wife decided to go and live in Australia. Perhaps he's still there."

' "Have you ever been married?" I asked.

'Tony smiled. "Never," he replied. "And I don't suppose I ever will." '

Dieter lay back on the grass and gazed up at the stars. His *Lederhosen* had rucked up, and I noticed that the skin of his lean thighs was still very brown and very smooth.

'That very evening,' Dieter continued, 'Tony and I arranged that if it was safe for me to visit the apartment he'd give me a sign at the end of his game of tennis by casually putting his right hand to the back of his head. For a whole year I used to visit Tony, the Englishman, in his apartment – at least three or four times a week. After a while, I came to look forward to the visits. You see, I'd grown fond of him. Apart from my mother, he was the only person who had ever shown any interest in me. Besides, by now, Tony was in love with me. And I soon found I enjoyed going to bed with him as much as he did going to bed with me. I no longer liked accepting his presents of money. But I needed the cash. Because in the terrible poverty and unemployment that had now spread over Austria, with little businesses going broke and factories closing down, my father was sacked from his job. One morning he left the house without a word to my mother. He never returned. We suspected that he had joined one of the secret Fascist organisations who would take on any tough – so long as he was ruthless. Anyhow, we haven't seen him since. As I told you, my mother is crippled from arthritis, and she cannot go out to work. Soon we had not enough to eat. So I lifted the floorboard in my room where I had hidden part of the cash Tony had given me and gave her most of it for the household – on the condition that she would never question me about where it came from. I only assured her that I had not stolen it. My mother took the money and said nothing, but I think that even then she must have suspected.

'When I began to give my mother money for the housekeeping every week, she must have known that I hadn't earned it on the tennis court. But since then I've talked with dozens of boys like me. They've all told me that their mothers *must* know for certain that they're on the game. A mother may be virtually sure that her son goes with men, these boys have told me, but so long as she doesn't know completely and utterly *for certain*, she will manage somehow not to be concerned about it.

'For another six months all went well,' Dieter continued. 'Tony had started giving me English lessons, and it gave me pleasure to see the pride he took in my progress. Now that my father had left the house, it didn't matter so much if I came home late. We were both of us happy. Then trouble began. Neither Tony nor his Austrian friend appeared at the tennis club for three days running. I was worried because they used to play tennis almost every day. Tony didn't have a telephone in the apartment, and I didn't know his office number. Even if I had, I wouldn't have wanted to disturb him at his work. I didn't want to go round to his apartment in case he was entertaining guests and my appearance might give away our secret. I suppose I could have written, but Tony had warned me against putting anything on paper that might be compromising. However, on the sixth day, I decided I must see Tony – whatever the risk. If there were people with him when he opened the door, I'd say I'd come to the wrong address and run off.

'My heart was thumping when I rang the top bell. I waited on the doorstep for so long that I was beginning to think he must be out. Then the door opened and Tony appeared. But I could hardly recognise him. His hair was untidy, his face was haggard and mottled; I could see that he'd been drinking heavily.

' "You can't come in," he said hurriedly. "Go quickly. I'll meet you at the Café Hirt. It's a small café in the third street on the right going towards the Ring. There's a back room. Wait for me there." Then he shut the door.

'I still couldn't imagine what had gone wrong. Half an hour later Tony appeared in the back room of the café. He was carrying a despatch case which he put under the table as he sat down opposite me. I was drinking lemonade as usual. Tony ordered himself a double brandy.

' "I daren't stay long," he said. "So I'll make it as short as I can. A week ago I had a visit from the police. They told me that they had been given information that I'd been entertaining a very young boy in my flat. He'd stay there for several hours, they stated, and he'd been seen going there over a long period of time. I'd been denounced, in fact. And I think I know by whom. It must have been someone in the building – because the police knew the exact time you'd arrive and the exact time when you'd leave. I believe I was denounced by that fat woman with dyed hair in the flat below mine. She's always complaining about something – I play my radio far too loud or my bath-water leaks into her kitchen. Anyhow the harm has been done. The police asked for your name and address. That gave me some hope – because it meant they couldn't have got hold of you to question you. I refused to give them any information about you. I told them that I refused to answer any questions whatsoever – except in the presence of my lawyer. I ignored their threats, and presently they left."

'Tony stared down at the table-cloth. "When I told you that you were the second boy I'd loved in my life, it wasn't a lie," he continued. "But there was one thing I didn't tell you because I thought it was better you shouldn't know. When Alec left me to marry his girl, I was terribly upset. I felt desperately lonely. I began drinking. One night in London I went out drunk and picked up a boy. He was about sixteen and obviously a prostitute, but I didn't care. I took him back to my flat. But the police were after the boy because he was not only a tart but a thief. He was arrested. He had made a note of my address. The police found this on him. They questioned him about me. He claimed I had got him drunk and seduced him. My flat was searched. They found evidence. I was prosecuted. It was thanks to a good lawyer that I was only given a suspended sentence which meant I didn't have to go to prison. But the episode was reported in the newspapers. It was to escape the scandal I eventually came to Austria. If the Vienna police find out about the case, then all the denials that you and I could make wouldn't help us. Besides, I know a bit about police methods in this town. If you don't talk they'll beat you up until you *do* confess. And I'm afraid that somehow they may trace you."

'Tony took a gulp of his brandy. His hand was shaking. "There's only one solution," he said. "I must leave the country. If I leave, they won't worry about you. So I've settled my business affairs. I've packed. I'm leaving tomorrow. I've brought a farewell present for you. I have only one question to ask you. It is this, Dieter. If I found a safe place for us to live together, would you join me?"

'I couldn't speak. I just nodded my head.

' "Thank you," he mumbled. "I hoped you'd say that. I've got your address. From what you've told me, I don't suppose there's any danger of your mother opening a letter addressed to you?"

' "No danger," I said.

' "Then I'll write."

'Tony opened his despatch case and handed me a thick envelope. "Put that in your pocket," he said, and he couldn't control the trembling of his voice. "By the time you've spent it, I hope I'll be able to send you a train ticket so you can join me, and we'll live together for good."

'Tony gave some money to the old waiter. "Stay here for a few minutes after I've gone, and then go straight home," he told me. "I won't say goodbye. I'll say *Aufwiedersehen*."

'Then Tony got up from the table and walked quickly from the room.'

Dieter sat up and clasped his knees with his hands. For a while he was silent.

'At the end of a month there was still no letter from him,' he said. 'At the end of two months the money he'd given me had been spent. After a time I gave up all hope.

'It was then that I started my search. I wanted to find another man like Tony – not only because I was short of money, but because I was lonely. I'd never been able to get on well with boys of my own age. Their jokes and conversation bored me. A man as kind and as intelligent as Tony was what I needed. And at last I thought I'd found one. I was strolling down the Kärtner Strasse and had stopped outside a shop that sold leather-ware. From the reflection in the window I saw a man standing near to me. He was well-dressed and powerfully built. For a wonderful moment I thought it was Tony. Then, as I turned to look at him, I saw the difference. His face was more pale and a little fatter, and perhaps he was a few inches taller. He had noticed my glance. He smiled at me. By then I was fourteen, and, as Tony had remarked, tall for my age. When I smiled back at him, I could see that the man fancied me from the way he was examining me. I felt that in his mind he was stripping me naked. He gave a little laugh.

' "Shall we go and have a coffee somewhere?" he asked. He spoke with a slight German accent.

' "All right," I replied. "*Ist gut*."

'The German smirked. "I think an invitation to coffee is the appropriate opening," he said as if he had not heard my answer. "I would invite you to my hotel, but at seven o'clock in the evening it might upset their sense of what is correct."

'I thought quickly. I had heard of a cheap lodging-house where

66

men could take under-age girls or boys.

' "I know of a place," I said.

' "With a clean bed, I hope," the German answered.

' "*Bestimmt*," I replied. "And we can walk there."

' "Splendid," he answered. "You walk ahead, and I will follow you. I think we might become close friends."

'Getting into the place was easier than I had supposed. As soon as we had reached our room, the German locked the door and took me in his arms. "How long can you stay?" he asked. "Till midnight if you like," I replied.

' "We'll see," he grunted and began taking off his clothes. He was bigger than Tony, but I wasn't afraid. I stripped quickly and lay down on the bed.

' "*Fabelhaft*," he muttered. "Now we can really enjoy ourselves." '

Dieter glanced at me and then turned away.

'He was very rough with me,' Dieter said. 'But I hadn't made love since Tony left. Only by myself. So I was excited, and I let him do what he pleased. We made love several times. Then he got up from the bed and began to dress. He had already paid for the room. He now took out his wallet again and handed me some money.

' "Thanks for the fun," he said.

' "When can we meet again?" I asked.

'He smiled at me. But I could see that it was a smile of contempt. "We can't meet again," he announced. "I leave for Berlin tomorrow." Somehow I felt he was lying.

' "But you said you wanted us to be close friends," I blurted out.

'He laughed. "And haven't we been close?" he demanded. "We could hardly have been any closer. And now I've given you the appropriate present, *aren't* we friends?"

'Perhaps there must have been bitterness in my voice, for suddenly he looked at me with open dislike. "I can't speak for other men," he said. "But so far as I am concerned I believe in the Chinese proverb. *No man bathes in the same river twice*. But I've adapted it to boys. And so far as I'm concerned no man should go up the same arse twice. *Gute Nacht*." And with that, he left the room.'

Dieter took out a crumpled packet of cigarettes from his pocket, lit two, and handed me one.

'You'd have thought I'd have given up after that. But I didn't. I still was determined to find another Tony. Besides, I needed the cash. But I never found a man who was interested in me as a person. They just wanted to lie with me, have me for one or two nights – and that was the end of it. Gradually I became more or less resigned to the treatment I'd get. Soon I came to expect it.

If they were especially brutal or unpleasant – and you can have no idea how vicious and brutal and dirty men can be in their tastes – I'd object. Otherwise I'd let them do as they pleased.

'My mother's illness was worse, and she was sent to hospital. I was worried. I went to see her whenever I could. But her illness had this advantage. I now had the house to myself. So at night when the neighbours were asleep I could bring back a client. I'd grown careless in my choice by now. Any man of any age – provided he looked as if he'd got money to spare – could pick me up for the night. But every morning when I'd open the letter-box I'd hope to find a letter from Tony. But I never did. In fact, I've never heard from him. Perhaps he had an accident. Perhaps in despair he picked up another boy prostitute in London and was arrested. I don't suppose I'll ever know. So I just carried on with my whoring.

'However, as you're aware, in the heat of summer men like our friend Gerald don't go to Vienna. The opera is closed, and there's nothing to do, so they come to places like Salzburg. By this time I'd left school and found work in a radio factory. At least it gave me a rest from endless patrols up and down the streets. So in the summer holidays I become a *Wandervogel* – "a bird of passage", I suppose you could call it. And my wanderings would generally take me to Salzburg.'

Dieter swung round and looked at me.

'Are you shocked?' he asked.

'Heavens, no,' I said. 'I expect I'd have done the same if I'd been in your place and had got your looks.'

'But you have got my looks.'

I laughed. 'What nonsense!' I said.

'What's more, you always did have.'

I stared at him. 'What on earth makes you say so?'

Dieter gave me a mysterious look and smiled.

'Tell me, Dieter. How can you possibly tell? And it's not true anyhow.'

'I know about you,' Dieter announced.

'How?'

'Can't you guess? From Gerald.'

'But you only met Gerald tonight.'

'Correct,' Dieter said. 'But how do you think he knew my name? Can't you see? I met Gerald in Salzburg two years ago. That first night before he took me off to a lodging-house of a kind, we had several drinks together. As usual, Gerald was drunk, and he began telling me his secrets.'

Dieter took a gulp of kirsch and handed me the bottle. 'Can't you remember what happened two years ago?' he asked.

'No,' I answered.

'But you must remember. You've just told me you were

staying in Vienna. It was in Vienna you first met Gerald. *Nicht wahr?* He fell for you. And a few weeks later he sent you a railway ticket to Venice so you could both meet there. True or not?'

'True,' I replied.

'In Venice, Gerald tried to have you,' Dieter continued. 'But you told him you could only go to bed with boys of your own age. *Nicht wahr?* So a few days later Gerald drove you back to Vienna, and left you there. From Vienna Gerald came to Salzburg. It was that very night I first met him.'

I gaped at Dieter. 'Gerald told you?' I exclaimed.

'Remember Gerald had by then become very drunk,' Dieter said. 'And I think he was still a bit in love with you. He couldn't stop talking about you. He even showed me a photograph of you. You'd been swimming, and you were naked. As soon as I saw the photo I was excited by it. I found it very attractive. I wanted to keep it. But Gerald wouldn't let me.'

Dieter was silent, and I began to wonder. Why had he wanted to keep the photograph? Why had he told me the story of his life in such detail? Was it possible? Could Dieter possibly be attracted to me? Perhaps. . . . But at that instant Dieter spoke, and for the first time the tone of his voice was bitter.

'You probably just pity me,' he said. 'And there's reason enough for pity. You've never done as I have. You wouldn't even go to bed with Gerald. But I've been to bed with anyone who wanted me – old men who needed special fondling to get a hard on, men who wanted dirty sex as a change from their wives, and boys who were just bursting for a fuck. And at the end of the whole performance, it just meant nothing to them – no more than their nightly piss before turning in. I loathe the lot of them. Sometimes I dream that I'll win a lottery and become rich. And then, I'd never let anyone touch my body again. Never.'

Dieter put a hand on my shoulder. 'I shouldn't have told you all that,' he muttered. '*Ich bin besoffen.* I'm drunk.'

I took out of my pocket the money that Gerald had left behind – together with all the money of my own I was carrying. I gave it to Dieter.

'Thanks,' he said. Then he examined the notes and looked up at me suspiciously. 'There's more here than Gerald left behind,' he announced.

'I don't think so,' I said.

Dieter's eyes peered at my face. Then he grinned. 'You're lying,' he laughed. 'Take some of it back. I won't take your money.'

'Yes, you will,' I said and tried to put the money in his pocket. But he was too quick for me. His hand grasped my wrist, but I was three years older than Dieter. Though I was laughing I managed to pull away his wrist. Then we began to wrestle. But

he too was laughing and I managed to press the money into his
shirt pocket. But while we had wrestled I had felt the softness of
his body, and the strength of him. We lay back exhausted on the
grass.

'You know you're the only person I've ever told about Tony,'
Dieter said suddenly. 'So I might as well explain the rest. I don't
want a lover to go to bed with. I want a friend. If I found a friend,
I'm sure the rest would follow. I'm certain of it. But I'm lonely.
You can have no idea how lonely I feel.'

Dieter took a sip of the kirsch.

'When Gerald talked about you,' Dieter continued, 'he said
that deep down you were a lonely person. Perhaps that's why I've
thought about you so much. Perhaps that's why I always hoped to
meet you – because I felt sure we could be friends.'

Dieter rolled over and pressed his face into the grass.

'Do you think I'm *ganz verrückt*?' he asked. 'Quite mad?'

'No.'

'Then listen to me, Robin,' Dieter said. 'I promise you I'm
not saying this because I'm drunk. Come with me to Vienna.
Come and live in my little *Wohnung*. I'd do my best to make you
comfortable. I'm certain we'd be happy together. You would
be the only person I'd go with, I promise it. We could live so
wonderfully together. I'd do all the housework. I'm used to it.
And while I was working at the factory, you could find a job –
translating or giving English lessons. Please, Robin. Come to
Vienna with me.'

I looked at this boy lying beside me. He was the most attractive
person I had ever seen, and there was a sweetness and gentleness
about him I have found hard to describe – together with an almost
heartbreaking wistfulness. Lying next to me was my nirvana. In
all of my life I would probably never have a chance like this
again. I could love Dieter; I loved him already. To live with him
would be to attain nirvana. Even if the bliss was only transitory it
would have been worthwhile. My spirit rose with the exaltation
of the existence I contemplated.

Then came the misty clouds of my conscience and of my eternal
guilt. If I left with this lovely boy I would always be fretted by
worries when I thought of my mother and my sisters who would
be concerned about me. I would fail to get a degree; I would not
pass my law exams. I would be living in an alien country without
any qualifications, and already war seemed inevitable. Moreover,
I had the sense to understand that if I left with Dieter for even a
fortnight of happiness in Vienna – which in my elated drunken
condition I was sure I could do by making excuses to my sister
Honor and by borrowing money from Gerald if he had not yet
left to join Willie in Bad Gastein – it would only make things
worse. For to leave Dieter after only two weeks would cause both

of us more unhappiness than the pleasure we had gained.

Gently I tried to explain this to Dieter. I could see his eyes give a little flinch of pain with each argument I produced. When I had finished he was silent. Suddenly he shivered. 'It's cold,' he said. 'Let's go into the hut.'

The stars were now pale in the sky. Dawn was approaching. For a while we watched the golden light spread over the domes and spires of the city.

'You've given me more money than Gerald,' Dieter said. 'Let's go into the hut. I wouldn't mind making love to you. I'm sure I wouldn't. In fact, I'm certain. And then . . . then perhaps you'd change your mind about coming with me to Vienna.'

I began to wonder if the hut was not a place he had used to take some of his clients when he needed money.

'Listen, Dieter,' I said quietly. 'You see from my eyes that I feel the same about you as you say that you feel about me. But we've drunk too much. I understand all you've told me about having to go to bed with anyone who will pay you. I've given you money. But I don't want to take advantage of the fact. Let's wait. Let's meet at the *Bier-Stube* this evening. Then we can try to make some plan. And if you still want to, maybe we can take a room some-where.'

Dieter gaped at me.

'But I thought you knew,' he blurted out. 'I thought I'd told you. I have to catch the first train. I have to report to my factory.'

Dieter was shaking with nerves. It was as if he had withdrawn from a deep dream to find himself in a waking nightmare of reality. He clutched at my wrist and looked at my watch.

'It's late,' he said. 'We must go straight to the station.'

'What about your clothes?'

'Clothes!' he cried. 'But I'm a *Landstreicher*. I've got no clothes here. If my shirt gets dirty I wash it – or some man buys me a new one. Come. We must go.'

Dieter scrambled to his feet and pulled me up. Together we hurried down the hill.

As we approached the *Bahnhof* he turned to me. 'I have my ticket,' he said. 'Come on to the platform. But don't watch the train leaving the station. *Das bringt Unglück.* It brings bad luck.'

The train was already waiting. It was crowded. Dieter held my shoulders, leaned forward, and kissed my lips. There were tears in his dark blue eyes.

'*Ach* Robin, *mein Schatz*, my dear Robin,' he said in a choked voice, 'if only you'd understood why I climbed the hill with you to the hut.'

The train gave a jolt as if preparing to move. Dieter sprang on to the steps of the carriage. At that moment, despite my drunken-ness, I remembered.

'I haven't got your address,' I cried.

'But Gerald gave me yours,' Dieter said.

He had let his floppy corn-coloured hair fall over his forehead – perhaps on purpose – so that it veiled his eyes.

'Dieter,' I said, 'promise me that you'll write to me.'

'Yes, Robin. *Mein Lieber*. Yes, I'll write.'

I could see that his cheeks were now wet with tears.

'Perhaps one day you'll understand,' he said. Then he began to sob. Abruptly he turned and disappeared into the over-crowded carriage.

He never wrote to me – or if he did, the letter never reached me. I never heard of Dieter or saw him again.

But I did understand. Even before I had walked up the hill and gone into the hut where, in a corner, I found an old blanket – and a soiled towel. I had understood it already.

I understand it now all the more. In fact, with each month and year that I live, I understand that perhaps I had irretrievably lost a chance of finding the nirvana I sought.

I returned to Cambridge to study law. Later I studied at a law school in London for the next three years. I think these were the gloomiest years in my life because I was now certain that a world war would break out at any moment. In fact, it was almost a relief when it came because one's imagination is always worse than reality.

The war, as a trooper in England and then as an officer fighting in tanks in the Western Desert, taught me that there were men from every walk of life who shared my homosexual inclinations. The war also determined me to escape from the prison of my environment and home – should I survive.

When I returned from the Middle East to London, I found that various friends of mine had discovered some sort of nirvana with a young companion who lived permanently with them in their flat. But, alas, two of them had been sent to prison for what was then an illegal relationship. Moreover, my parents were still alive. I adored my mother and my sisters; they often visited the little house in Chelsea close to Cadogan Square which my mother had found for me. A boyfriend such as Dieter, if I could ever find him again or if he had survived the war, seemed impossible. Yet I felt young, ardent and vigorous.

I had developed an intense interest in the Arab lands; from time to time I would take on assignments as a journalist in the Middle

East in order to escape from the prison which my existence in London seemed to have become. When I was only twenty-two years old, Willie started a conversation with me with the words: 'Now that you are positively middle-aged . . .'. I was now thirty-one. I felt I wanted to discover my own nirvana before I grew too old.

It was while I was staying in Alexandria with my friend and benefactor, Eric Duke, to whom my novel *The Servant* is dedicated, that I heard of a place which might offer a chance of nirvana to me. It was an oasis in the Libyan Desert, politically part of Egypt, and lay about three hundred and fifty miles west south-west of Cairo across a vast stretch of desert. In those days it was very hard to reach. Siwa's very remoteness had helped preserve customs which had survived from the days of Herodotus – and before. One of its more unusual customs was the marriage of a man to a boy.

Now, I have already quoted Freya Stark's review of the short book I eventually wrote about Siwa. I must now quote a few more lines from it.

The article in *The Observer* was headed, RETICENT TRAVELLER. 'It is strange, when one thinks of it, how we hesitate over sodomy . . . when contemplating the history of Egypt,' Freya Stark had commented. '*The fact is we would like Robin Maugham to let himself go a little more.*' (My italics)

However, my family and their friends were still alive. What Harold Nicolson called 'the nursery governess' who he maintained peered disapprovingly over the shoulder of every English writer of a certain class, was still over-looking mine. I could not help feeling reticent.

But in the last few years my whole life has altered, and I can now fill in the parts of the text which the 'nursery governess' suppressed. I can fill in all the gaps. Moreover, I can also use portions of the text of my book which is very little known.

As I moved around Egypt, I began to hear fascinating stories about Siwa. Not only was it very beautiful, but homosexuality was considered as normal as heterosexuality. In 1926, for instance, it seemed that an English official had expressed a desire to visit the oasis. Accordingly the Egyptian Minister for the Interior had mounted an impressive expedition to ensure the English official's safety across the sea of sand. They then set forth. After an arduous journey they had reached 'the town' – as the Egyptians called the village – and had found all the inhabitants happily celebrating a wedding.

'What an auspicious moment to arrive,' had declared the conventional official.

'Most charming,' the Egyptian official had agreed.

They approached closer. The bridal procession came to a halt. They were introduced to the bridegroom and the bride. It was

74

The town of Siwa.

then that the full horror of the spectacle struck them. The bridegroom was a man of forty and the bride was a boy of fifteen.

Indignantly the expedition returned to Cairo. Promptly the finest preacher who could be spared from the mosque was sent out to convert the Siwans from their vile habits.

A few years later another expedition was mounted to visit this distant oasis. Once again they arrived with the same Egyptian Minister of the Interior. And once again a marriage was in progress. But this time the procession was still more magnificent than previously, and the bridal couple was carried under a canopy covered with a golden cloth. Yet again the procession came to a halt. Once more the expedition was introduced to the bridegroom and the bride. This time the expedition discovered that the bridegroom was none other than the Imam himself and his bride was a boy of fourteen.

I knew that my young Egyptian friends sometimes exaggerated, and these stories seemed to be too good to be true. But I was so fascinated by what they told me that I decided to take the trouble to look up the authorities.

'*The feast of marrying a boy was celebrated with great pomp, and the money paid for a boy sometimes amounted to fifteen pounds, while the money paid for a woman was a little over a pound besides the clothes which do not exceed two or three pounds for this abnormal marriage,*' says Steindorff in his *Amonsoase*.

'*Their passions are easily roused . . . ,*' says T. B. Hohler in his *Report on the Oasis of Siwa*, published in 1900, '*and the morals of either sex are said to overstep all limits of decency.*'

(Even in modern days I am amused to read that '. . . *even in the twentieth century its local customs were still thriving including homosexuality to the point of an all male marriage.*')*

Though it would mean obtaining endless permits from Egyptian officials, I determined to go to Siwa. A friend of Eric Dukes', Dimitri Papadimos, known to his friends as 'Taki', of about my own age, who had been in the Greek Airforce during the war was longing to photograph Siwa. The photographs which illustrate this section were all taken by him. So we met and made plans to go there together that very winter. The problems of transport were overcome and through the help of a kind Egyptian colonel we were lent a 15-cwt truck and a driver.

I now went to the English Library to look up Siwa in the *Encyclopaedia Britannica* and the *Dictionary of National Biography*. The oasis is some six miles long by some four or five miles wide. The population is nearly four thousand. The inhabitants are of Libyan (Berber) stock and have a language of their own. The town is built on two rocks and resembles a fortress. The oasis

*Robin Lane Fox: *Alexander the Great*: Allen Lane, London: 1973.

owes its distinction to the oracle temple of Ammon. The Oracle of Siwa was one of the five great oracles of the ancient world.

It was a universal belief in the ancient world that there is a capacity in the human mind to divine the will of God. This capacity is not equally developed in all men. Very few persons are distinguished from the mass. These are able to understand the methods by which the gods reveal their intentions to men. For the divine will was revealed to the interpreting medium in two ways – by inspiration and by signs. In the first method the divine influence overpowered the soul of the medium and took entire possession of it for a time. . . . The second method, of revelation by signs, required a distinct art of interpretation. There was a belief that at certain places the god gave revelations more frequently than at others. Such places were generally characterised by some marked physical feature. A warm spring gushing out of the desert enhanced the divine qualities of the Temple at Siwa. At these places there were established regular institutions, with a staff of priests and prophets, to which the neighbours resorted for counsel. Practically the oracles were worked by the priests.

The oracle certainly lent political importance to the Ammonians (as the Siwans were called). Kings, Ambassadors and Generals landed nervously at Mersa Matruh to begin the long desert journey. Nervously, because the oracle was ruthless and honest. Lysander tried to bribe it without success. Siwa soon became worth conquering. In 525 B.C. Cambyses planned an expedition against it. But Herodotus tells us that they had only *'reached about half way when, as they were at their midday meal, a wind arose from the South, strong and deadly, bringing with it vast columns of whirling sand, which entirely covered up the troops, and caused them wholly to disappear.'**

The panoply and pay-chests and skeletons of forty thousand men lie, perhaps marvellously preserved by the dry air of the locality, in the vast sea of sand which has mingled with the dust of their virility.

But how, I wondered, did oracles gain their repute? *'In 500 B.C.,'* I read, *'Siwa and the other oases were subjected to Persia, and in the following year Cimon the celebrated Athenian general, sent a secret embassy to the oracle. The oracle was greeted by the words, "Cimon is already with me," and on their return it was found that Cimon had himself perished in battle. The foretelling of Cimon's death augmented considerably the reputation of the oracle.'†*

But how was it done?

I know an old fortune-teller who appears at small parties. She sits in an upstairs room, and guests queue up to visit her. Often a

---

*Herodotus: *History*. Book III, Ch. 26. J. M. Dent & Sons, Ltd.
†C. Dalrymple Belgrave: *Siwa: The Oasis of Jupiter Ammon*: Bodley Head.

person leaves the room shattered by her perspicacity. I have examined her technique. When you first go in, she plays with cards or with a crystal according to her mood. She knows that this stage is complete mumbo-jumbo, but it gives her time to examine her victim. During this period, Mrs A relies on her stock-in-trade patter and is liable to issue any innocuous hack prophesy such as 'Tomorrow as ever is you'll meet a girl with brown eyes whose name begins with a D'. Meanwhile she is covertly investigating you. She is a trained detective. Your manner, your clothes, your hands, your shoes, your eyes – all reveal something to Mrs A. Then begins the second stage which is a summing up of her intelligence survey supported by shrewdness, intuition and guesswork and sometimes by information volunteered by previous visitors. 'Your cousin died last week. You're thirty years old. Your wound is troubling you less now. But you ought to rest more. You've been abroad a lot lately I should say.' And so on. But what is confusing and rather alarming is that during either the first stage or the second, Mrs A will suddenly receive an accurate transmission of thought or a genuine flash of foresight, which she will intersperse into her patter. 'Your father lives in America,' she told one English guest. 'He will die next week.' He did. Thus Mrs A employs the ambiguous banalities of her trade, her keenly trained faculties of intelligence and, on rare occasions, the real powers of a medium with which she is endowed. Perhaps the great oracles worked in the same way.

Alexander the Great had such faith in the oracle of Ammon that in 331 B.C. he left his headquarters at a critical moment in Egypt to undertake the dangerous desert journey from Matruh to Siwa. Alexander asked whether Ammon would bestow upon him the lordship of the world. The priest replied that he would. The purpose of his journey had been achieved. Alexander now had reason for wearing the tortuous horns of Ammon. He was divine. In a secret session, later, the oracle revealed to Alexander a message which he swore he would only repeat to his mother. The message was never retold. For Alexander died before reaching home.

Towards the end of the third century B.C. the fame of the oracle declined. With the advent of Christianity, Siwa became a place of banishment for political criminals. The light which had cast its beam across the world was extinguished.* Siwa was left like a derelict lighthouse in a sea of sand.

We set out along the road from Alexandria which runs west like

*'The oracle was reported dumb by Pausanias, c. A.D. 160,' says the Encyclopaedia Britannica.

a blue carpet rolled unevenly towards the desert. Presently, a strong wind swept up clouds of dust which poured over us from the south. A veil covered the desert. Then the wind subsided, and like a moor of purple heather the Western Desert lay serenely in the evening sun.

At night we slept by the truck.

Gradually the brown desert changed as we began to descend from the high limestone plateau. The track ran between boulders and vast slabs of dull red rock. The wind dropped. We were painfully bumping down a valley flanked by cliffs layered by the winds like a cake and by giant boulders lashed into odd shapes. As we descended, the air grew milder and the crags more fantastic, as if we were passing from consciousness into a dream. Then, in the distance below us, between two dun-coloured cliffs, we saw the green palm-trees of Siwa Oasis.

The town is built on a rock and surrounded by bright palm groves which rise out of the vast expanse of desert like an emerald set in a wooden box. Our truck moved slowly along dusty streets, flanked by dun-coloured houses built one above the other on the rock-side. White-robed men and swarthy ragged children stared at us curiously.

The empty rest-house which the Mamur, the Governor of Siwa, had told us we could stay in was perched on a hill one kilometre away from the town. It was kept by a young Siwan called Ahmed to whom we gave money to buy us food for supper – eggs, flat bread, a tiny chicken, dates, olives and sweet lemons, our daily meal while we were in Siwa. Then we stepped out into the clear, cold night and walked along a track until ahead of us, pale grey in the moonlight, we saw tiers of mud-houses, rising like battlements above a fortress, and lofty minarets tapering into the deep-blue Libyan night. There was silence. No lights showed through the tight-shuttered windows, as if the place were deliberately secretive. The narrow, unlit streets were empty. Inside the town it was very dark. Suddenly we heard a choking sob, then a man's laugh.

The next morning the Mamur showed us the town.

'All the habits of the Siwans today,' he said, 'come from what happened in the past. The old town, as you can see, is built on a rock. The Siwans who were quite rich from their dates and olives were so afraid of raids from the Bedouin tribes in the surrounding desert that when the population increased, and the rock became crowded, they built one house on top of the other. A father would build a storey on top of his house for his son; when he got married, his son would build another for his son and his wives, and so on.

(*Left*)
View from a
rooftop of the
crumbling houses
of Siwa.

A view of the
town of Siwa.

The houses, just as today, were made of mud mixed with salt, which hardens to the firmness of cement, until it rains which fortunately is very seldom. They use palm trunks for beams, and you can see them projecting from the ends of the houses.'

Gradually, we learned, the town became like a giant hive, with each cell joined by a steep, dark passage. In this confusion of lanes and black tunnels, unmarried men caused trouble in the harems, so there was a rule that no unmarried men might remain inside the walls of the town after sunset. The unmarried men were called 'zaggalas'. (It is a Berber word meaning 'bachelor'; the Siwans are the remnant of an old Berber race now intermixed with the blood of light-skinned Arabs and the blood of jet black slaves brought by the caravans.) The zaggalas slept at night in roughly thatched shelters outside the walls, and they were responsible for the defence of Siwa. If raiders approached, they sounded the alarm and went out to attack the enemy. The zaggalas were fierce and abandoned. At night they would lie in their shelter singing wild songs and drinking lubki which is got from the heart of a palm-tree. As soon as a boy reached puberty, he was sent out to join them. 'And he soon became like the rest,' said the Mamur.

We now understood the habits of the Siwans. For if the zaggalas, 'fierce and abandoned', spent their nights 'singing wild songs and drinking lubki' with boys who had just reached puberty the result would seem inevitable. But not quite – as we discovered when we learned their unwritten law. If a zaggala fell in love with a young boy and wanted to marry him, by their law he had to warn the boy who, if he did not fancy the zaggala, would run away into the palm groves. The zaggala would run after him in pursuit. If the zaggala caught up with the boy and seized him, then he could make love to him there and then and later take him back to his shelter outside the town walls. If by the following night the boy had been so overwhelmed by the charms of the zaggala that he wanted to stay with him, then he would remain with him in the zaggala's shelter during the night that followed without making any attempt to escape from his embraces. Eventually they would get married.

'But they also marry girls – sometimes as young as nine or ten. But the marriage is seldom consummated the first night,' the doctor told us. 'This is a good psychological rule. If I remove my wife's virginity the first night, I teach her that marriage is only the bed. And if I am ill or away on travel, she will seek the bed elsewhere. But if I flatter her and am sweet to her and teach myself to love her, she will know that marriage is not only that. But I wonder how the Siwans have found out this psychological rule. Some men do not consummate the marriage for days, some for months. But, of course, the man sleeps with the girl in his arms during this time. And on occasion he may get excited and penetrate her, and then if the girl is very small she may die of an internal haemorrhage. But death is taken very lightly by the Siwans. And they change wives frequently. I know one girl here of twenty-five who has been divorced nineteen times, the poor thing. But she seems quite happy.'

The following day we were shown round the market by a merchant who came to Siwa only during the date season. He was a lean, hawk-nosed man with sallow skin, furtive eyes and a jovial manner. He showed us the large date market of Siwa in a wide, open square surrounded by a wall. Groups of ragged children squatted by the mounds of dates spread across the market, sorting them into different qualities. The poorer sort are crushed into a solid mass and eaten by the Siwans or sold to the Bedouin. The finer kind are put carefully into baskets or tins and sent by lorry to Cairo.

Siwan dates are exceptionally rich in sugar, and provide the main source of wealth and nutriment in the oasis. The rule in the market is 'you can eat as many dates as you like for nothing, but you may not take any away'. The dates were warm and sticky and delicious.

'They even give the dates to their animals,' the merchant said. 'Siwa is so rich in dates. And rich in olives too. But they have little modern machinery and still press out the olive oil by hand. They cling to their customs. They will not alter them. They refuse to change any of their habits. For this reason the men still make love to boys. And their women are badly neglected. The other thing is a habit they have got from their ancestors, like smoking. They will kill each other for a boy. Never for a woman. But now the marriage to a boy is illegal. Yet it still persists.'

I walked away into the gardens in the outlying oasis of Zeitoun and found a dozen zaggalas digging out an irrigation trench. They used hoes, as large as spades, and they picked out the earth and threw it on the bank with a single movement. A pale, thin man strained his hoe into the earth with a shuddering groan, as if each thrust tore out his entrails. I was glad when they stopped for a rest. The variety of racial stock in the oasis was illustrated by these men as they lay sprawling on the rich ground, smoking home-made pipes. They were light-skinned Berbers with wide mouths, hawk-nosed Arabs, dark-eyed smiling Sudanese, lean Egyptians, blubber-lipped Negroes. They were all friendly. Their wages were a few piastres a day, eked out to them in rations and small cash payments.

'They give us money in little bits,' their leader, a hairy Negro, said. 'If they gave us a lump sum, we would not return to work

A 'married' couple.

until it was spent. We'd sing and drink.'

'And why should we work except for money?' cried his friend, a young dark boy called Sayed who lay beside him. 'And why do we need money except for tobacco and tea and sugar? We make our own drink.'

'What about a wife?' I asked.

Sayed's eyes glittered beneath their long lashes as they turned towards his friend.

'A good wife costs you ten pounds or more,' he said. 'But for fifteen piastres you can have a girl for a short time.' Sayed touched the Negro's cheek. 'That is – if you want one,' he added.

Towards sunset that afternoon, I returned to the rest-house which was still empty except for Taki and me. Taki was still taking photographs, so I was alone. The door to the room which belonged to Ahmed, the caretaker, was half open. I looked in because I wanted to make sure that Ahmed had bought us fresh fruit and eggs for our supper. Ahmed was in bed with a boy of about fourteen. The boy was stretched face downwards, his face buried in the pillow. Ahmed was straddling him.

I was extremely surprised and a little shocked. For Ahmed had married a twelve-year-old girl only a week previously. He had insisted on taking Taki and me to his house to see his bride on the day after the marriage.

Ahmed's house was a two-storeyed mud cottage supported by thick palm trunks which jutted out into the street. Ahmed had hung the jaw-bone of a donkey on one of the projections to keep away the evil eye. We entered a small low-ceilinged room on the upper storey. It was carpeted with gay striped rugs and gazelle skins strewn with patchwork cushions. Two little windows were placed low on the wall so that a person could see out of them as he reclined on the floor. Three brightly painted marriage chests were the only furniture in the light blue room; these contained the women's clothes and jewellery. We were introduced to Ahmed's parents. His mother was fifty years old. Her worn, sallow face was alive with humour, and she moved her tiny hands with a wonderful grace. Each time she rose to show us one of the necklaces or ear-rings (of which she was very proud) her wizened husband gazed up at her with love in his eyes. We heard some shuffling and giggling outside, and Ahmed came in leading his young sister Hanouma who stared at us coyly. We wondered when we would be allowed to meet Mabrouka, his latest wife. 'She is ever so small,' Ahmed would say with a blush, 'and I have only had her for a week. She is not used to me yet.' At last he decided to let us see her, and he took us to a tiny courtyard where

86

Mabrouka was waiting. She was a shy little creature with enormous eyes deepened by kohl and a broad mouth set sulkily beneath a fleshy snub nose. She looked bewildered and hurt, like a trapped animal in a cage.

'I paid ten whole pounds for her,' Ahmed had told us proudly.

But here was Ahmed making love to a boy. I turned to go. At that moment Ahmed heard me and looked round. He smiled at me in greeting and then, when he saw that I was gazing at the slenderness of the boy, his expression became at once amused and lascivious.

'*Auz el walad?*' he sniggered. 'Would you like to have the boy?'

As Ahmed spoke, the boy raised his head from the grubby pillow and turned to examine me. For an instant there was silence. As usual, my desire was in conflict both with my silly romantic notions and my sense of a decision which must essentially be sordid. Then, in his turn, the boy gave me a wide smile which showed his gleaming teeth. While Ahmed still straddled him the boy's smile remained set – without a muscle of his face moving. It was as if I were staring at an erotic postcard. Then his lips moved and from between them his tongue protruded and slid wetly from one side of his mouth to the other, while his eyes expressed a furtive though definite invitation. Almost imperceptibly he nodded his head. Next, as if to show me his attractions, he began to writhe between Ahmed's thighs.

'Would you like him?' Ahmed asked hoarsely.

Suddenly I remembered Dieter's words: 'It means no more than a piss before going to bed.'

'Would you like him?' Ahmed repeated.

'Indeed I would,' I answered, trying to speak lightly. Then a lie which would spare the boy's feelings came into my head. 'But the fact is I've a young friend visiting me later.'

Ahmed grinned. 'As long as you're happy, *ya sidi*,' he murmured and leaned down and kissed the boy's neck.

I am divided in two by Siwa. My Western half is worried that springs which could turn the desert into fertile grounds are wasted. He begins to calculate the cost of transporting labourers from the Nile Valley, the difficulty of building a new village for them (the aloof Siwans would have no truck with foreigners), the type of irrigation needed, and the capital required. He is irritated by the laziness and ignorance of the Siwans, by their obstinate refusal to change their habits, by their acceptance of pain, by their dirt and diseases. He is appalled by the brutal way in which the Siwan men seem to use their girls and boys. He is shocked by the almost universal lack of gentleness or shame.

A young Siwan girl.

(*Right*)
Two Siwan sisters.

But lurking behind him is the other half, an alien Eastern person, who watches the Siwans lolling in the sun, waiting until their money is finished, idling until they are forced to work, and sympathises with them. This person dreads the rectangular brick factories for the dates that civilisation may bring, the splutter of pumps for straining oil from olives, the blowing horn of the foreman's car, the wailing of bazaar music on the radio, the struggle for existence, the strain for advancement, the grasping of money. He is afraid of the petrol-stations and policemen. He is ardent and lawless. If the choice is between freedom and comfort, he prefers freedom. He does not want Siwa to be exploited, because he knows it would bring clerks and supervision and controls. He prefers to see the palms nodding serenely over the rough careless men and the light fading behind the dun-coloured village until the deep Libyan night seals the village in silence.

My Eastern half is in agreement with the author of the book I

The palm groves of Siwa.

have been reading. 'We Westerners,' the author maintains, 'are fearful of being reduced to acknowledge that the labour, the thought, the agitation which have place among us, often augment not the happiness of the individual, and are of doubtful utility to the collective body. . . . Impatience, activity, and sanguine hope, are habits of a European. . . . The habits of the Oriental, on the contrary, are indolence, gravity, patience. His ideas are few in number. . . . They are, however, generally correct.'

Thus writes W. G. Browne – the first European to reach Siwa since Roman times. He visited the oasis in 1792. But Browne's visit to Siwa was a flop. He got there; that was all. His servants' plan of disguise was to blame. 'My attendants,' he writes, 'had thought proper to make me pass for a Mamluk. Not having any intimation of this until it was too late, and unable as I then was to converse in Arabic, it was almost impossible to remain undiscovered.' Browne's views on Siwa are thus hardly profound. 'The complexion of the people is generally darker than that of the Egyptians. Their dialect is also different. . . . The dress of the lower class is very simple, they being almost naked.'

90

But Browne was a brave traveller. Dysentery and the rebuff were soon forgotten. His 'design' was to penetrate into the interior of Africa. In May 1793, ignoring the warnings of Moslems and Christians alike, he set out from Egypt for Darfur (in the Sudan) with the annual caravan. He reached Darfur safely and found lodgings in a house in the town where he lived while waiting for an interview with the Sultan whose permission he needed to join an expedition for slaves. While waiting in this house there occurred the incident which altered his life (he was twenty-five years old at the time). It is a curious incident; and I give it in Browne's own words.

'The slaves of the house used frequently to collect round me, as if to examine a strange object – I joked occasionally with them, without any other view than that of momentary relaxation. One day as I was reading in the hut, one of them, a girl about fifteen, came to the door of it, when, from a whim of the moment, I seized the cloth that was round her waist, which dropped and left her naked. Chance so determined that the owner of the slave passed at the moment and saw her. The publicity of the place precluded view of further familiarity, but the tumult which succeeded appeared to mark the most heinous of crimes, and to threaten the most exemplary vengeance. The man threw his turban on the earth and exclaimed, 'Ye believers in the Prophet, hear me! Ye faithful, avenge me!' with other similar expressions. – 'A Caffre has violated the property of a descendant of Mohammed;' (meaning himself, which was utterly false). When a number of people was collected around him, he related the supposed injury he had received in the strongest terms, and exhorted them to take their arms and sacrifice the Caffre. He had charged a carbine, and affected to come forward to execute his threats, when some one of the company who had advanced furthest, and saw me, called out to the rest that I was armed, and prepared to resist.

It was then agreed among the assembly that some method of punishment might be found, that promised more security and profit to the complainant, and would be more formidable to the guilty. The man whom I have already mentioned as my broker was to take the slave, as if she had really been violated, and agreed to pay whatever her master should charge as the price. The latter had the modesty to ask ten head of slaves. He was then to make his demand on me for the value of ten slaves.'*

How often one has suffered from a similar 'whim of the moment' in the Orient, and how often in occurs at most inauspicious moments! All the same it is an odd story. And what follows is still odder. In a rather off-hand way and without his usual precision, Browne tells us that as a result of this incident he 'suffered a constrained residence in Darfur of nearly three years'.

But I wonder if Browne was not glad of an excuse to stay in Darfur. We know that he was in no hurry to return for there was

---

*W. G. Browne: *Travels in Africa*: London: 1799.

little Browne liked about Europe. 'In Europe, education is the art of moulding the soul to the times,' he writes. 'Advancement is the object; and to obtain it activity is required. This end is gained; but in the art of directing the powers of his mind to the attainment of his own happiness, or to the public utility, or of preserving his body sane and vigorous, the man remains still a child.' Evidently, Browne felt constrained and uneasy in European society. 'The ingenuity of man in contriving his own happiness,' he writes, 'is in no part of the world more conspicuous than in Europe. Our mutual intercourse is so beset with forms, that it becomes doubtful whether it be a good or an evil; and the individual, not unfrequently, leaves a company dissatisfied that he ever entered into it. Whenever a number of persons meet together, eating and drinking seem to be a necessary bond of union; and they often do not separate without that kind of festivity which impairs the health of each, and creates dissensions, as it were, by its mechanical operation.' What a good description of a cocktail party!

Browne preferred the tranquil and easy society of the Arabs. He detested 'the fashions to which we are slaves' in Europe. 'A certain dress is to be worn,' he complains, 'a certain establishment kept up, under pain of indelible ignominy; and the man whose circumstances disable him from complying with this terrific mandate, with timid irresolution hides his head.'

Browne did not enjoy Western society and I suspect that his three years in Darfur were not as constrained as we might think from his book. He admits he was neither imprisoned nor personally ill-treated. Perhaps his 'broker' who was 'to take the slave, as if she had already been violated' allowed him to see her again. 'The passions, indeed,' says Browne, 'are to the mind what motion is to the body; and the absence of either causes and marks, in each respectively, symptoms that may be termed morbid.' We may assume that there was no morbid absence of passion in Browne. His philosophy of life was clear-cut.

'*No man who reflects on his past enjoyments and sufferings can doubt but that the latter, by their intenseness, duration, and frequency, have been decidedly predominant. To render them more equal, that is, to be less miserable, or to make life tolerable, either the number of pleasures must be augmented, according to the system of the Epicureans, or that of pains must be diminished, according to that of the Stoics. The Orientals strive to attain the one object like ourselves, by sensuality; and here it is not to be conceived that they are happier than we are; but the other they gain in a more complete degree than ourselves, and are much more exercised in the stoical system, which seems the most effectual to the purpose.*'

I wondered how Browne spent the rest of his life. I returned to the *Encyclopaedia Britannica*. Yes, there it was. In 1800 he left England and spent three years in visiting Greece, some part of

Asia Minor and Sicily. No details. Then came the last blunt sentence. 'About the end of the summer of 1813 he left Tabriz for Teheran, intending to proceed to Tartary, but was shortly afterwards murdered.' No more.

I turned to the *Dictionary of National Biography*, which provided me with some new bits of information. Browne was descended from an old Cumberland family. He was educated privately before entering Oriel College. After his journey to Greece he spent ten years in England where he was 'intimate with several men of similar tastes'. He was grave and saturnine, I discovered, 'with a demeanour precisely that of a Turk of the better order'. Beneath this reserve he concealed an ardent enthusiasm, his attachments were warm and durable, he acted from the highest principles of honour, and was capable of great generosity and kindness. In politics he was a republican, in religion a free-thinker.

But why was he murdered? 'He proceeded in safety as far as Tabriz,' says the *D.N.B.*, 'which he left for Teheran towards the end of the summer of 1813, accompanied by two servants. According to one account these men returned a few days afterwards, declaring that Browne had been murdered by bandits. According to another, the discovery was made by the Nehmandar, or officer, to ensure his safety, whom Browne had unfortunately preceded. His body could not be recovered, but his effects, excepting his money, were restored to the English ambassador, and after some time his bones, or what were represented as such, were brought to Tabriz and honourably interred. There seems no good reason for the suspicions entertained of the Persian government, and it remains a question whether the motive of the murder was plunder or fanaticism exasperated by Browne's imprudence in wearing a Turkish dress.'

Or was the fanaticism exasperated by one of Browne's whims of the moment? We shall never know.

Browne, William George, English traveller, born 1768, died in 1813.

But did he die? What is the evidence? The reports of two servants, his effects, *excepting his money*, and some bones. (If Browne preceded him, the *Nehmandar's* account must have been secondhand.)

Browne had spent ten years in Europe. He was forty-five years old, in the full vigour of life. He had a good constitution and 'much indifference to personal accommodations'. He was sick to death of Western society. His whole life showed that he had constantly sought to find his own personal nirvana. May he not have arranged his escape from Europe for ever? Think how easy it was. He had only to bribe his two servants, who were probably fond of him, sacrifice a few of his personal belongings, and purchase some bones. 'Social man,' he had written, 'has been too

93

long employed in counteracting nature, not to have moulded all to his dwarfish intellect.' Perhaps Browne had had the courage of his convictions. Perhaps he went back to nature.

I like to believe that he slowly determined on his plan to attain his nirvana during the last five years he spent in England. I like to think of him, awkward and taciturn, balancing a tea-cup on his knee in a stuffy drawing-room, turning the plan over in his mind. What did he need? A wild locality, reliable witnesses, a few relics, and a safe refuge until the little fluster caused by the news of his death had blown over. He could reasonably expect a further twenty years to enjoy his existence. But I do not think he worried much about death. 'The European,' he wrote, 'dissatisfied with the present, and only supported by the hope of what is to come, attached beyond measure to the advantages which his anxieties have been prolonged to acquire, has already, even at an early age, fixed for himself a period short of which he thinks it *hard and unjust* to be deprived of life.'

He had fixed himself no such period. But he was determined to discover his nirvana. He was tired of nations which 'formed their disciples on the narrow view of that community'. He disliked living in a land where 'nature is distorted and paralysed by authority'. For the rest of his days he wanted to lead a life 'free from ligatures' among natural people. So he escaped, or so I like to believe. And I like to think that in his nirvana, as he threw away his Western clothing, he thought of it as a symbol of the conventions he was finally shedding before he could plunge into the life from which he had previously been debarred by the Western garb of his mind.

While he was lusty, I am sure he had no regrets. But as he grew old and weak, did his mind remain in the Oriental nirvana he had described? 'The Orientals,' he had said, 'are not much disturbed at the thoughts of death, but resign life without a sigh. Their mind is tortured when the blossoms of hope are suddenly torn from it; but their gradual decay is not incompatible with a kind of tranquillity.'

Was he tranquil as he withered in an alien land? Or was his mind racked by the fear of death as he yearned for the green hills and grey sky of Cumberland?

One evening Taki and I were in the living-room of the rest-house, eating our supper of boiled eggs and fruit, when the pi-dogs began barking outside. Then we heard voices in the kitchen. Presently Ahmed came into the living-room.

'A young Senussi soldier from the Libyan army has just arrived,' Ahmed announced. 'He got lost on a patrol. He has been wandering in the desert for two days. He saw the light of this house far away and he made straight for it. He is very tired. May he stay here in the rest-house?'

'Of course,' we replied.

'I have given him water to drink, for he was very thirsty. But I have finished my meal,' Ahmed continued. 'And I must go home to my new wife. So may the soldier join you to eat? And can he sleep in the spare room?'

'Certainly,' we answered.

Ahmed left, and presently returned with the soldier and some more food.

'This is Salem,' he said. 'I'm afraid that like me he speaks no English.'

The soldier salaamed and smiled at us nervously. He had washed away the sand from his hands and face, but his calico tunic was coated with sand. He was surprisingly young – and extremely attractive, with his smooth oval face and large brown eyes fringed by long, curling lashes. Ahmed brought up a chair for him.

'Welcome,' we said in Arabic. '*Tfaddal*. Please sit down.'

'*Mammoon giddan*,' he said. 'Thank you very much.'

His voice had a slight huskiness which I have often noticed among Bedouin.

We offered him wine and a cigarette, but, as we had expected, he refused. The Senussi form a strict Moslem sect. The Senussi Bedouin will neither smoke nor drink. However, we were glad to see that as soon as his shyness at meeting us had left him, Salem began to eat hungrily. Meanwhile Taki and I carried on a banal conversation in our halting Arabic, and once, when Salem was not looking, Taki gave me a wink, for Taki had sensed intuitively that I was fascinated by the young soldier. After we had finished our meal, we made coffee.

'I am quite exhausted,' Taki said presently. 'So I shall retire to bed. Goodnight to you both.' He took a paraffin lamp from a side-table and walked up the stairs to his bedroom. At that moment I turned and saw that the soldier was looking at me. Then he smiled, but the smile was wholly unlike the sensual leer of the boy whom Ahmed had offered to me. Salem's smile was without any guile or sensuality; it was an open smile of friendship and affection. It was also completely innocent.

'I am grateful to you for your hospitality,' he said solemnly.

'*Afwan*,' I answered. 'It was our pleasure.'

'I was foolish to get lost,' Salem announced. 'Of course, I could have found my directions by the stars, but the sky was overcast.'

'Had you no compass?'

Salem smiled. 'I once had a compass, but I lost it.'

'Have a little more to eat?'

'No, thank you. I am full, praise be to Allah,' Salem said.

95

'And now,' he added, 'I would like to wash myself before I go to bed, for I have not washed all over for three days.'

'I will show you to your bedroom,' I told him. 'And I'll show you the bathroom. The shower works, but I'm afraid the water is cold.'

Salem grinned. 'I am used to cold water,' he said.

I gave him a lamp, took another lamp for myself, and led the way up the stairs. The spare room was separated from mine by the bathroom. I made sure that there were enough blankets on Salem's bed, for winter nights in the Western Desert can be very cold. I showed him how the shower worked; I said goodnight to him, and went to my room. Though I was a little weary, I was too excited to sleep. I put the lamp on a table by my bed, and in order to distract myself from the thought of the boy washing himself under the shower next door, and in order to try to find relief from my desire, I took up at random one of the books I had brought with me to read on the journey. It was *Urne-Burial* by Sir Thomas Browne.

'*A great part of Antiquity contented their hopes of subsistency with a transmigration of their souls,*' I read. '*A good way to continue their memories, while having the advantage of plural successions, they could not but act something remarkable in such variety of beings, and enjoying the fame of their past selves, make accumulations of glory unto their last durations. Others rather than be lost in the uncomfortable night of nothing, were content to recede into the common being, and make one particle of the publick soul of all things, which was no more than to return into their unknown and divine Original again.*'

Suddenly the door which led to the bathroom opened, and Salem appeared and stood there motionless. He was naked except for a towel wound round his waist. His body was lithe yet wiry and beautifully formed. He looked very young. His tawny skin seemed to glow in the light of the lamp he was carrying.

'I saw from under the door that your lamp was still shining,' he said in his soft, husky voice. 'So I knew you were still awake.'

I was silent, for I could think of nothing to say.

'I hope I haven't disturbed you,' Salem muttered.

'Not at all,' I answered. 'Why don't you come in?'

'If I do not disturb you, then I will come in for a moment,' Salem said with a shy smile. 'Before I ate food and took my shower I was tired. Now my tiredness has gone.'

Salem came into the room, closing the door behind him, and put down his lamp on a table. He sat down on a decrepit wicker chair. He was silent. I tried to make conversation.

'How old are you, Salem?' I asked.

'Sixteen or seventeen,' he replied. 'I am not sure.'

'What made you become a soldier?'

'There was a drought. My tribe became very poor. There were

too many mouths to feed. In the army there is always food.'

'How long have you been in the army?'

'Three months.'

'Do you enjoy the life?'

'Sometimes. But I miss the people of my tribe and my friends.'

'Surely you have made friends in the army?'

Salem stared down at the floor. He frowned. 'Sometimes a man has tried to make friends with me,' he said. 'But I did not like him.'

'Have you a girl in your tribe you are fond of?'

'When I have no money, how can I afford to buy a wife?'

'Have you been to Tripoli?'

'Once, yes.'

'What about the girls you can find there?'

'But one of those girls will go with any man for a night if she is paid. Besides, they say that some of them have disease.'

'Then what do you do when you feel desire?'

Salem smiled. 'You are a man, so you must know,' he answered. Then he looked up at me. 'How old are you?' he asked.

'Thirty-one.'

'That is a good age – thirty-one.'

'Why?'

'Because by then your mind has learned something about life, yet your body is still young.'

'But surely you must have learned quite a lot about life?'

'We Arabs have a proverb which says "*Addounia sammounn essoumou el insanu tadrigian*". The world is a poison which poisons the soul of man gradually. I am not yet poisoned. Nor are you, I think. But in many ways I am still a child. I know little about the world. What is worse, I still have the fears of a child.'

'What fears?' I asked.

Salem gazed at me with his large eyes. 'I am afraid to be alone,' he told me. 'These last days when I was alone and lost in the desert I was so frightened I thought I was going mad. I was very much afraid.'

'So would most of us be,' I answered.

'Perhaps,' Salem said. 'But I have another fear which is so childish you will laugh at me.'

'I won't laugh, I promise you.'

'Why do you think I came into this room?'

'Tell me.'

'Because I am afraid to sleep alone in a room,' Salem said, his head bent towards the ground.

For an instant I thought that Salem might be making a discreet preparation for an 'advance' to have sex. But then he looked up at me, and his dark eyes were as always completely innocent. What he next said subdued my excitement.

'I looked at the other room and I knew I could never sleep alone there,' Salem told me. 'You see, in our tribe the unmarried men and boys sleep in a tent together. In the army we sleep in barracks. So I am used to hearing the sound of men breathing or stirring in their sleep. I have never slept alone in a room. And now you may laugh at me. But it is the truth all the same.'

I tried to conceal my disappointment; I tried to make my voice sound sympathetic yet casual when I spoke the only words which it was now possible to say.

'There's room in this bed,' I said.

Salem smiled at me in gratitude. 'I sleep very quietly,' he stated. 'I mean, I do not snore or move about.'

'Don't worry,' I answered as I made room for him in the bed. 'You must be cold.'

'Thanks,' Salem said. Then he rose from the chair, blew out his lamp which was on a table beside him, crossed the room, and got into the part of the bed that was now empty. He lay on his back with his hands folded above the blankets. He was motionless.

'Shall we say "goodnight"?' he asked.

'Yes,' I replied. '*Leiltak saida.* Sleep well.'

'Thanks,' Salem repeated.

There was silence. Salem did not stir. I wondered if I should put out the lamp which was still alight. But I knew that I could not sleep; I wanted to read for a while to calm my desire. I looked at Salem. His eyes were closed; he was breathing steadily. I turned back to *Urne-Burial*.

'*Egyptian ingenuity was more unsatisfied, contriving their bodies in sweet consistencies, to attend the return of their souls,*' I read. '*But all was vanity, feeding the winde, and folly. The Egyptian Mummies, which* Cambyses *or time hath spared, avarice now consumeth. Mummies is become merchandise,* Mizraim *cures wounds, and Pharaoh is sold for balsoms.*

'*In vain do individuals hope for immortality, or any patent from oblivion, in preservations below the Moon.*'

The words were very beautiful and moving. They should have swung my thoughts away from the bed in which I was lying. But I was still intensely aware of the boy who was only a few inches away from me. He was lying completely still as if he too had been 'contrived in sweet consistencies'. I looked at him in the light of the lamp. His lips were a little parted which gave his smooth face a childish expression. The blanket covered only the lower half of his body; the skin was stretched tight over his broad shoulders and hairless chest. Then I began to examine him more closely. Salem had told me that he slept quietly and never moved in bed, but though his chest rose and fell as he breathed, I began to wonder at the stillness of his body. Suddenly I understood the reason for it. His quietness was not the result of sleep; it was an act of conscious will, for though his eyes were closed Salem was awake. For a while I hesitated. Then I could endure the doubt of my hope no longer. I stretched out my hand and put it on Salem's shoulder. His skin was very warm. He did not move. Perhaps I only imagined that I saw his eyelids flicker for an instant. I kept my hand on his shoulder for a while, then, as if by no deliberate act of my own, my hand slid down to feel the smoothness of his chest. At that moment his whole body seemed to give a start, and at the same instant he turned swiftly, and his arms clasped me and pressed my body against him, while his lips slid across my face until they came to my mouth.

Long after my energy was exhausted, Salem continued with his love-making. It was as if he had learned to make love but had never practised the art he had acquired, so that the fountain of his desire had been pent-up under the ground and now that it was released flowed endlessly. Towards dawn he went to sleep with his head on my chest and his arms still holding me.

When we came down into the living-room that morning Taki had already had breakfast and left, for he liked to take his photographs in the early morning light. Ahmed brought us coffee and toast and leered at us knowingly. But Salem gave no sign that he had noticed the leer; he was smiling at me happily across the table and talking so fast that I had to ask him to speak more slowly, for I could not understand his Arabic.

'You must learn Arabic, and you must come and live with me in my tribe,' Salem told me.

'*You* must learn English, and come and live with me in London,' I answered.

We had reached that stage in the intoxication of a new love during which the difficult problems of the real world vanished, and all plans seem both possible and wonderful. As we walked round the oasis that morning a part of me was uneasily aware of this fact, but I managed to disregard it. For though we may never attain a permanent state of nirvana in our lives, at a moment when an opportunity for a temporary period of nirvana presents itself we can enjoy it completely only by forgetting the past and ignoring the future and living each minute in contemplation of the joy of the present.

I took Salem to see the ruins of the Temple of the Oracle of Jupiter Ammon. Then we went to bathe in the warm waters of Ain el Hammam where a spring spurts up from the earth and forms a round pool which irrigates the groves of date palms.

As I watched Salem's lean body frisking in the sunshine I knew that I could not wait for nightfall before I made love to him again. I could not wait for that mixture of fierceness so strangely combined with tenderness.

We spoke little at lunch in the rest-house. Suddenly our eyes met and we smiled contentedly, for at that moment we were both aware that our thought was the same. Presently, in silence, we climbed the stairs that led to my bedroom.

Three days passed in a trance of happiness. But during the fourth day I noticed at times – if only for a few seconds – that the happiness glowing on Salem's face would vanish. At the same instant he would lower his long curling lashes as if to shut out some vision that confronted him. Then I realised that for a moment the future had pierced through the protective dome of contentment that covered his present nirvana.

An hour before sunset that day Salem suggested that we should visit once again the oasis of Zeitoun. For a while we walked quietly admiring the beauty of the place. Tall palms and giant olive trees flourished their branches over sugar-cane, pome-granates and sweet lemons. The spring wells up in a pool of gleaming water and reflects the delicate fronds of the palms which surround it like a group of bathers. Green stalactites of weeds wave slowly in the pool. Then Salem spoke.

'You know that I must go back,' he said. 'They may send out a patrol to find me. And if they discover I have stayed here with you for several days without making any effort to return or to get a message through to our headquarters, I would be horribly punished.'

'There must be something we can do,' I replied. But even as I spoke, I was aware that my words were futile.

'What can we do?' Salem asked in his husky voice. 'Let us admit the truth to ourselves. Even if I could get away from the army, you would never be happy for long living in our goat-skin tents. Even if I could reach London, I could never live for long in a town, for I am still a Bedouin.'

I was silent. The dome protecting our nirvana had been shattered.

'Another thing,' Salem added. 'I could not bear to say goodbye to you. So one day you will find I have gone. But you must remember that I shall always remember you. And I shall pray to Allah for your happiness.'

When we are deeply moved our words – the actual words we use – are very banal. It is the expression of our face and the grief in our voice that convey our feelings, so I will not attempt to repeat – even inaccurately – the words I then said to Salem. The only sense I made was to tell him I would give him my spare compass.

As usual that evening Salem had his shower and came into my room with a towel round his waist which he hung neatly on the wicker chair and got into bed with me. That night his passion was fiercer than it had ever been. And later, when it was all finished and he thought I was asleep, he ran his hands over my body from my head to my feet as if he were blind and could not see me by the faint light of the lamp that had been turned down low. Then he gave a long sigh. For a while he lay still. Presently he blew out the lamp. Soon I went to sleep.

In the morning he had gone.

Ahmed told me that he had taken provisions for his journey from the kitchen.

Taki had taken all the photographs he wanted; he had to return to Cairo for another assignment. I decided I would return with him – at least for a while – for I needed to clear my mind before I made any decisions for the future.

On our last night in Siwa a fantasia took place in the little hall of the rest-house. Two dozen zaggalas appeared towards ten in the evening. They entered in a compact mass, as if controlled by one communal spirit, and sat in a close circle round the hall – little smooth-cheeked boys, stocky Berbers with shaved scalps, gigantic Negroes, all of them workers from the groves. They had been drinking the fomented palm juice called lubki, and their eyes were wild as they began to dance, moving slowly round a large Negro who sat on the floor playing on a rough wooden flute, never pausing for breath. At first, their deliberate, jerky steps as each followed the other round the circle seemed ridiculous. Then they began to sing stridently, the half-broken voices of the adolescents mingling with the strong bass of the Negroes. I wrote down the tune thus:

The words of each refrain were in their own Siwan language.

'This one is about love,' Ahmed whispered to me later. 'This is what they are singing: "My love is like a flaming torch, and sometimes I take him to my breast".'

Leathery, black, naked feet, deeply scarred by the palm fronds, slapped the floor to the rhythm of two drums, one bass, one tenor. The dancers moved, following their leader, in a small circle round the musicians, now swaying and bowing, now crouching and springing up into the air, now shuffling one foot after the other, now bending and twirling. Suddenly a dancer would grab the man ahead, and they would be clasped together for a moment in a sexual embrace before returning to their place in the ring. Then the music stopped abruptly, and the sweating men and boys fell limply to the floor. During this pause the Negro

A Zaggala.

with huge limbs who appeared to be their leader took a double reed flute which he played while the others listened casually.

I watched the tough lean zaggalas sprawling together against the wall. They were utterly relaxed, I noticed; there was no tension in their bodies at that moment. But on their faces was an expression which at first I found hard to decipher. Later in the evening I understood the reason for it. They were devoid of any feeling of guilt, the cross of Western civilisation; and therefore they were free from our worst worry. They were careless.

We may at times protest against the doctrine that all pleasure is sinful. We may believe that the teachings of Christ suggest loving-kindness rather than unrelieved guilt. But the drops of propaganda for the sinfulness of pleasure which were spilt over us by teachers and pastors in our youth have left a scar that throbs. The pure well of our pleasure in life has been poisoned. Guilt, the Church's secret weapon, stealthily attacks each person in the West; and it is a force which, by sapping the strength of the individual, has weakened our resistance to domination by the State. We feel that it must surely be wrong for us to be happy by ourselves, therefore we settle down with a sigh to being corporately gloomy. Pursuit of happiness is abandoned.

The drums began throbbing; the dancers stirred, rose languidly and formed into a circle, one behind the other. The drums' beat grew more insistent. Then with a shout the men burst into their chant.

Ya Haoul il lah   Ya Haoul il lah

Ya Haoul il lah   Ya Haoul il lah

Over and over again the same four words echoed around the room, 'Oh power of God, oh power of God'. The drums beat louder and quicker, and the men sang with all the power of their lungs. In the field of work their faces had been stolid. Now they were alight with passion. As they moved faster, their gestures became larger and more intense, as if speed increased their desire

Mosque in Siwa.

for expression. 'Ya Haoul il lah. Ya Haoul il lah.' The circle of their dance and the four words had a hypnotic effect; the original meaning was forgotten. The syllables had become an incantation. Round and round the circle men pranced and leaped and swayed. The beats of the drums were quiet at the beginning of each phrase, and then, as the tempo grew faster, they would swell into loud thuds, until, when the climax of din and speed had been reached, the beats would grow soft, as if exhausted by their orgasm; but soon clamour would rise and swell again.

Tearing off their clothes, dancers flung themselves into wilder movements. A boy would break away to perform a frantic solo belly-dance until pulled back into the jerking circle by his friend. A gaunt Berber seized the pipes; the tune continued, and the great Negro, released from his toil, plunged into the ring in an ecstasy of strength. Sweat trickled down his hard black limbs. Men's bodies as well as their eyes soon revealed rising passions. They quivered with the intensity of their excitement. And then the last strip of cloth was dropped or was torn from their loins. They were rigid in their exaltation; their organs like their muscles were extremely well-developed.

'Ya Haoul il lah. Ya Haoul il lah.' The chant was bellowed now, as if it were a protest against all restrictions, against the need to work and the need to live in bonds of flesh and the need to grow old and die. It was a plea for release from human bondage. The zaggalas were pouring their virility into the dance as a libation to freedom. Tomorrow might be painful, but tonight they could experience the culmination of joy.

But for all the excitement and elation that I enjoyed as I watched their last orgasms, I realised that even if I married the most beautiful boy among that frenzied group and even if I lived in an ecstasy of union for a while, I knew that my Western self would still be weakened by my sense of guilt. As yet I was neither strong enough in mind nor in custom to endure the East for any length of time. I must return, for a while at least, to my existence in 'Western civilisation', to my own form of bondage.

Since the laws regarding homosexuality have been changed in England, it is possible for two men to live openly together without the stigma which had been previously attached to it. Thirty years ago, men who set up a household together were immediately suspected of being 'strange' or 'that way'. With the climate of change, more general tolerance and less prejudice, I am aware that a form of marriage between two men is now possible and even socially acceptable. One does not have to travel as far as Siwa to find a 'married couple'.

I have recently written at length about this subject, so here I will be brief. I believe that heredity has far more effect on the individual than has environment. Heredity determines the type and strength of a tree, and the climate will affect its growth. But the tree will remain an oak or a cypress. People – both male and female – have been created by the genes and chromosomes of their parents. Within each person flow male and female traits in varying degrees. But the normal person, I maintain, is a bisexual, largely formed by his heredity and slightly modified by his environment.

The Zaggala leader.

107

Ask yourself at the age of fifty: 'Where did my life go wrong?' The answer is: 'Probably before I was born.'

If a man is predominantly male in his outlook and his partner is predominantly female in her outlook there is a chance that the union will flourish. But the ties that bind the homosexual couple together are very much weaker than those of a man and wife. The latter have probably got children to cherish and educate; they have the approbation of their neighbours, and a firm position in society. Another important tie is in their legal security, for unless some other provision has been made the one will inherit from the other.

However, the most important danger to a homosexual marriage is the homosexual tolerance of promiscuity. There are no clubs where married men go to ogle each other across a bar-counter; there are dozens in every big town where queers can congregate. 'I know of one girl here of twenty-five who has been divorced nineteen times, poor thing,' the doctor told us in Siwa. Transpose the words 'girl in Siwa' to 'boy in London' and it would be no exaggeration.

However, despite all the difficulties that confront them, a marriage in Europe between a man and a boy or between a man and a man can still result in a perfect, enduring and beautiful relationship.

Siwa had for the time being quenched my desire to discover nirvana; I was overdrawn at the bank; I decided that – like the rest of the world – I must try to find contentment in work. I took a job writing film scripts and I began to adapt plays. At that time Melville Gillam was running the Worthing Repertory Theatre, and it was he who gave me my first chances. The late Henry Sherek and his wife Pamela would come down for the opening of these 'try-outs'. I liked Pamela at first sight. Her warm personality and graciousness and generosity of character were most attractive – and, indeed, they still are. But at first I was awed by Henry. I was alarmed by the sheer bulk of the man, for he was enormous, and even his wonderful sense of humour could not remove my apprehension of him. However, he took options on my plays *The Leopard* and *Mr Lear* and on a play called *Rise Above It* which he eventually produced on television.

Rise Above It was staged in Berlin before Henry produced it on television. He flew to Berlin to see the play and, as soon as he arrived, he persuaded me to leave with him at dawn the following day – a Sunday – to go to Paris to get seats for a new play called *Monsieur Masure*.

'If you like the play,' Henry told me, 'I'll buy it for you to adapt for the London stage.'

'Splendid,' I replied. 'But why do we have to leave at dawn?'

Henry gave me a stern look. 'To lunch at the Ritz, of course,' he answered. 'I always lunch at the Ritz if there's the slightest chance of doing so.'

Since we were leaving Berlin on a tourist class night flight we did not suppose we would get any breakfast on the plane. We ate a large breakfast in our hotel. However, as soon as the plane took off an ample breakfast was served.

'This,' Henry says in his autobiography *Not In Front Of The Children,** 'caused Robin to come out of his disgruntled coma and show very slight signs of life. . . . After breakfast, and only to make Robin laugh, I shouted to a passing steward "Really, this being Air France, we fully expected caviar and champagne".'

Within what seemed a few seconds the steward returned. With him was a bottle of *Veuve Cliquot* and a mound of caviar. It was not until we changed planes at Frankfurt, where Henry decided to have yet another breakfast, that we were actually sick.

However, by the time we had booked into our hotel and had a bath we felt better. We took a taxi to the Ritz and were deposited on the Place Vendôme side. I had never entered the Ritz in Paris with Henry before; it was indeed an experience. Already colossal in size, he seemed to grow in stature. Moreover, every single member of the Ritz staff knew him.

'*Bonjour, Monsieur Sherek,*' said the doorman.

'*Bonjour, Monsieur Sherek,*' said the hall-porter positively beaming with joy. '*C'est un plaisir de vous voir.*'

'*Bonjour, Monsieur Sherek,*' cried sleek flunkies as Henry made his majestic way (with me following) to the restaurant at the far end of the hotel.

With a '*Bonjour, Monsieur Sherek*', we were ushered to the table Henry had reserved for us. As we sat down the *maître d'hôtel* came up, and his '*Bonjour, Monsieur Sherek*' was the most effusive of all. We were handed two enormous menu cards. Henry glanced briefly at the menu and then put down the card with a sigh.

'When I was a young man,' he said to me, 'my ambition was to be like the E. Phillips Oppenheim hero who was known by name to every head waiter in Europe.'

Henry paused and gazed at me sadly.

'I have achieved my life's ambition,' he continued. 'And you see before you a ruined man.'

I loved the play *Monsieur Masure*; it was extremely funny, but I realised that in order to have a success in England and America the three characters would have to be changed, the scene would

*Henry Sherek: *Not in Front of the Children*: William Heinemann, London: 1959.

have to be moved from France to a cottage in Kent in England, and the arrangement changed from two to three acts.

Henry, Pamela and I met the author Claude Magnier and his wife at a pleasant club. I told Claude that I admired his play greatly. Then quietly but firmly, I told him that I would not take on the adaptation unless he gave me *carte blanche* to make whatever changes I wanted. To my amazement, he agreed. I wrote the play which I called *Odd Man In*. Henry's casting was magnificent. The play went into rehearsal at the St Martin's Theatre in the West End of London.

On the night before the opening I had one of the strangest experiences of my life.

I had realised that the dress rehearsal would be an ordeal, so on my way to the theatre, I stopped at the house of a doctor who was a friend of mine, and he gave me a calming injection. He unfortunately forgot to tell me that on no account must I touch any alcohol for the next twenty-four hours.

From my point of view the dress rehearsal went splendidly. The three actors, Donald Sinden, Muriel Pavlow, and her husband Derek Farr all gave superb performances. Unfortunately, after the rehearsal was over and we had listened to Henry's notes over supper at The Ivy, I met a young married couple I knew and they persuaded me to go to a party with them out in the wilds beyond St John's Wood.

The party was fun, but I suddenly realised that I was getting slightly drunk. I explained to my friends that I had had an injection from the doctor that day to help me get through the evening. I insisted that the moment had come for me to go home. But each time I got to the door I was dragged back by some guest or other and given another drink. Finally I escaped from the room on the pretext that I was going to the loo. By this time I was feeling very odd.

I walked out into the street and took in great gulps of fresh air. Looking vaguely around me, I realised that I had no idea where I was. I moved unsteadily along a road which led past a deserted park in a region which seemed quite empty of private houses. There were a few closed garages and deserted factories. As I was walking along by the park railings, I was disturbed by a faint crying noise. I looked down to see a small kitten at my feet which was mewing piteously. I knelt down to examine the kitten to see if it had been hurt, but I could find no sign of any injury. So I stroked the kitten's head and got up and moved on. But the kitten followed me, still mewing pathetically. There were now park railings on one side of me; the broad road was flanked by stores on the other.

Suddenly, a large black Jaguar, driven fast, came up the road towards me. The driver saw me and with a scream of tyres turned the car round in the broad road so that it drew up beside the pavement opposite me.

In the front of the car were two men with badly scarred faces. The elder one, who was driving, was about forty. He looked pale and fleshy, and he was stoutly built. The younger man was about twenty. He was lean, with a finely chiselled face and a pointed nose, which made him look rather like a fox. Sitting at the back of the car were two flashily-dressed girls of about sixteen or seventeen, one blonde and one dark. Both were extremely attractive. The blonde girl had a small, pert face and large blue eyes: she was so heavily made-up that she managed to look like a rather dissolute baroque cherub. The dark girl had slanting eyes and an olive complexion. She was almost certainly Eurasian.

The driver, who looked like a gangster, leaned out of the car window and shouted out to me.

'What's the way to the Barnet By-Pass?'

'I'm awfully sorry, but I don't know,' I replied. 'I'm lost myself as a matter of fact.'

Then I felt impelled to share my worry about the kitten.

'But I wonder if you could help me,' I continued. 'What in heaven's name do you think I ought to do with this kitten? It's obviously lost, and I can't find any sign of any house it could have come from. Do you think I ought to take it home with me?'

The occupants of the car – the two gangsters and their flashy girls – leaned out and looked at the kitten, which was still mewing.

'Is he hurt?' the blonde girl asked.

'I don't think so,' I answered. 'But you have a look.'

I stooped down, picked up the kitten, and handed it to her. The blonde examined the kitten, and so did the two thugs.

'He seems all right,' the younger gangster said.

'You'd better leave him here,' the blonde said finally. 'Otherwise he'll never get home. Goodnight.'

The thick-set gangster jerked the Jaguar into gear, and the car roared away into the night, moving in the opposite direction from that in which it had originally been driving.

I swayed a little. The combination of the doctor's injection and whisky were now having a most unfortunate effect. I was holding the kitten in my left hand, and with my right hand I wiped the sweat away from my forehead. Alcohol and my doctor's drugs obviously didn't mix. I knelt down on the pavement to put the kitten down. I stroked the kitten's head and then got up. As I rose unsteadily to my feet, a heavy hand fell on my shoulder. I looked up and saw a large, heavily-built policeman standing over me. The policeman had the face of an overgrown school bully. He held me in a hard grip.

'Let me go,' I said.

'Not likely,' the policeman replied. 'I'm taking you into custody for being drunk and incapable.'

'What nonsense,' I said. 'You must be out of your mind.'

But even as I spoke, I could hear that my voice was becoming slow and slurred. I struggled violently to get away from my captor. Suddenly the policeman hit me hard across the face. I staggered back to my feet, and the policeman hit me again.

'Now I shall take you in for being drunk and disorderly,' the policeman said.

It was 3 a.m. My play was opening that very evening. With a ghastly clarity, I could see the headlines in the papers if I had to appear in court that morning on a drunk and disorderly charge. I felt sick and appalled.

Suddenly there was a screech of brakes. It was the Jaguar back again. The gangsters' black car drew up beside us. The two thugs got out of the car and walked – very slowly and very deliberately – across to us.

'What's going on here?' the large thug asked the policeman. 'What are you doing to our friend Sid?'

I was sober enough not to gape at them.

'I'm taking him in for being drunk and disorderly,' the policeman answered flatly.

'Now copper, take it easy,' said the thug. 'We've been with Sid all evening. And we can tell you just what he'd had to drink.' He turned to his foxy friend. 'Can't we, Ron?'

'Of course,' Ron answered. 'Now, George, let's just go through the whole evening.'

'Well,' George began, 'in the pub our friend Sid had two pints of bitter. Then he had a small whisky with his supper, and a half pint of bitter after it. And that's the lot. Isn't it, Ron?'

'That's all he had,' Ron, the smaller gangster, confirmed. 'I shouldn't take him in if I were you, copper,' Ron continued. 'If you do we'd have to come in as witnesses. And if we did, we'd have to say what we saw you do to him just now.'

The policeman looked at the scarred faces of the two men. Then without a word he turned on his heel and walked away – leaving me alone with my rescuers. I tried to thank them, but I could hardly find words to do so.

'You just don't know how grateful I am to you,' I ended up.

'You look as if you could do with a drink,' George, the larger gangster, said. 'Hop in the back and we'll take you into town. It's too late to make Oxford tonight.'

I got into the back of the car with the two wildly attractive little girls, and the car drove off.

They took me to a club in Soho.

Over drinks I learned about their background. Both George

and Ron had been in prison for 'grievous bodily harm'. Both the girls had been in various institutions and approved schools. Elsie, the blonde girl, had only escaped a few months previously. All four of my friends were gangsters – but only small-time gangsters, they explained to me. They were only very small fry in the big underworld of crime. When the Soho club closed, we went and drank at a pub in Covent Garden which stayed open all night for the porters. It was at this pub, at seven in the morning, that George, the hefty leader of the group, confessed they had done a burglary that very night. That was why they were in a hurry to leave London – in case the police were after them. The loot was still in the boot of the car.

There was now one question which perplexed me so much I knew I must ask it.

'Why ever did you bother to try and help me?' I asked them. 'Why did you take such a terrific risk?'

'Because we don't like coppers,' said George.

'Besides,' scar-faced Ron explained, 'we'd sort of taken a liking to you.'

'But why?' I asked.

'Well,' George explained. 'Anyone who can be all that fond of a pussy-cat can't have much wrong with him.'

'That's right,' the other three of them agreed solemnly with conviction.

As I stared at them in amazement, suddenly I had an idea.

'If you can stay tonight in London,' I said, 'can I leave you four tickets for the opening of my play tonight?'

'You can,' they answered. 'And you can leave the four tickets in the name of Brown.'

The tickets in the name of Brown were collected. But I shall never know if the four of them attended the opening of *Odd Man In*. The play was a success. Later it toured Australia and the United States for a year. I shall always remember my four unexpected deliverers and their odd code of morality with gratitude.

I soon got over my awe of Henry Sherek and we became close friends. When Henry retired and he and Pamela went to live in Geneva, they often asked me to stay with them. They were both gourmets; with them I enjoyed the best meals I have ever known in my life and the most splendid company. I still miss Henry very much.

As I have said, I was at times driven by my conscience to forsake all thoughts of nirvana by working on efforts such as the fight against slavery. I had already bought a slave outside Timbuktu to show that slavery still existed. I now decided to revisit Zanzibar from where I suspected slaves were shipped to the southern shores of Arabia.

My technique for discovering where slaves were bought and sold was generally the same. I would go to a *louche* bar where I was likely to be accosted by some pimp. After a few drinks I would confide in him that I wanted to buy a boy or a girl as a servant to take away with me. The pimp, on one occasion, led me to a place where slaves were to be procured.

The bar was reached through tiny narrow winding streets with roofs projecting so close that they almost touched. Sunshine never percolated into these narrow alleys. A doctor once told me that the children who lived in these teeming streets suffered from

On board a dhow in Zanzibar harbour.

diseases caused by a deficiency of sunlight even though outside the dark foul-smelling alleys the sun would be blazing down on long stretches of white sand and turquoise water. I made my way through a labyrinth of streets in which the paint flaked off the sides of the houses, leaving them black and striped with patches of their previous layers of colour – red and light blue, green and yellow.

Presently I reached the bar. I knew it was near the harbour for the stench of the street was overlaid by the delicious smell of cloves, and it was close to a row of small thatched mud huts – each of which was used as a brothel. The bar consisted of one room only, furnished with rusty tin tables and metal chairs. Advertisements for various brands of beer were plastered on the shabby walls. And at that bar I met Fadi. He was half African and half Arab, very tall and slim, with receding hair and rosebud lips. After some conversation and several drinks, Fadi took me down to the harbour where an Indian dhow had just come in from Bombay. The vessel was of about 150 tons and had a crew of only eight. Four of them were young boys who were paid only sixty rupees a month. But this sum was paid to the boy's father in almost all cases; in effect, the boy was virtually a slave. The dhow had taken two months on its journey from Bombay. There was a dazed look in one of the youngest boy's eyes; he was obviously doped.

A crew member from a dhow in Zanzibar harbour.

'If you are interested in one of them,' Fadi told me, 'I can easily arrange it.'

I took photographs and then left the dhow and went with Fadi to another bar. Fadi had informed me that he could seldom afford whisky, so I ordered large whiskies because I wanted to get him to talk. Eventually he did. He revealed that slaves are smuggled into Saudi Arabia, Jedda, Aden, Mukalla and Muscat by dhows in the following ways.

A boy or a young man is offered a lump sum of about thirty pounds to work for a 'friend' of the dhow master (known as the Nahoda) for two months. The dhow master promises that after the two months' work the young man will be returned to Zanzibar. Since a house boy in Zanzibar gets only three pounds a month he jumps at this opportunity. He is prepared to leave his home secretly; he is taken in a rowing-boat to the dhow that very night. When the dhow reaches the port in Arabia, officials discover that the man has no passport or immigration papers. He is an illegal immigrant in fact. The man is therefore informed that he cannot be employed at the thirty pounds a month because his papers are not in order. He is told he will have to work in order to earn money to pay back his passage to Zanzibar. He is then engaged by the Nahoda's 'friend' who is, of course, a slave dealer. In the slave market he is sold to the highest bidder. He never gets back to Zanzibar.

The second method relies on the fact that in Zanzibar it is an established custom for a boy's father to bring his son to some large Arab family and offer the boy's services for two or three pounds a month, according to his age, *and* it is apparently usual for the father to state that the monthly wages should be paid direct to him rather than to his son. So the Nahoda goes to the father of a boy he fancies and says he will take him on as crew at five pounds a month. The dhow, he says, will be away for a year: he will therefore pay the boy's father two-thirds of the boy's wages in advance. He pays the father forty pounds. The boy seldom returns.

Thirdly, a fully-grown African labourer is offered a free passage to Arabia on a dhow in exchange for a promissory note to repay the Nahoda out of the wages the man will get from working in the prosperous oil fields. The man is told that Saudi Arabia is the richest country in the world – so rich that even the poor there are wealthy. When the dhow reaches Jedda the African labourer gets no chance of finding a job. He is prevented from making any contact which would allow him anywhere near the oil fields. The Nahoda holds his promissory note to repay him for the passage. The man becomes the Nahoda's property.

The last method is the most unpleasant of all.

Asian families, especially Indian families in Zanzibar, swarm with children. Although provision is made for registration of births in Zanzibar, the enforcement of it is lax. Many babies are never registered at all. Indian girls and boys are very much in demand by the rich Emirs and Sheiks of Saudi Arabia. Therefore the Nahoda and one or two of his crew go round the poverty-stricken shanty towns of the Indian quarters where the families live in huts patched up with mud and roofed with flattened petrol cans. When the men produce bags of sweets, they manage without any difficulty to persuade tiny children of three or four years old to stray from the shanty town where they live and wander into the palm groves. As soon as the child is out of sight, it is quickly gagged and trussed and put into a sack. At night the sack is

stowed at the bottom of a rowing-boat which is then rowed out
to the dhow at anchor. The parents of the stolen child sometimes
report the child's loss to the police. But they fear that they or their
families may be suspected of having sold the child, and their suspicion of authority is innate. Also, Indian families are very numerous. After a while the disappearance of the child is accepted as an
evil stroke of fate.

When the dhow reaches Saudi Arabia the child is smuggled
ashore and taken to a particular farm inland. There, over a period
of four or five years the children are fattened and specially trained
in the art of pleasing an Arab master. A child from this particular
farm which caters for the Emirs and Sheiks with special tastes
may fetch five or six hundred pounds.

The Immigration Department both in Zanzibar and in Mombasa is vigilant, efficient and alert. But with a hundred dhows in
harbour and dinghies moving to and from each of them how can
the Immigration Officer in charge keep watch over the lot of
them? Moreover, in the watches of the night it is usually an
Arab or African subordinate who is on duty. These subordinates
are pathetically underpaid, and they are only too easily bribed to
look the other way.

After a few weeks, I had got the proof I needed; I had taken my
photographs; and I had written my report to the appropriate
authority. I decided to relax for a while.

One evening after dinner I was strolling along a wide street
with beautiful old Arab houses on either side of it when I was
accosted by Fadi.

Dhows in Zanzibar
harbour.

117

'Do you want to go down to see the dhows?' he asked.

'No, thanks,' I replied.

'What *would* you like to see?' Fadi asked.

'Nothing in particular,' I answered.

But Fadi, as I had found, was irrepressible. Somehow he contrived to produce a gleam of excitement in his bloodshot eyes.

'I know a girl,' he announced. 'She is about sixteen, and very slim and beautiful. She is half Arab and half African – like I am. She is the daughter of a friend of mine who is away from Zanzibar. Her name is Zara. She is so beautiful that if you see her I know you will want to sleep with her. And I think she will want to go with you, for she is fond of going with a white man though she seldom gets the chance.'

At that stage, I managed to persuade myself that my reason for going to see the girl was disinterested – almost that of a sociologist. So once again I followed Fadi through the dusty narrow lanes. We stopped outside a single-storeyed Arab house.

'You must give me money,' Fadi whispered to me, 'because I must pay money to bribe the old woman who looks after the girl when my friend is away.'

As soon as I had paid Fadi, he knocked on the door. A grille was slid aside and a wizened face looked out. The old woman and Fadi now began to whisper urgently to each other in Arabic, speaking so fast I could not understand a word. Presently the old woman opened the door. We walked into a dimly lit hall.

'Wait here,' Fadi told me. 'The woman will go and tell the girl you are here. If you like the girl and sleep with her,' Fadi whispered to me, 'you will give her a present when you leave.'

'Certainly,' I agreed.

After a few minutes the old woman opened a door at the end of the hall and beckoned to me.

'Now I go,' Fadi whispered to me. 'So you give me a tip.'

I gave Fadi his usual tip and he slipped quietly away.

I followed the woman into a small bedroom lit by an oil-lamp. Lying naked on a mattress in the corner was one of the loveliest girls I had ever seen. She lay on her back with her arms folded behind her head. Her young breasts stood out from her slender body. In her hair was a white gardenia. Her skin seemed to be more African than Arab; her limbs were dark and gleamed like polished ivory. The girl gave me a smile of welcome. The woman sidled from the room. The girl stretched out her arms to me. I bent down and kissed her. She held me for a moment and then gave a little laugh.

'Take off your clothes,' she murmured.

She watched me as I undressed and hung my clothes over the back of a chair.

'I like you naked,' she said. Then she smiled and beckoned to me. 'I am waiting for you,' she whispered.

I lay on the mattress beside her. Her hands began to stroke my back; she brushed her breasts lightly against my chest.

'You smell good,' she told me. 'Your smell excites me.' Then her polished thighs parted. 'Take me now,' she said. 'Please, now . . .'

Shortly before dawn, as I walked back to the little hotel in Zanzibar where I was staying, I began to wonder if my bisexuality was not becoming stronger than my homosexuality, for the hours I had spent with Zara had delighted and deeply thrilled me. I felt elated and utterly satisfied. I wanted to go back to her the following evening. Vague ideas of installing her in some little house as my mistress entered my exhilarated mind. After all Fadi had said that his friend was away in Aden for at least three months, and the old woman had shown how easily she could be bribed. I could imagine myself living in a state of entrancing nirvana with little Zara who had shown by every word she had spoken, by the passionate love she had made to me, and by her frantic appeals for me to return again, that she was indeed fond of me.

That afternoon an English friend of mine who worked for a small shipping firm flew in on the plane from Mombasa. I will call him Walter. He was about my age but looked older because his hair was grey and he was very thin. Over drinks that night in the hotel, I told him about Zara. He finished his whisky helped himself to another, and then stared at me for a while in silence.

'I'm so fond of Zara,' I continued, 'that if it were possible to arrange and if she would consent I'd find a house outside the town and install her as my mistress.'

Walter smiled. 'I think the girl would agree. Without any doubt, I think she would,' he said.

'What are you smiling about?' I asked.

Walter's smile became even more mysterious. 'I am not sure that I'm right,' he said. 'And if I *am* right, I'm not certain if I should tell you.'

'Drink down your drink,' I told him. 'And stop being so mysterious.'

Walter finished his drink and gave a sigh. 'You were let into the house by an old woman?' he asked.

'Yes.'

'The girl's room was through a rather badly lit hall? And she was lying on a none too clean mattress over in the right-hand corner of the little room?'

'Yes,' I replied. 'Just what are you trying to tell me?'

But Walter was not perturbed by the anger in my voice. 'You

see, I never knew the girl's name,' he began rather absently. 'But now I'm fairly sure she must have been your little Zara with whom I spent such an exquisite evening last time I was in Zanzibar.'

Walter stopped speaking and looked directly at me.

'What nonsense!' I exclaimed indignantly. 'Here in Zanzibar there must be hundreds of houses which fit the description; and there are probably hundreds of girls lying in bedrooms in them. Why in heaven's name should you suppose that the girl you had was Zara?'

Walter gazed at me calmly.

'I'm not sure,' he answered. 'But if the girl was Zara then I think I can repeat to you some of the phrases she used. However, I may say that I'm only doing this to stop you from making a complete idiot of yourself.'

'Carry on,' I said grimly.

'Did she ask you to undress?' Walter enquired.

'Obviously.'

'Did the girl say "I like you naked"?'

I managed to appear unconcerned.

'Yes,' I replied. 'As it happens, she did.'

'And did she by any chance say to you "You smell good"? Did she tell you that your smell excited her?'

'Yes,' I answered.

Walter repeated a whole sequence of remarks which Zara had made to me. I realised that they were simply the stock phrases of her profession. Walter stopped speaking. He refilled his glass with whisky. Then he gazed at me in silence for a moment.

'Have I said enough?' Walter asked.

'You have said enough,' I answered.

'You mustn't blame the girl,' Walter said. 'These are the speeches that she's been taught to make to every client. I've only told you the truth because I didn't want you to get hurt later. You may have worn better than I have. But the fact remains – we're both middle-aged. And what a girl like Zara would like – if she were given the chance – would be a very lusty young lad of her own age.'

'Right,' I said. 'I'm very grateful to you. Now let's order another bottle of whisky and get really drunk.'

'Splendid,' said Walter. 'But you needn't look so glum. Remember that there are both girls *and* boys who actually prefer men older than themselves.'

'Thank you for the consolation,' I replied.

Later that night when I went up to my room in the hotel I tried to forget my experience with Zara. I could not.

When I had been twenty-two my uncle had said that I was positively middle-aged, and since that obviously inaccurate remark I had stopped worrying about my age. However, I took care to remain slim and fit. I now crossed the room and looked at the mirror – above which hung a naked electric light bulb. I examined my face dispassionately. I observed the wrinkles of my forehead and the deep lines that ran from my nostrils to the sides of my mouth. And as I watched them I realised that the boy whom Gerald Haxton had loved was gone. Gone was the youth whom Dieter had wanted to take to the hut above Salzburg. Gone was the young man whom Salem – the Senussi soldier – had briefly loved.

I was then forty-seven years old. I was middle-aged; and there was nothing I could do about it – except to adapt myself to the fact.

And in 1973 I am nearly sixty years old. Here I am, alone in my cabin – for William and I are the only two passengers on board this cargo boat, and each of us has separate accommodation – and I am travelling in search of yet another nirvana, this time in Ceylon, or rather just off its coast. Like many other travellers I was attracted to Ceylon the very first time I arrived there. The second time I came there, some friends of mine drove me south from Colombo along the palm-fringed coast, past straggling villages of mud-huts, past green and turquoise lagoons. Eventually we reached the Rest House of Weligama. From there, less than a hundred yards away from the Rest House, across a shallow stretch of sparkling sea, was the island of Taprobane – a mound, covered with a tangle of palm trees through which a house could be vaguely glimpsed.

The tide was low; we were wearing shorts. So we waded across to the island and scrambled on to a decrepit landing-stage. At the far end was a padlocked gate. We called out, and from a mass of thick undergrowth, which dripped with orchids, a man appeared. We told him that we were visitors and would love to see the island. With a pleasant smile, he unlocked the gate. Together we climbed up a hundred steps that led along a narrow winding path, passing stone benches and pieces of broken statuary, until we reached a terrace surrounding an octagonal house – twenty-five yards wide. First, we wandered round the terrace of the summit which is only one hundred and thirty-five feet square. The pillars on the terrace reminded me of Capri. From the terrace the overgrown, brightly coloured garden dropped abruptly to the sea. Trees festooned with all kinds of orchids and bougainvillaeas seemed to sprout from its declivity. And when we reached the terrace we found that from each side was an amazing view. To one side, we could see the bay outspreading its arms towards the ocean until they were lost in the haze of the far distance. To the other side, the sea, streaked with an amethyst-purple, glittered in the sunlight. No land lay between us and the South Pole. The beauty of the island was fantastic.

The house itself had been built by the Count de Mauny in 1926. He was a remarkable man. The Count was born in 1866 and in 1898 married The Lady Mary Byng who was the eldest daughter of the 4th Earl of Stratford and was a Maid of Honour to Queen Victoria. He first visited Ceylon in 1911 as a guest of Sir Thomas Lipton and immediately fell in love with the place. He made several further visits between then and 1919. The Count made one more visit to England in 1923 and spent the next eighteen years of his life in Ceylon. In about 1925 he made his headquarters at the Weligama Rest House from which he gazed longingly at the island opposite – which was then called the 'Island of Doves'.

The Count de Mauny and his son decided to approach the owner who had cleared the very top of the island of a few coconut trees and had imported a supply of cut-stone blocks before abandoning the idea of building for financial reasons. The island was purchased. This is how the Count de Mauny describes the building of the house.*

'The house is the picture, the garden the frame; they must be in keeping with each other, happily married, so to speak, if the *ensemble* of picture and frame is to be as perfect as human imperfection will allow. Sometimes the gardens are laid out to suit the house; or the house may be built to suit our ideal of a garden. The latter was my case. I knew, from the first, what the garden should be; to please me, it would have to conform with the lie of the ground, harmonise with the surroundings, and make the best use of the space allotted to it. The house should do the same, and by its complete adaptation to and harmony with the gardens it should realise the *ensemble* of which I dreamed.

'Had I left Taprobane as I found it – a granite rock, some boulders, a few coconut-palms, and thickets of scrub – the house must have been a mere week-end shooting and fishing box, with walls of dried mud and a *cadjan* roof: merely a living-room, open at both ends, one bedroom with bathroom on either side, and a "godown" for kitchen and servants' quarters. It could have been made a nice little place, for a little taste can make any house attractive. But it could never have become the fulfilment of my aspirations. It might have been a camping-place, but never "home", the achievement of my creative faculties.'

'The house, being a home for the tropics, had to be in tune with the East, in its style of architecture, its colouring, its dimensions,

*Count de Mauny: *The Garden of Taprobane*: Williams & Norgate, London: 1937.

its proportions and internal dispositions, and the details of the carvings and mouldings. Above all, it must not overwhelm the island by its exaggerated size and proportions; indeed, it should have a certain semblance of lightness, an effect obtained by an adequate appearance of height – as in the castle which crowns Mont Saint-Michel. The central dome, rising above roofs and gables, was to play this part. The gardens, being the setting of the jewel, had to emphasise the façade in some places, and to cast the shade of their trees on others.'

Many years later Paul Bowles visited the island, and 'explored the place'. This is what he wrote: 'It was far better even than I had expected – an embodiment of the innumerable fantasies and day-dreams that had flitted through my mind since childhood. . . . The hot smell of the sun on the flowers, the sound of the sea breaking on the big rocks. . . . More than ever the island represented an unfulfilled desire, an impossible wish.'

Eventually Paul bought the island and lived there with his wife for many happy months.

With these thoughts in our minds, we now entered the house the Count de Mauny had built. The first thing I noticed was its splendid spaciousness and marvellous views – from the centre of the hall you could see through every bedroom. The next thing my practical side observed was – as Paul had remarked – the 'im-practicability' of the place. There was no privacy at all, but this could be remedied without destroying the essential character of the high-domed 'Hall of the Lotus'. Next I admired the furniture.

'Every piece of furniture,' says the Count, 'has been made by local craftsmen, from models inspired by French artists. It is what it was intended to be, an object-lesson, testifying to the remarkable skill of Sinhalese craftsmen in woodwork, wrought-iron and brass-work. A few specimens of the genuine Dutch style give a finishing touch to the furnishing of the hall.'

I walked out on to the loggia and gazed at the thick clusters of flowers that tumbled down the steep sides of the island as if they were about to fall into the sea. By then – like Paul – I felt an intense 'wish' to inhabit the place.

Accordingly, when I returned to England after that particular journey I met the son of the Ceylonese owner of the island who happened to be in London and made a vague agreement with him as to the price I would pay. Friends of mine in Ceylon had told me that I had a good chance of getting a permanent visa to live there and I had decided that, if necessary, I could live there by myself. I would learn Ceylonese; I would make friends – as Paul had done – with the people in the neighbourhood of Weligama;

I had at least three novels floating around in my head which I wanted to write, and hundreds of books I wanted to read. I would lead an orderly and tranquil life. On the island of Taprobane I would find my nirvana.

Our journey on the M.S. *Tiber* of the Wilhelmsen Line had been arranged by a friend of Mr Wilhelmsen himself. The ship did not ordinarily carry passengers, and the space and the peace of the deck outside our two cabins was as enjoyable as the kindness of the Captain and his officers and the excellence of the food. However, one disadvantage of travelling on a cargo boat in these days is that the ship can get held up outside a harbour for two or three weeks before it can find a berth in which to unload. But this did not worry us because I was dictating my novel *The Sign*. For exercise we played hectic table-tennis on deck, and we were both reading books on Buddhism.

The *Tiber* eventually docked at Karachi, where we spent some time on shore. On our third morning in Karachi we had drinks with the British Consul-General and his wife, and we lunched with a Saudi Arabian student who had attended a lecture I had given at the American School the previous day. Shortly after three o'clock we took a taxi from outside the Inter-Continental Hotel and asked the driver, a thin middle-aged Pakistani, to take us to the East Wharf gate of the harbour.

At the gate we produced our shore-leave passes. But the pompous looking official dressed in a khaki uniform who appeared to be in charge of the customs post was not interested in them. Instead, he shouted in Pakistani at the driver. We presumed that he had directed him to reverse away from the post, for this was what the driver did. The taxi stopped about fifty yards away from the gate. The pompous security guard who was wearing two chevrons on his arm then strode over to the taxi and began punching our driver viciously in the face. He was promptly joined by another and younger guard in khaki who was also wearing two chevrons. Presumably they were both police corporals. Together they dragged our driver out of the car, knocked him to the ground, and then began kicking him in the groin with their heavy boots.

William shouted at them in protest, and I got out of the car to try to find someone in charge. But by then a mob had gathered. I had to push my way through the crowd to reach what seemed to be the main office. As I moved, a third guard approached me with his right arm raised to attack. I was clutching my passport and I flicked his hand hard with the edge of it. I burst into an office where fortunately there was an officer sitting. Rapidly I explained that our driver was being kicked to death. Promptly, the officer went with me to the taxi where the driver was still lying groaning on the ground beside his cab while the two corporals continued to kick him. The officer shouted out an order. The two corporals stopped their assault. The taxi driver somehow managed to crawl back into his driving-seat. The mob was dispersed. The driver was allowed to drive on his way along the wharf to our ship.

From conversation with officers on board the *Tiber*, we gathered that the trouble probably started because our driver did not offer the corporal a bribe to allow him to drive us to the ship. But there had been no conversation between our driver and the corporal. And since our driver – when ordered to back his car – waited patiently for the corporal to approach him, he was obviously ignorant of the custom of bribery.

However, this was the only unpleasant incident while we were in Karachi, and we were most hospitably entertained. The agent of the shipping line kindly suggested that we might like to stay for three or four nights in a small beach hut that he owned a few miles out of Karachi in an area where some hippies had founded a colony.

I have met hippies all over the world – from Karachi and Ibiza to the largest communes in Morocco. Though people disapprove of them, their influence on the world cannot be dismissed, and their ideals and hopes to abolish the evils of class-distinction and racialism are wholly admirable. And if a young person wants to 'opt out' of society, why should he not be permitted to do so? In the Middle Ages in Europe the young men who wished to 'opt out' of a world which they considered evil became monks or friars; they were protected from the enmity of society by the might of the Church; some of them eventually became saints.

I cannot, however, sympathise with what would seem to be their cult of being dirty. So filthy did the hippies become in the town of Ibiza that the Spanish authorities began to fear that they would discourage the lucrative tourist trade. Accordingly the Governor issued an edict which in the English translation ran as follows.

> People may be expelled from the island of Ibiza
> for one or both of the following reasons:
>   1: Economic frivolity.
>   2: Being of hideous aspect.

Wearing no shoes or sandals counted as being both economically frivolous *and* of hideous aspect. Shoals of hippies were put on a boat and transported to Barcelona.

However, most of the hippies with whom I made friends lived either in Essaouira, formerly called Mogador, or in Marrakech.

Essaouira was founded in 1760 by the Sultan Sidi Mohammed ben Abdullah – first because he wanted to punish the port of Agadir which was in revolt against him; secondly because he wanted Southern Morocco to have a harbour for commerce and as a base for the Corsairs who were privateering against foreign vessels. He gave his authority for designing the new town to a French prisoner called Theodore Cornut. Now the Sultan wished to attract European merchants and also Jews who had commercial relations with England. Accordingly the old town is divided into various districts; it has a mellah, a medina, and two kasbahs. The town was beautifully set out with living quarters for Arabs, English, and Jews. Each district had its own small market to cater for the special tastes of the inhabitants, but there was a large central market where all could meet. Essaouira, in fact, was the first attempt at community planning in Morocco and enjoyed a reputation for tolerance. It still does.

When I was there in 1970, wondering vaguely if I would find a nirvana there, I discovered that the hippies had taken over a village called Diabet on the outskirts of the town as their head-quarters. There they lived six or seven to a room, or they camped out in the sandy crumbling ruins of the old royal palace nearby. Each morning the hippies trooped into town, looking as if they had borrowed a film company's wardrobe for a fancy dress ball. Some were disguised as flamboyant pirates, complete with moustaches and cutlasses, others were dressed up like Andalusian gypsies with huge ear-rings and castanets. They would shop – and then buy their kif. They would sit down outside the café in the main square and drink black coffee.

The inhabitants of Essaouira accept the hippies because they represent a permanent source of income, and because – in the town – they are gentle and orderly. Many of the young Moroccans think that the hippies are a different nationality.

'*Vous êtes Français?*' I was asked as I sat at the café.

'*Non.*'

'*Americain?*'

'*Non.*'

'*Hippie?*'

And in a way the Moroccans are right to think of the hippies as a separate race, for they have become a race apart. They look different; they have their own customs; even a language of their own is developing. More important, their code of ethics and their way of behaviour are completely different. Meeting these quiet, soft-spoken young people lying on their blankets in the dunes, contemplating the lovely mimosa trees around them, you cannot help feeling sympathy with them.

'We hippies adore natural things,' a young man told me. 'We live crudely on a small budget. We believe in free love. But a male and female hippy will try to look alike, and a male hippy often presents himself as sexless. Some of the men, of course, are bi-sexual. We live in a kind of a-sexual *dolce vita*.

'If our society works well,' he continued, 'we don't care which way the balls swing between a man's legs – because we can *see* their bodies and we can dance in front of each other. And that's it. Being *aware* of each other's bodies is enough. We are adults playing the games of children. We are being childlike in our adult behaviour – like children playing at doctors. We have lived with adults; we have been shown the actions of adults. But we have reached a point when we dare to believe that we are adults by the very fact that we do not perform actions normally performed in adult society. You could say that we are going on a pilgrimage to find a place in the world where we can treat each other in a way which we believe enables us to find true belief and a true society. At this moment, we are going through the stage of finding out and testing our true beliefs. We are still in transit.

'The parties we have on the beach aren't orgies. We make friends with each other simply. There's a greeting, and an accept-ance of the greeting. We smoke a pipe or two of kif. Generally, there's a guitarist, a drummer, a tambourine-player, and some-times a flautist down there. The rhythm of their playing is pleasant, yet in a way desperate because we are all trying to break through – trying to find just one single thing. Hallucinatory drugs are our short way to heaven and allow us for a while to believe that we *have* found it.'

In the afternoon the young hippies – both boys and girls – lie in the sun among the mimosa trees and smoke their pipes of kif, which is made from the flower leaves of hemp grown in Morocco in the mountains above Ketama. Until some years ago Ketama was a barren region. Then the Sultan visited it. He was appalled by the terrible poverty he saw.

'What can I do to alleviate the misery of your people?' he asked the local chieftain.

'Grant us permission to grow the plant from which comes kif and hashish,' the chief answered.

The Sultan gave his permission. The district now prospers.

Throughout the ages man's need to escape from the reality of his everyday life has led him to search for some means of reach-ing some kind of dream-world. Hallucinatory drugs have been used from time immemorial. Thousands of books have been written on the subject. Here, I will only say that kif or hashish which both come from the hemp plant are generally agreed to be the least harmful.

I wondered if I could attain a temporary nirvana through hashish. I went out into the mimosa groves one afternoon with two hippy friends of mine. The hash, which was dry and brown coloured and smelled of hay, had already been cut up and mixed with tea. We had had a very light lunch and no liquor. We reached the dunes at 2.30 and each of us drank two cups. At 3.00 we had our second cup which was stronger and much darker. We were lying in a small clearing between large mimosa trees. Half an hour later I began to feel slightly light-headed and amused by everything. Soon, I began to feel wonderfully relaxed. It seemed to me that I could hear all sounds with an unusual clarity – the rustle of the sea, the birds singing in the trees. Presently I was conscious of a vivid sense of awareness. This was accompanied by a sensation of complete irresponsibility. I was extremely conscious of my body which seemed to glow with vitality, yet I felt no sexual desire, for nothing seemed to matter. What I did would be of no importance, and in any case I did not want to do anything in particular. Though full of ardour I was at the same time marvellously relaxed. And I was conscious that I was seeing everything very distinctly. I was intensely aware of the beauty of the incredibly bright yellowness of the mimosa blooms on the branches above my head, and through the branches I could see an almost incredibly blue sky. This was a delight. But at the same time I experienced a profound sense of detachment from the whole scene, which in some way I found strangely disquieting. An odd vision swung into my mind. I was in a vast ballroom, and I could see in fantastic detail all the pictures on the walls and the great chandeliers hanging from the ceiling. But there were no people

in the room. I was all alone; my loneliness dismayed me. Suddenly I was frightened. Yet I was still conscious of the presence of my two friends. Vaguely, I could listen to them talking. Yet I was still very much alone; my solitude now became alarming. I then noticed that the sun had dipped beneath the yellow branches. I was cold, but I was unwilling to make any effort to move until I became aware that my friends were speaking to me. They were suggesting we should walk back to their car.

I was glad to go.

But the child-like quality that hippies seem to encourage in themselves and in each other has two dangers. They can be easily influenced by a really strong character, and they are fascinated, like children, by new experiments.

The hippies of Diabet, for instance, believe they must go through a 'spiritual and organic experience' in order to find out the true meaning of their principles. Recently they decided that LSD could help them reach a fuller understanding of life. So they planned an 'acid party' on the beach.

In the moonlight, they performed a Rites of Spring dance. All of them were naked, and as the evening progressed they got very high and very wild. The hippies thought they were alone. But they were being watched by a Moroccan hidden in the dunes. The man watched them with a loathing of their immorality – a loathing mixed with envy of their well-made, fine young bodies. For he was a hunchback, and his left leg was withered and useless. He watched them, and he waited.

Essaouira
(formerly Mogador).

At about 3.00 a.m., the hippies drifted back to the village. They left behind an American and his girlfriend who was so far gone she couldn't move. Presently the boy wandered off. As soon as the boy had left, the hunchback crawled slowly and silently towards the girl who was lying face downward in the sand. Slowly he took out a dagger and plunged it between her shoulders.

The girl screamed. The boyfriend rushed back to her. He saw the hunchback slithering away into the dunes. He saw the girl's wound. The boy then ran off and collected his friends from the village. Someone hurried into town to fetch an ambulance. The rest formed a circle round the girl who was now unconscious. They examined her wound. It looked as if she was dying. So the hippies decided they must sing a spiritual chant to liberate her spirit before death. As they chanted the girl regained consciousness.

'We are liberating your spirit,' they told her.

Weakly, she nodded her head. As the chanting continued the girl began, in a feeble croaking voice, to join in. She was still singing when the ambulance arrived.

My hippy friends' explanation that the use of drugs is the hippy 'short way to heaven' is, I am certain, true. But so are the stories of the ghastly misery that can be caused by the drugs they use so freely.

Recently, a young girl from London arrived at Diabet. With her spectacles and thin face she was not beautiful, my friend told me. But she had a lovely body. She also possessed a large number of LSD tablets. One evening when she was already high on LSD she went out into the dunes alone. After she had walked some way she met four young Moroccans. They were aged – so it came out at the inquest – between sixteen and twenty-two. They were labourers from an inland farm. Jackson tells us in his *Account of the Empire of Morocco*, published in 1809, that the sensuality of the Moroccans 'knows no bounds' and 'such is their wretched depravity that they indulge in the most unnatural and abominable propensities, in short, every vice that is disgraceful and degrading to human nature, is to be found amongst them'. Certainly in my own travels I have found the Moroccans admirably 'permissive' in their attitude to sex. So I do not expect that the four young farm labourers were wholly innocent. They had probably smoked hash which is fairly easy to obtain in the district. But it is certain they had never taken any of the stronger hallucinatory drugs.

The girl gave them a slack smile. But it was not her face that attracted their attention, it was the slimness of her young body. The girl smiled at them again and beckoned to them to follow her. She led the way to a concealed place in the dunes. Then she reached into her shoulder-bag and brought out some LSD tablets which she handed round. Even before she began to take off her clothes the boys had become excited. The girl indicated they should take off their clothes. When they were all naked she handed round more tablets. Presently she began fondling each of them in turn. But it seems that she refused to let them have sex with her. Instead, on her LSD 'trip' she began to crawl on all fours idiotically grinning at them. Soon she began to howl and make weird sounds. The boys decided this must be a game. Already the drug was working on them. They too began crawling about on their hands and knees and howling like wolf-dogs. The game thrilled them.

But suddenly it was a game no longer. They *became* wolf-dogs. They clutched at the girl, tearing her skin, and gripping her arms and legs. Then, one by one, they raped her – while the other three held her down. But the medical evidence at the inquest showed that the girl had not died because she had been raped; she had died from loss of blood. Her breasts had been gnawed away.

But in spite of the horrible incidents that sometimes occur, there is still a certain pastoral charm about the hippies of Diabet. The scene in the famous city of Marrakech some one hundred and twenty-five miles away is very different. The hippy colony in this largely Berber town in which Saharan and African Negro influences have always intermingled had been started eighteen months before my visit in 1970. A famous American hippy called Lee had announced that Marrakech was 'the appointed city for all hippies to rally and turn on and tune in and drop out'. Pop fans will remember the popular record by Crosby, Stills, Nash and Young called *Marrakech Express* that helped to publicise 'the great get-together'.

Almost all drugs which need a prescription in Britain are sold openly in the chemist shops of Marrakech; several of these drugs include preparations which contain opium. A popular slimming cure that is on the market contains liquid methadrine – known as 'speed'. Large supplies of LSD are brought in by visiting hippies. At sunset the hippies and the Morrocans congregate in the well-known square called the Djemaa el Fna. Crowds form round the jugglers, snake-charmers, acrobats, dancers, and storytellers. An unlikely selection of celebrities from Field-Marshal Lord Auchinleck to Mick Jagger and Marianne Faithfull stroll around inspecting the scene.

By now the drums have started to throb. The whole square seems to quiver and vibrate. I noticed that the hippies began to draw together as if for mutual protection from the excitements they had experienced and excitements hovering on the fringe of their vision which were yet to come.

In the square I met an English boy called Michael whom I had known in Ibiza. He had drifted from Ibiza to Tangier where he met Timothy Leary who was then 'the apostle of LSD'. Leary had recently been jailed in America for drug offences. He gave Michael LSD; his 'trip' lasted eighteen hours. Michael still takes the drug.

'I enjoyed the experience,' he told me. 'It made me understand more about myself and more about other people. And it made me feel very much *aware*. But I don't want to take too much of the stuff. It can burn out your brain.'

Michael, like many of his hippy friends, came to Marrakech for the 'great get-together' and, like them, he stayed there because he enjoyed 'its spontaneity, music and pleasure'.

'Back in England or America everyone is on the defensive,' Michael explained. 'But here you can make a direct contact with a Moroccan with your eyes. And it's here one can rediscover the *animal* that lies in every person. But the place takes a bit of getting used to. When the hippies first came to Marrakech they felt lost. The food is different. They're a long way from Mum and hot baths. And they just can't put things together. The conditions in some of the hotels they live in are like the Black Hole of Calcutta.

'Some of the hippies find it too much. And they disappear – but heaven knows where, because so many of them have cut their ties with home. Many of them run out of money. After a while, the managers of these seedy hotels make an official complaint, and the police throw the hippies out. Then comes the real misery because they haven't realised – quite apart from anything else – that the town is like an oven in summer and can be very cold in winter.'

Some of the stories I heard while I was in Marrakech were terrible.

A few days before my visit, an English girl appeared at the main police station. Her dress was stained and torn; she had no shoes; there were lice in her hair and her skin was filthy. The drugs she had taken had destroyed her mind. She was lost. She could not remember how long she had been in Morocco. She could not even remember her name. She was taken to hospital.

The previous year an American boy of twenty died from an

overdose of amphetamine. In the squalid room in which he had been living, the police found a girl of the same age. Her mind was gone; she had 'flipped'. She was taken off in an ambulance.

A young English girl became obsessed by the virility of the young Moroccans she went to bed with. After a few months she met a Moroccan of about thirty who was tough, handsome and unusually ardent. She lived with him for a while and fell desperately in love with him. He enjoyed sleeping with her because she was very blonde, and dark-skinned Moroccans are violently attracted to blonde girls and boys. The girl became a Moslem and married her Moroccan lover. The Moroccan now keeps her locked up in his house – together with his other three wives.

A French girl became a methadrine addict. But gradually her money began to run short and she was thrown out of her hotel. She found a room quite close to the Djemaa el Fna. But she needed money to pay for her 'speed'. One evening in the square a prosperous-looking Moroccan accosted her and offered her a sum of money if he could sleep with her for the night. She accepted. The money he gave to her kept her in 'speed' for a week. When the money ran out she went once again to the square. But by now she was beginning to look a little shabby. This time her client paid her less. Her deterioration continued. Soon she became a full-time prostitute. When I saw the girl her hair was done up in the traditional fashion of a Moroccan prostitute and dyed red. She wore a cloak and some cheap beads. Her forehead was tattooed. Her face was smeared with make-up. Any Moroccan could have her for the equivalent of twenty-five pence.

However, these grim stories are exceptions, and after all such events occur regularly in London or New York. But in London or New York the hippies would not be so far away from adequate 'care and protection'.

In Morocco many hippies lead an enjoyable existence – until their money runs out. As Michael had pointed out to me, the hippies can make 'a direct contact with a Morrocan' with their eyes. I have joined groups of hippies both in the square and in old crumbling Arab houses which they have rented in the outskirts of the town. I have been amazed at the contact they have made with Moroccan strangers using only a few words of common language. It is at once fascinating and moving to witness the ease with which these young boys and girls overcome the language barrier.

But the friendship of the hippies with the young Moroccans has had an effect on which no one had reckoned. For many of the Moroccan youths are beginning to discover that *they too* are hippies at heart. Like the visiting hippies whose parents may be well-to-do dentists in Detroit or solicitors in Surbiton, the Moroccan students are beginning to abandon the values and standards of *their* middle-class parents. No longer are they impressed by the fridgidaire and the washing-machine in the kitchen and the hifi set in the living-room. The Moroccan students have told me in all sincerity that they are beginning to rediscover the old Berber values of simplicity and leisure. Without meaning to, the hippies have had a profound influence on a great many Moroccans.

Recently some two hundred students had protested in Rabat because a Moroccan who had committed a political murder and had fled to Spain had been repatriated by the Spanish authorities and executed. Their demonstration, inspired by the liberal ideals they had learned from their hippy friends, was so violent that the police closed the gates of the central square in Rabat and opened fire. Over a hundred students were killed.

These students are now considered martyrs to the cause of freedom by young Moroccans and hippies alike. The joint movement still continues.

I smoked hashish with my hippy friends in Marrakech. I had no nightmares, and I did not feel ill next morning as I expect I would have done if I had drunk half a bottle of whisky. While I was smoking I felt a peace inside myself and a friendliness to all around me.

'Dreams are excursions to the limbo of things,' we have been told, 'a semi-deliverance from the human prison.'

Moreover, De Quincey went further. He first took a tincture of opium because he had a toothache. 'I took it,' he writes, 'and an hour later, O heavens! what an apocalypse of the world within me! That my pain had vanished was now a trifle in my eyes, swallowed up in the abyss of divine enjoyment suddenly revealed. Here was a panacea for all human woes; here was the secret of happiness about which the philosophers had disputed for so many ages; happiness might now be bought for a penny, and carried in the waistcoat pocket; portable ecstasies might be corked up in a pint bottle; and peace of mind sent down by the mail.'

If nirvana can be obtained from the distillation of the poppy, surely those of us who seek an escape from 'the human prison' should take it. Unfortunately prolonged use of opium caused De Quincey other effects. He suffered from dark fantasies and terrible dreams, from periods of physical and mental collapse, and, later, from a perpetual struggle against the violent demands of his addiction.

But what of hash – to use the popular word for the various products of the hemp plant? Many doctors now argue that 'pot, hash, marijuana' – or whatever the products of cannabis resin of the hemp plant may be called – should be made legal. Has hash any worse effects than excessive drinking? Now, heavy hash smoking and heavy alcohol drinking (I am not talking about the complete alcoholic or the total drug-addict who both present problems of their own) have the following in common. First, and most important, is that every individual is affected differently by the same amount. Thus, for instance, I know people who can get drunk on half a bottle of wine. But when I would be at Chartwell or Chequers entertained by Winston Churchill I would note with admiration the amount of liquor he would daily consume without ever getting drunk. The same applies to hash. Each person's tolerance is different. Moreover, each person's will to survive is different. Some have already given up hope and will drink methylated spirit or take heroin if they can get hold of it. Others have a job, an ego, ambition and pride. These will *not* be so easily led astray. They will drink in moderation and their intake of drugs – if any outside those medically used – will remain consistently small; used, in fact, in the same way as the moderate drinker uses alcohol.

The second similarity between alcohol and hash is that the effects of euphoria and the escape from the prison of life are roughly similar – in that with both they are only transitory. Both can produce a condition of euphoria for a length of time – but there is equally always an end to the period of elation. 'The human prison' is returned to.

However, there are distinct differences. First, if, say, in London you buy a bottle of whisky or gin you can be virtually certain that the contents are unadulterated. But the hash that you buy from a 'dealer' has passed through several hands and several countries before it has reached you and may have been mixed with opium to make it stronger. Next, in most countries the smoker of hash risks large fines or harsh prison sentences. This in itself tends to lend hash the well-known glamour of flirting with danger. (Here it must be added, that this glamour is a very strong reason for making hash legal. For if hash were openly sold in smart packages in government supervised shops, the glamour felt by the young would vanish.) The regular hash-smoker is also somewhat prone to a form of proselytising. 'I've smoked hash, for the last five years,' says the older man to his girlfriend. 'As you can see, it's done me no harm whatsoever. Why not have a "toke"?' The glamour may also partly account for the *slide* from hash to stronger drugs. A heavy drinker of whisky or gin, for instance, will not suddenly get the idea of drinking 'meths'. He may change to vodka by day and brandy by night, but he very seldom hankers after raw alcohol. But my personal experience of young people – especially children – who begin on hash is that they *may* 'graduate' to stronger stuff – which can be the first step towards a humiliating and terrible death.

Perhaps I am too much aware of the dangers of drugs because a dozen years ago I went as a journalist to Hong Kong. I have seen many slums in my life but nothing as horrible and grim as the Walled City of Kowloon on the Chinese mainland. The streets are so narrow there is barely room for two people to pass. Often the so-called streets are no more than cracks between dilapidated houses filled with refuse and stinking excrement. The stench is loathsome. There is no sanitation, no drains of any kind, and no electric light. And no licence is required for the shops that sell adulterated liquor, or for the shops that sell contaminated food. This is because the Walled City does not come under the regulations of the Hong Kong Government. For the same reason no

Marrakech, in a hippy commune.

permit is required for the innumerable dentist-shops facing the outer road of the enclave where unqualified dentists practise on the cheap in dirty little rooms with unsterilised instruments. For the same reason old men and women – cheap sweated labour – crouch at machines in dark airless hovels making shuttles for looms at ten cents each. For the same reason, tiny children squat in the filth making matches, picking them up with an old bit of broken comb to put them into the matchboxes. Fourteen hours' work may bring them the equivalent of sixpence.

It is believed that twelve thousand five hundred people live in this foetid enclave. I suspect the figure is far more. But it is *known* that in the enclave there are seventy substandard factories and seventeen shops that sell polluted food to the inhabitants. It was from this enclave that tiny girls were procured for the Europeans who enjoy sex with children. Inside this enclave the underground Communist agents can meet in safety. In this enclave are the heroin divans.

With trepidation I went into a heroin divan.

It was a low-ceilinged windowless room, lit by a single paraffin lamp. Crouching on the floor which was strewn with litter and old sacks were five addicts, gaunt hollow-cheeked wrecks of men in tattered clothes, with their arms and legs wasted to thin sticks. They looked at me dully as I came in. I was with a Chinese friend, and there was no danger in me seeing them at that moment, for they were waiting, waiting with quivering hands and yearning eyes, waiting for the drug-peddler to arrive and put an end to their ghastly craving – for a while.

One man in every six in Hong Kong is a drug-addict. For every ten men or women sent to prison for an offence unconnected with drugs, at least six are discovered to be secret addicts. As soon as their supply of drugs is stopped, what the doctors call 'withdrawal symptoms' set in, and the addict has to confess his addiction. These are frightening facts and some explanation of how this terrible condition has come about is called for.

For centuries the Chinese of all classes smoked opium perfectly legally. It was a normal habit like smoking tobacco is with us. The fortunes of some of the great British merchant houses in Hong Kong were made by importing opium into China. However, the Chinese were not too happy about the British – to them little known Barbarian merchants – smuggling the opium into China. In 1839 the Emperor of China tried to stop the illegal importing and trade in opium. The British defied him, and the Opium Wars – in which China was defeated – were fought. The opium – grown on the fertile plains of Bengal – continued to be shipped in, sold to the Chinese who remained tranquil and subservient. But after the Second World War the Government of Hong Kong made a determined effort to suppress opium-smoking. The result has been unfortunate. The traffickers and drug-addicts have turned from opium to heroin, because heroin is far easier to smuggle and much easier to take and because heroin doesn't leave a tell-tale smell as opium does. But heroin, which is a derivative of morphine, which in its turn is extracted from opium, is infinitely stronger and more harmful. Heroin can kill. And heroin doesn't require the paraphernalia of the brazier and a pipe and tongs that opium does. At its easiest, all you need to take heroin is a syringe. You can take it quickly and easily at home.

Many of the Chinese start taking heroin for the sheer excitement of it or to give themselves a thrill during the sexual act. Heroin gives the illusion of exhilaration and wellbeing and seems to prolong and intensify the period of orgasm. The thrill is so acute the man or boy tries it a second time – and then a third. By the fourth dose he has found it impossible to stop. Within two or three months he is a slave to the habit, and a slave to the drug-peddler. He deteriorates physically and mentally. All form of self-control is broken. Honour and decency are swept away. He will lie, beg, cheat, steal, blackmail or even kill to satisfy his craving.

But the Hong Kong Government is doing its best to combat the horrors of heroin addiction.

I drove into the New Territories – on the Chinese mainland – with the Prison Commissioner, to see the Tai Lam Prison which holds seven hundred drug-addicts on a steep hillside below the giant Tai Lam Chung dam. Working under the supervision of prison officers the former addicts have made dining-rooms out of barrack-blocks and offices out of stores. They have built concrete steps up the muddy hillside and laid conduits to carry the torrential summer rains. But it isn't the appearance of the place with its well laid-out grounds and sixty-foot long swimming-pool that is important. It's what is being done for the inmates that counts. I was taken by the Indian Medical Officer to see the hospital where the worst cases that arrive are given complete rest. On either side of the brightly-painted block lay haggard emaciated men with withered limbs and frighteningly haunted eyes.

'These men are still suffering from withdrawal symptoms,' the Medical Officer told me. 'They have involuntary seminal ejaculations. They are in almost constant mental anguish, and we give them tranquillisers. Twenty per cent of them have tuberculosis. When they get better they will be given a daily treatment and a special diet including milk, eggs and vitamins. They will be put on light duties. They will be able to sit around in the garden without working. But as soon as the men begin to get fit, they are put to work in the open air, working on making new buildings, cutting fire-breaks, planting young pines for the Forestry Department, gardening, creating a new estate where reformed addicts will be given grants to live.'

I saw the prisoners on various working-parties. They were stripped to the waist in the bright sunshine. It was hard to believe that these healthy-looking men, with their bodies well-covered with flesh, had once looked like the ghastly pathetic burnt-out wrecks in the hospital. But it was true. The photographs complete with each man's case history are the proof.

For various medical reasons which I will not list here, most of the time – apart from my hours of work – I drink too much. Though I have been able to stop myself smoking cigarettes, I have not been able to stop myself drinking. I have an uneasy feeling that if I started to smoke hash with any regularity I might 'slide' into stronger drugs as various of my friends seem to have done. Lastly, I am still haunted by the spectacle of the skeletons in the den in Kowloon who were still alive and craving for a momentary end to their torment.

I have now lived for six such happy weeks on the M.S. *Tiber* that sometimes we have wondered if one could not find a form of nirvana in the existence one leads on a cargo boat. After all, one is splendidly detached from the worries of everyday life. Good and plentiful food arrives at regular intervals without any effort on one's part. The cabins are clean and bright, and all around is the open and seemingly endless blue sea.

When the engines start as the ship leaves harbour the whole vessel shudders, at first rather languidly, then presently begins to pound and shiver rhythmically, beating with such an insistent though gentle rhythm that odd poems come into one's head. As one gazes down from the deck, the movement of the ship through the waves gives one a spurious sense of purpose, and this sensation of an almost spiritual advancement in one's soul ends, disappointingly, when at last the engines stop. After a month on a cargo boat, the ship becomes a womb one is unwilling to leave. The instant one sets foot on shore – even for a day or two – one feels immediately apprehensive and nervous. For once again there is a need to make decisions – where to go, what to buy, where to eat, when to return to harbour. The glory of life for a passenger on a cargo boat is that he has no decision to make from dawn to dusk.

But what of the officers and crew?

On the *Tiber* – because William and I spoke no Norwegian and some of the officers with whom we ate spoke English with a slight difficulty – we were all at first shy and diffident. But as the

An opium den in Kowloon (Hong Kong).

days passed by, they grew used to us and would talk to us and among themselves. But with the exception of the Captain, the Radio Officer, and the First Mate, they seemed reserved. Some remained almost completely silent. As with all men, each individual reacts differently to life at sea. The Captain, I believe, had found his own nirvana on his ship. One afternoon he came up to the little table on deck at which I was working. There was bright sunshine and a mild breeze. The Captain stood for a while in silence staring out at the horizon and the white flecks on the rippling waves. He took in deep breaths of happiness. Then he turned and smiled at me – almost ruefully. 'This,' he said, 'is really living.'

However many of the officers have joined the merchant service simply because it is so well paid in Norway that if they work for nine months they can then afford to have three months holiday on land, both officers and crew work briskly and efficiently. The ship was immaculate. But I did not detect any enjoyment in their lives. Some of them would not even go ashore at ports of call such as Karachi.

'Why should I bother to go on shore to visit the place?' the young Second Mate enquired. 'I despise the Paks because they are dirty and they lack any ambition.'

'But they may be happier than you are,' William suggested to him.

'How can they be?' the Second Mate replied. 'I am working on this ship to make myself money to better myself socially. Karachi is just dirty and hopeless.'

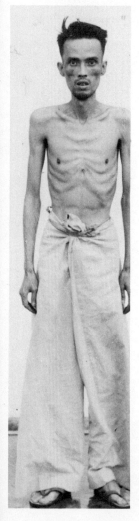

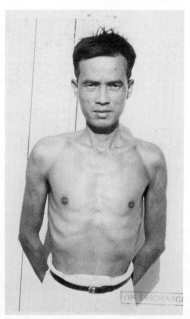

(*Left hand picture*)
A heroin addict from the Tai Lam Prison, Hong Kong. Before the cure.

(*Right hand picture*)
After the cure.

Our sadness in leaving our friends on the *Tiber* was diminished by the pleasure of being met at Colombo by two tea-planter friends, Christopher Worthington and John Burgess. Both were on leave; each had his own car. After two or three days at the Mount Lavinia Hotel bathing and buying provisions in Colombo, John Burgess had to drive back to his tea-plantation. Christopher, William and I began our journey to Taprobane.

On the way we spent the night at one of the most famous houses in the Orient which was built by a gentle giant of a man called Bevis Bawa whom I had known for many years. Bevis has found his nirvana; indeed, he created it.

Bevis' father was the eldest son of an executive lawyer who, when he died, left his aristocratic French middle-class wife and hoard of children penniless. Bevis' father had to start from scratch to keep the wolf from the door. With brilliance and hard work he rose to be the most eminent lawyer of his day.

Bevis' mother was a third cousin of the Duke of Argyll who

Bevis Bawa.

was considered the black sheep of the family because he married a Ceylonese woman. The lady's father must have been a pleasant eccentric for he once sent a gift of white mice to Queen Victoria to prove that something white could come from a black country. Bevis weighed fifteen pounds at birth; when he was shown to his mother she cried, 'Take it away,' and went into a swoon. But Bevis' father was delighted, for the child had an unusually long neck, and six-inch collars were then in fashion.

'A fine neck for high collars,' said the father and from that moment Bevis was brought up in luxury. Bevis now stands six foot seven inches and wears no collar at all.

He had a Portuguese nanny whom he adored. She wore a long-sleeved white jacket, he remembers, a rustling silk flared skirt and a chain of gold beads. Each day young Bevis would be sent in one of the family rickshaws to Galleface Beach. The rickshaw-wallah was a tall, dark Indian who wore a vast red turban upon which was a large B in polished brass – standing for Bawa, the family name. Bevis loathed school and was brought up by a series of governesses and tutors. For ten years he was an only child. But he was not lonely, for in his parents' house in those days there were eighteen servants. Bevis would play with their children; they were his only friends. 'They shared my joys which were few,' says Bevis, 'and a kid's problems which are many.'

As Bevis grew up his career became diverse; he was in turn painter, writer, editor, and A.D.C. to three British governors of Ceylon before its independence.

But meanwhile the event had occurred which changed his whole life.

'When I was seventeen years old,' Bevis told me, 'my mother said, "Go, son, and make of life what you will." I had selected a plot of land on a rubber plantation which she gave me, and she built me a small house.'

The house has become a fantastic series of rambling courtyards, patios, loggias and long terraces. The garden, or rather the inter-locking series of gardens, has become the most beautiful in Ceylon. Rare and fantastic plants and birds abound in its wonderful greenness.

'The plantation has gone,' Bevis said. 'But what remains of my estate still provides me with my few needs. The gardens and the house have been built by the love and loyalty of my Ceylonese* helpers combined with their deep knowledge of true values. Though I pay them salaries, I consider them friends. It is with

*Bevis actually used the word 'Sinhalese' which strictly means the indigenous inhabitants of Ceylon as opposed to the Tamil and Moslem communities who came in from Southern India. A Sinhalese will now also refer to Ceylon as Sri Lanka, but I have found it simpler to use the words Ceylonese and Ceylon.

their help that I have been able to create Brief.'

'Why did you call the place Brief?' I asked him.

'Well, as you know, the nearest village is called Bentota. And I thought that Bevis Bawa, Brief, Bentota, sounded rather pleasant.'

We gazed out over the gardens.

'Since childhood I've been a collector,' Bevis told me as we sat comfortably in leather-backed chairs on his largest verandah. 'A collector of many things from match-boxes and labels, to stamps and coins. From first editions to antiques. But suddenly I felt that such hobbies made one conceited and selfish, and, above all, a bore. So I turned to nature, which can be enjoyed by all humanity – the poor, the rich, the young and the old. Nature enables one to forget the nonsensical barriers created by man.'

One of the gardens at Brief.

Bevis turned to his handsome young Ceylonese friend and companion called Doolan.

'Please forgive me, my dear Doolan,' he said. 'But I seem to have lost my walking stick again.'

Doolan promptly fetched the stick from a corner and gave it to Bevis with a smile of affection. Bevis rose with dignity from his chair and began to walk slowly down the steps that lead to the garden. At the age of sixty-five and as a result of the operation that nearly killed him together with his acute diabetes, he leans heavily on his stick and walks with a distinguished stoop. His face is drawn, his cheeks are hollow. But his marvellous sense of humour, good spirits and kindness have never left him. He now waved his stick around at the wonderful flowering trees whose petals were scattered on the lawn.

'Trees do not hate,' Bevis said. 'Their very stance is elegant and beautiful to watch. Though man delights in destroying plant life and the greenery around him, I have never known plants to let down man.'

We were walking along a path flanked by a long pool of lotus blossoms.

'The whole of my garden,' Bevis told me, 'is a collection of many small gardens thought out in various moods and at various times during its forty-year growth. A number of them have altered almost beyond recognition. But my gardens have now reached the end of their progress and they now rest in peace – perhaps looking back with happiness on their forty years of growth, perhaps rather sad that they can no longer move on to a further change of mood.'

It is hard to give any idea of the richness, variety, and magic of the place – the Japanese garden; the vista from the largest verandah of the gently descending terraced lawns dotted by streams, and sculptures, and bordered by formal hedges; the secret bowers; the fern garden; the profusion of orchids; the walled gardens outside each bedroom; the long drive of exotic trees – an avenue of palms like a colonnade of Corinthian pillars; the pervading scent of frangipani.

When the *Ceylon Sunday Observer* came to interview Bevis and photograph his wonderful estate, their article was headed: THE LAST OF THE MASTODONS. But for my part I find Bevis completely timeless, being neither old nor young in spirit or in outlook. However, I agree with three points the *Observer* made in its article. They reminded their readers that there are now no locks on any of the doors at Brief – though when Bevis arrived there the place was known as a criminal area, and still is. Secondly they described him as being truly democratic in an aristocratic way. Lastly, they pointed out – most correctly – that Bevis considers life too short to collect enemies, and so he suffers fools, knaves, liars and blackmailers with as much gladness as he can summon.

On the last day of my stay at Brief I stood yet again with Bevis at the end of his verandah looking out at the wonderful view. For a long while Bevis stood in silence contemplating his life's work. Then he turned to me with his usual gentle smile which

now seems to me to be a smile of apology for his infirmities.

'I have outlived many of the trees I planted,' he told me. 'Younger ones have taken their place and are probably as happy in their growth as those that have gone before them, and perhaps they're certain of their future. They live for the day – as indeed I do in this haven.' Then he turned to me. 'I shall miss you,' he said. 'But I know what you are searching for, and I am certain you are right to search for it.'

Bevis was silent. Once again he was gazing at his gardens sloping down the incline of the terrain to the paddy fields beyond. When he spoke again his voice was even softer than usual.

'People think I am lonely here at Brief because I do not need the endless rush of a city like Colombo or New York. I do not need the modern inventions, the pollution, noise and squalor with which the human race has burdened itself, calling it progress. I shall be happy if I can live surrounded by this beauty until I die.'

Bevis is the only person that I know who from his industry and from the genius of his imagination and his talent for friendship with people of all classes and colours has created a perfect work of art. Though he is far too modest to admit the fact, Bevis has found his own nirvana.

Early the next morning Christopher, William and I set out for the island of Taprobane. We had seen the way in which one man had found and made his nirvana; we now had hopes that on that very day we should discover at least the possibility of finding another one. We drove through Galle and stopped briefly to admire the Portuguese fortress of the lovely old town. As we drew closer to our destination, Christopher, a tea-planter in charge of two thousand labourers and the practical one among us, began enumerating the difficulties that anyone who lived on the island would face. First, there was a rumour that the well had run dry, but he knew a firm of contractors who could construct a pipe under the sea from the mainland water supply. Secondly, the house could be maintained far more cleanly and economically if it had electricity. An underground cable could be run over the short distance that separated the island from the mainland. Lastly, in case of illness or emergency, it would be perfectly simple to lay a telephone line. All these lines would have to be under the sea because at high-tide the fishing boats used the narrow strip of water between the island and the mainland for a shelter.

We were all excited.

'I sought for happiness,' the Count de Mauny had written when he was in Ceylon, 'and there were times when I told myself I had found it, but a *few steps* further on it was still more *beautiful*. Was I not looking for one spot which, by its sublime beauty, would fulfil my dreams and hold me for life? I sought, and in the course of my endless seeking destiny one morning made me discover the "Isle of Dreams". My rock was nameless. . . . I christened the island TAPROBANE – the old Greek word for Ceylon.'

But as we approached, we were confronted by our first disappointment. A new main road had been built between the Weligama Rest House and the beach. The road had been raised to protect it from the tides, so that from the Rest House the island was no longer visible. As the tide was low we waded across to the island. The iron landing-stage had been broken up by waves. However, since Christopher had telephoned to the Rest House that we were arriving that morning, the caretaker, a Ceylonese with a wrinkled face and a pleasant smile, was waiting to welcome us. We scrambled on to the remains of the landing-stage and he helped us up on to the rocks and led the way through the glorious garden with its casuarina trees and Temple flowers, cannas and hibiscus, up the hundred steps to the house which, as I have said, occupies the whole of the top of the mound except for a narrow terrace surrounding it. With its broken balustrades and pillars it might have been an old house in Capri. For an instant we gazed at the white orchids, tumbling in profusion down the side of the little island, and at the wide sea to the south beyond. Then we

entered the house which I had last seen nine years before. And we
stared around us in dismay. The lovely old Portuguese chests,
Dutch furniture and French tables had gone. They had been
replaced by cheap chairs and tables. The place was derelict. We
could see daylight through the roof. Worse, most of the rooms
had been partitioned from the octagonal Hall of the Lotus with
ply-wood. The kind caretaker told us that the rooms had been
thus partitioned because the owner of the house ran a small
package tour in a mini-bus. Taprobane was one of the night stops.
We went into some of the bedrooms. The stained old mattresses
were foul and musty. We walked downstairs to the servants'
quarters. The disused rooms were black, filthy hovels. We returned to the terrace, and looked towards the mainland. The
'breaking surf and curving palm-fringed shoreline' which had
remained in Paul Bowles' head and had determined him to live
on the island had been ruined by the main road which ran across
it. The whole long stretch of beach had been wrecked, and to be
able to swim or wade to the beach is essential. For – though cool –
the house itself was smaller than I had remembered it, and the
terraces surrounding it are too narrow and overwhelmingly hot.
There is no beach at the base of the island, so one must depend
upon the mainland 'palm-fringed shoreline' with the main road

running through it. An old lorry, belching thick clouds of black diesel smoke, came thundering along and disappeared into the distance. I remembered Bevis Bawa's words: 'I do not need the modern inventions, the pollution, noise and squalor with which the human race has burdened itself.'

For a while we were silent as these dismal thoughts floated in our heads like dark fish in an aquarium.

Then Christopher spoke.

'I'm afraid it won't do, Robin,' he said.

But I am obstinate, and I still refused to be convinced. I left the two of them gazing gloomily at the main road. There was no reason to examine the garden again, for the trees and shrubs and flowers were among the most beautiful I have ever seen. But I explored the house once more, and with a lurch of sadness I realised that to restore it – even to make it liveable in – would cost far more money than I could afford.

I rejoined William and Christopher on the terrace.

'You're right,' I said to Christopher. 'I'm afraid it *won't* do.'

Sadly we said goodbye to the caretaker and scrambled from the rusty landing-stage on to the rocks and into the sea. As we waded breast high back to the shore William held his camera above his head and took pictures of the island. We lunched at the

Rest House where the staff were as friendly as ever. Then we got into the car and said goodbye to the island – probably for ever – and began the long drive to the Rest House of Hambantota where we were to meet John Burgess that night. We sat on the terrace, drinking whisky, and watching the brown and black bodies splashing merrily in the shallows of the turbulent sea with its dangerously pounding surf and white breakers.

The Island of Taprobane.

I had now realised that the place in which I had – perhaps over-romantically – hoped to find my nirvana was impossible for me. But I was still in one of the countries I loved most in the world, and Christopher had already suggested that we should come and stay with him on his tea-plantation in Lindula. So we decided to drive up-country staying a night or two with some of Christopher's friends on the way; for he believed that in the splendid country which lay between the coast and the uplands I might well find the nirvana for which I was seeking.

It was a happy journey. For reasons that will become apparent, I do not wish to describe in detail the various planters I met, nor their comfortable bungalows and enchanting gardens with views which as Sir Emerson Tennent – a Member of Parliament and Civil Secretary to the Colonial Government of Ceylon between 1845 and 1850 – says 'combine sublimity and beauty'.

When I arrived at Christopher's bungalow with its deep terrace overlooking a broad lake covered with water lilies and was greeted by his house servants whom I had not seen for nine years, it was like coming home. After a day or two of rest, I began writing my notes; later I continued to work on my novel *The Sign*. I led the form of life which seems to be the only way of living I can adopt when I am writing a novel. I work all morning; take a walk before lunch; lunch, and in the afternoon correct what I have written in the morning. I take a walk before dinner, dine early; and I am in bed by nine thirty.

Here, perhaps I may pause to say that though I'm afraid I've inherited few of the merits of my father's intellect, I have certainly inherited to a certain extent one of its few defects. My father had what is known as a 'lawyer's brain'. He could master some subject of which he was almost ignorant by means of hard work and research. His brain seemed capable of assimilating for a period of time an extremely complicated subject. Thus, when he appeared as Counsel in the Marconi case his knowledge of wireless astounded all present. Yet a few months later he was practically unable to comprehend the workings of the simplest radio. Now, I find that my memory of the facts I have acquired extends for perhaps a longer period, say for two or three years – but gradually the knowledge seeps away until I can remember hardly any single fact of what I once used to know so well. Thus, when I was learning to be a tank commander in 1940, I passed out with a 'distinction' from Bovington where we had been taught the intricacies of a tank mechanism. Yet today – perhaps due to my head wound from the Western Desert – I can remember not a thing about the inside of a tank, hardly even of an ordinary motor car. So it is with my research. For this reason if I am writing a historical novel which requires research material – such as *The Last Encounter*, my book on General Gordon – I write down notes in a manuscript book, for I know that in a year or perhaps even a month I shall have forgotten what I learned and even the title of the book I read.

However, for some reason that I have never been able to understand, I have the most fantastic gift for being able to remember dialogue.

Accordingly I set to work promptly on my novel *The Sign* – which was then called *AD 20*. We led a pleasant life, and I felt that in these surroundings I had reached as close to nirvana as ever I could.

However, many miles below us on the coast, Ceylon – or Sri Lanka as it is now called – seemed to be perishing. 'Sri Lanka's economy,' wrote the *Ceylon Daily Mirror* on 6 February 1973, 'is truly in the red and its total collapse imminent . . . Sri Lanka is in desperate financial straits.'

The Island
of Taprobane.

But, I was immersed in my work; I was delighted to be in the company of Christopher and William; I was entertained by the tea-planters I met; I rejoiced in the beauty of my surroundings.

I tried to live for the present.

While I was up-country during my various visits to Ceylon, I met many tea-planters, and I suggest that I could give short descriptions of several of them. But just as in my autobiography I invented one single boyfriend to represent the various boys who had lived with me during the period about which I was writing, so in this book I have decided that it would be both wiser and kinder if I created a composite picture of a tea-planter. So I have invented a complete character.

I will call him Jack Phillipson.

I met Jack Phillipson in the club of the district where I was staying up-country in Ceylon. I had been made an honorary member. There were few people in the bar-room that evening. I went to the counter to order a whisky. Standing next to me was a tall man who turned to me with a pleasant smile.

'Good evening,' he said. 'It's good to see a new face here once in a while. Heaven knows there are few of us left. Fifteen years ago there were four hundred European planters. Now we're only twenty. Have a drink or two with me?'

'Thanks,' I replied.

As the squat Ceylonese barman poured out our drinks, I examined the planter. He was about forty, and at first sight he looked like the hero of an early safari movie made in Africa. He had a 'rugged, handsome, virile face' – as his publicity agent would have proclaimed – and a genial yet stern expression. You could hear his crisp word of command, 'Bring out the machine-guns.' Yet when I observed him more closely I detected flaws in the picture I had formed of him. His cheeks were slightly flabby; his eyes which should by rights have 'gleamed a crystal blue' were a little bloodshot, and his chin, which should, of course, have been as firm as marble, quivered slightly as he talked.

'Cheers!' he said: and went on: 'This country's tea finds its way to most parts of the world. It accounts for two-thirds of Sri Lanka's export earnings. But it won't for long. Not at the present way things are going.' He scowled at me as if I were the government economist responsible. 'What's your name?' he asked.

I told him.

'Mine's Jack Phillipson,' he said. 'But everyone calls me Jack, so you'd better as well.' He sipped his whisky and then turned to the barman. 'Now look here, Asoka,' he said. 'I seem to remember we've had this argument before now. You're a very good fellow, but you've a poor memory. When I say I want whisky, I don't mean a teaspoonful. I want three measures. So be a kind man and fill up our glasses, will you?'

The barman grinned. Evidently he liked my companion. Our glasses were filled up. Jack raised his glass to me and drank.

'Of course, one needs discipline on a tea-estate,' he told me. 'A tea bush should be plucked every seven or eight days. The women mainly do the plucking. The men are responsible for replanting, draining, road maintenance, spraying and pruning and the rest. The men get about three rupees and fifty cents a day. That's the equivalent of over four shillings. The women get two rupees and eighty cents a day. What's more the coolies . . . sorry – we have to call them 'labourers' nowadays . . . the *labourers* live in their lines rent-free with a free plot of land for cultivating a garden or keeping cattle and goats. There's a school for the children who get free food-stuffs paid for by the estate. There's a dispensary and a maternity ward complete with midwife. So what more do they want? Answer me that one.' Jack raised his glass and finished it. 'But I can tell you what *I* want,' he announced. 'Asoka!'

'This round is on me,' I said.

'Impossible,' Jack replied. 'You're not a member, and only members can buy drinks.'

'I'm an honorary member.'

Jack laughed. 'All right,' he said. 'You win. But for heaven's sake let's go and sit down. These bar-stools are quite desperately uncomfortable.'

As we moved to a small table at the other side of the room I reflected on the tone of voice in which he had said the words 'quite desperately'. The accent had been more like that of a television comedian than an Empire builder. I decided that Jack Phillipson was an odd mixture; I also decided that at all costs I must steer the conversation away from the manufacture of tea.

'How long have you been out here?' I asked.

'Here? Ever since I chucked up my pathetic studies in London to become a chartered accountant. I never felt at ease in England – to tell you the truth. You see, I was born in India. My father was a bank manager in Bombay.'

One of the 'boys' brought our drinks.

'I was sent to school in England, of course. And I loathed it. I just couldn't wait for my holidays in India.'

Jack sipped his drink and then smiled gratefully at Asoka.

'Well done,' he shouted. 'Exactly right. Positively brilliant.'

It was at that moment I decided that Jack was already a bit drunk.

'The climate in Bombay can be ghastly. But for all the humidity and heat the place has a distinct advantage. Can you guess what?'

I could think of several advantages, but I decided to be wary. 'No,' I replied.

'Promise you won't be shocked?'

'I promise.'

'Girls,' said Jack. 'Girls of every age and size. *Now* are you shocked?'

'Not at all.'

'Good,' Jack said. 'That means I can make a further confidence. In those days my parents had plenty of Indian servants, and the servants had children. I slept with my first Indian girl when I was fourteen. She was the same age as I was. Her name was Rashmie. Well, I'm not a poet, so I'll just put it in one word. It was ecstasy. Ecstasy. I couldn't believe that so much pleasure could exist on earth – or that I could ever experience it again. But I did. Indeed, I did. The very next night we met at the same place. And so it went on till I had to go back to school.

'Next holidays Rashmie was still there. And it was just as wonderful. Of course, by then I'd done the usual playing around with other boys at school, but it wasn't the same thing. I suppose in a way I was in love with Rashmie. Then while I was at school came the break up. My father was posted to Borneo. I never saw Rashmie again.'

'Well, the years passed by. At times I'd go to Borneo, and I'd find a girl there. But when I started my work for my accountancy exams I decided I'd better start looking round for an English girl. And at last I found one who was perfect. Nineteen, slim, blonde, pretty, sensual-looking – the lot. She worked as a typist in an office close to the college where I was pretending I'd make an accountant. We made friends, and at last, after a theatre and supper one night, I took her back to my room.'

Jack took a large drink of whisky.

'Now what I'm going to tell you at this very moment you're going to find hard to believe,' he continued. 'It's this. It just didn't work. There I was naked in bed with this beautiful girl – and it was no good. I couldn't do a thing. Hopeless. And very shaming. Of course, I told her some yarn about the enervating life I'd led in the tropics, but I don't think she believed me. Anyhow, we never met again.

'Well, I don't mind telling you I was worried. Then, a few weeks later, I'd been to a cinema, and I was walking back alone through Soho, when I saw a young Indian girl standing in a doorway. She was obviously a prostitute. I smiled at her. She smiled back and beckoned to me to come into the house. I followed her up some foul-smelling stairs to a room with a double bed. She told me her price. I agreed. She kissed me – expertly, I don't mind telling you. And we stripped. And it was perfect. Ecstasy. No trouble at all. In fact, I went back to the girl several times.'

Jack beckoned to Asoka who brought us two more drinks.

'I tried another English girl,' Jack continued. 'Fatal. Hopeless. No good at all. By then I'd analysed the differences between white and black girls. So far as I'm concerned it's very simple: it comes down to two things. The texture of a white girl's skin is soft but somehow unpolished – sometimes quite rough, whereas a coloured skin is smooth as ivory. Secondly, coloured girls give all of themselves. At the climax of love they've no thought in their head except sheer animal delight.

'So there I was,' Jack said, with a dramatic emphasis in his voice which would have been more effective if his words had been less slurred. 'There I was. And I couldn't think of any solution. What's more, I was determined I wasn't going to remain chaste for the rest of my life. My father had retired to England and taken a house in Mayfield. And I wasn't going to find a coloured girl in Mayfield very easily. And if I *did* my dear parents wouldn't be best pleased. There was only one thing to do – and I did it. I chucked up accountancy and came out to Ceylon. I worked hard. In no time I'd got a good job as an assistant superintendent.'

Suddenly Jack stared at me with his bleary eyes as if he had never seen me before.

'Did I ask you your name?' he enquired.

'Yes.'

'Do you mind repeating it?'

I repeated it.

'But I don't know what you're doing here,' Jack said, grinning at me strangely. 'You're not a member. And do you know what they do in this club if they find someone in its noble, though delapidated precincts who is *not a member*? Well, first of all they execute him. They execute him with a sword which once belonged to a governor of Ceylon – whose name escapes me – and is now kept constantly sharpened by my good friend Asoka. After the non-member's head is cut off, the procedure is too ghastly to be related.'

'I'm an honorary member,' I said.

'Ah well,' cried Jack, 'that's a very different kettle of fish.'

He stretched out his hand, and I took it.

'I'm delighted to meet you,' Jack said. 'And if you would do me the honour of dining at my bungalow next Tuesday I should be delighted.'

'Thank you.'

'I'll come here and collect you at 5.00 p.m. Don't forget. 5.00 p.m. – because then we can see the sunset from my verandah. I seem to have become a little bit pissed, but I shan't forget – and don't you forget either.'

'I won't.'

Very slowly he got up from the table.

'Would you do me a favour?' he asked me.

'Certainly.'

'Could you possibly tell me the day of the week?'

'Saturday.'

Phillipson beamed at me with pleasure.

'Saturday,' he repeated. 'Saturday. That's exactly what it should be – because, and it's a most important because, because Saturday evening is my night for getting drunk. Goodnight to you. I have enjoyed our conversation greatly.' Slowly Jack Phillipson swayed towards to door.

'Asoka!' he bellowed. 'My dear old Asoka, be a good fellow and help me to my car. And call for my driver.'

Jack opened the door of the bar. As he staggered into the corridor, Asoka appeared. Jack leaned heavily on his shoulder and made his way towards the portico of the club.

The following day I met a friend in the club and asked him about Jack Phillipson.

'Of course Jack was drunk,' he said. 'Last night was Saturday. We should have warned you. Dear old Jack always gets drunk on a Saturday night. Regularly – every Saturday night, and generally makes a fool of himself. But when you dine with him on Tuesday, don't be taken in by that bluff act of his. He's far less stupid than you might think.'

Punctually at five o'clock on Tuesday afternoon Jack appeared, greeted me as an old friend, and shouted for Asoka. He looked the glamorous – if slightly ageing – film-star I had seen when I first met him at the bar.

'Let's have one for the road,' he said. Over drinks we discussed Ceylonese politics and tea.

'I can't even sack a coolie – I mean, a "labourer" – for half-murdering another man without having to appear in Court to explain why I've sacked him. It's not easy running a plantation these days,' he concluded.

On the drive to his estate Jack was silent. I was glad because I could watch the hills and distant blue mountains. Presently we reached the tea country. At a distance the slopes looked like vast banks of moss stretching to the horizon; closer they reminded one of some fantastic tapestry work upon which the workers on their way home – mainly Tamil women – appeared like white dots. And far away, like immense castles, were the tea-factories.

The car drove briskly down the drive and stopped under the porch of a two-storeyed house. Three house-boys were waiting to greet us; behind them hovered inquisitively the cook and a night-watchman.

'Like a swim?' Jack asked, pointing to a pool at the end of the lawn. 'Or shall we just take a stroll and then have a drink or two?'

'Let's take a stroll,' I replied.

Large orange multi-coloured bougainvillaea trees sprang from the long stretch of amazingly green lawn. Far away rose the blue and green foothills of a mountain range. The herbaceous borders gleamed with flowers. A low privet hedge stretched the whole length of the lawn; from it the land fell abruptly into a thickly wooded valley.

'It's magnificent,' I said.

'I love the place,' Jack answered. 'Except when I'm sick to death of the sight of it. Let's go and have a drink.'

The drinks were as strong as at the club. And while we drank, the sky became dark red and scarlet as the sun dipped away from our sight.

Tea Estate, up-country Ceylon.

'One trouble of living alone,' Jack said with a smile after his second drink, 'is that you become terribly garrulous. You'd suppose that if you lived alone, and a stranger came to visit you and dine, you'd want to listen to what *he* had to say. Not a bit of it! After a few drinks you want to tell him about your *own* business problems. After a few whiskies or beers and some

163

brandy you want to tell him the whole story of your life.'

'I think I know the reason,' I replied. 'When we meet our friends frequently during the week, we use each one of them, or at least most of them – perhaps without knowing it – as a kind of confessor. To *this* kind woman we tell of some event that has occurred to us in which we may have behaved badly – perhaps with some justification. She, in her turn, will tell us of a quarrel with her husband during which she behaved not *quite* like a bitch, but almost. To *that* benevolent man we will confess we lost our temper with a shop-assistant who had no change for a five pound note. He in his turn will admit he was unpleasant to his secretary that very morning.'

I finished my drink. Jack poured me another.

'So by half-truths and half-lies we manage to confess our sins,' I concluded. 'But if we live alone we lack a confessor. Suddenly a friend – or even a complete stranger – appears. We pour drink down him – and down ourselves – and promptly begin our confessions.'

Jack laughed. 'So you'll see why I asked you to dinner,' he said.

'You told me you came to Ceylon – or should I call it Sri Lanka – to find a beautiful girl with a dark skin,' I said. 'Did you?'

'Yes.'

'Is she here now?'

'No.'

'May I in my role of confessor ask "why not?" '

Jack leaned back in his chair. The mountains were now black against the horizon.

'It began when I was an Assistant Superintendent,' he said. 'In those days, as I told you at the club, there were nearly four hundred white planters up-country. Now there are a bare twenty. Even after the war there were parties four or five days a week – if you wanted to go to them. After dinner there was bridge and dancing to the gramophone and plenty to drink. It was all very pleasant. But my trouble persisted. I couldn't fancy the planters' daughters – or their wives, come to that. And I didn't fancy the Ceylonese boys – as some did on the sly.

'At a dance one night I'd drunk a bit too much because I didn't much like my hosts, and I'd been persuaded into going to their bungalow against my will. I went out on to the verandah and strolled round to the far side of the house where the nursery quarters were. The night was deliciously cool. As I turned the corner I saw a Ceylonese girl. She was about seventeen. She was wearing a length of coloured cloth round her waist and a short tight-fitting bodice which left her midriff bare. She was obviously the children's *ayah*. The girl heard me move and looked round. She was very beautiful. She saw me staring at her, and turned

her head away. But she did not move. I walked towards her and smiled.'

' "Are the children asleep?" I asked quietly.

' "Yes."

' "I haven't seen you before. How long have you been here?"

' "Three weeks."

'She had turned her head towards me now and she was gazing at me timidly. I could see the softness of her skin and the sensual gentleness of her mouth.

' "Are you happy?" I asked.

'The girl was silent. Then she lowered her head.

' "You're not happy. Why?"

' "The other servants . . . they do not like me – perhaps because I am Singhalese – they are Tamil. They will not talk to me. I like the children, but they are too young. The eldest is only five."

' "Why did you come here?"

' "My father didn't want me to work on the estate, picking tea. He is a building work contractor. He has high ambitions for me. We are a large family and poor. He makes four hundred rupees a month. There are many mouths to feed."

' "Do you sleep here?"

' "I sleep with the children."

' "What is your name?"

' "Lalitha."

' "My estate is sixty miles to the north," I said. "Only three hours in my car."

'There was silence. I knew I would blame myself all my life if I lost this opportunity.

' "Would you like to look after my house on the estate I run?" I asked. "I am lonely."

'The girl was staring at me with her large dark eyes. I wanted to make my approach to her subtly, but I couldn't. There was always the danger that someone would walk round the verandah. I couldn't delay.

' "Are you sure that you want me?" she asked.

'It was the sudden look of desire in her eyes that decided me. I went up to her and kissed her on the mouth.

' "I want you to sleep with me," I said.

'Her eyes stared at me steadily.

' "For one night, perhaps."

' "No."

' "For a week or two, then?"

' "I've told you. I want you to come and live with me."

' "As your mistress?"

'A slight breeze wafted the sound of a fox-trot from the living-room. With it a sense of reality returned into my mind. I could imagine the self-righteous fury of the planters' wives if I invited them to sit down at table with a former coloured servant. But if I chose to lead an overt yet solitary life with Lalitha, I knew – I'm speaking of the days fifteen years ago, remember – that I'd risk losing my job, and I'd just been promoted to be superintendent of an estate, still further away.

' "Yes." I replied. "You would have your own room. And you would sit down to table with me when we were alone. And you would always share my bed."

'I knew my words sounded harsh, but I was determined I must be firm from the beginning.

' "And where would I eat when you had company?"

' "In your own bed-sitting room."

' "I understand," she said.

' "I doubt if you do," I replied. "But I think you will in time. Having a girl is a sin among us idiots – though few of us worry much about it. I'm not afraid of what the men will think. It's the malicious gossip of their wives that can do us harm."

' "But when we are alone, I can dine at table with you, as if I were your wife?"

' "Certainly."

' "You have drunk a little," Lalitha said. "Will you still feel the same when you wake up in your house tomorrow?"

' "I swear it."

'I slipped my hand beneath her bodice and held her breast. She gave a small shudder, then she kissed my mouth.

' "Lalitha," I said, "are you sure you would like to live with me?"

'Her eyes stared at me solemnly. "Yes," she said. "I want you. I want you very much."

' "What will your father say – if you tell him?"

Up-country Ceylon.

167

(*Left hand picture*)
Nuwara Eliya,
Ceylon.

(*Right hand picture*)
An up-country
view, Ceylon.

' "He will disown me. He will say I am a disgrace to the family, and I will lose face for good. He will throw me out of the house forever." Lalitha smiled. "But he will say nothing, if he is given enough money. He is very much fond of money." '

Jack smiled at me. 'And that was how it all happened,' he said. 'Do you think I was a complete fool?'

'No,' I answered. 'You were prepared to be fairly discreet. You were lonely. The girl was – from what you tell me – enchanting. I'd say you were very sensible. But how did it work out? Why isn't she here now?'

'To put it in a phrase, she was heaven in bed, and hell out of it.'

'What was wrong?'

'In the last decade we've had a social revolution out here,' Jack answered, 'so I don't expect you realise that the ambition of many Ceylonese girls in those days was to marry a white man. It now sounds plain daft. But that was Lalitha's ambition – as it gradually turned out. But I couldn't face the problems of marriage to her: possible loss of my job: having to leave her alone at home when I went to the club or to a party: half-caste children. And then. . . . Well then there was another thing. I've told you it was sheer bliss in bed. And so it was, and I honestly believe she enjoyed it as much as I did. At the instant of our wild fulfilment, when she was giving soft cries of pleasure and pain, I knew that at that moment I possessed her body completely. Her body, indeed yes. But her mind was far away from me. And I knew that any white man who could give her the excitement I did *and* who would marry her – or promise to marry her – could take her away from me. What's more, I was right.'

Jack filled our glasses.

'How were you right?'

168

'It was very simple. There was a man called Jennings who owned a garage here. Something went wrong with one of my lorries. He came out himself to put it right. That day I had to attend a tribunal over an accident. When I came back to the bungalow, Jennings had mended the truck and gone. Lalitha told me she had given him lunch and a drink before he left. All seemed well – except that my house-servants, who all, of course, knew that Lalitha was my mistress, seemed for once uneasy in my presence.'

Jack turned on more lights on the verandah. His voice was deliberately casual as he spoke.

'A week later I found I had caught the clap,' he said. 'Well, I hadn't been unfaithful to the girl, so there was only one person from whom I could have caught the disease. But I said nothing. I wanted to make certain. I had a store of antibiotics in my dispensary. I knew the amount to take. Two nights later I was in the club. I was with a group of friends, when suddenly Jennings came into the bar. He was such a puny, dull man that I couldn't understand why they were all staring at him. For a moment there was silence, then they all began slowly but loudly to clap their hands together. After an instant they began to laugh. It was then that Jennings saw the point of their joke. He tried to smile.'

'I thought a doctor was supposed to be discreet,' he said. 'He is,' they laughed. 'But the local chemist isn't – or so it would seem.'

Jack slapped at a mosquito that had settled on the table.

'I suppose the end was what you'd expect,' he said. 'I drove straight home from the club. Lalitha was in our bed as usual. She was awake. I told her that Jennings had got drunk at the club and had boasted to me that he had been to bed with her. Lalitha denied it, then cried. Next, she claimed that Jennings had raped her. Why hadn't she called for the servants, I asked. And why hadn't she told me? Next, she said he'd made her drunk. She used every excuse possible. But I knew. For I could remember the evasive looks of my house-servants.

'I gave her some money – quite a lot, in fact. I asked my head-servant to drive her back to her family. She left that night. "You'll be sorry," she said. "Mister Jennings wants to marry me. And then the servants will no longer be able to jeer at me and call me whore." '

Jack took a long drink of whisky.

'When it came to the decision,' he continued, ' "*Mister* Jennings" wasn't so keen as my darling Lalitha had supposed. I'm told that her father made him pay a decent sum of money. Lalitha now runs a bar in Notchena, a low part of Colombo. She's a tart. And that's the end of my first confession.'

Jack had stopped his story abruptly. A house-boy came in to

169

announce that dinner was ready.

We entered a dining-room which might have belonged to a country house in England: Chippendale furniture, well-polished early Georgian silver, flowers in a bowl on the centre of the table. Both the food and the wine were excellent. Jack was a pleasant host. We talked of plays and films he had seen when he had last been on leave in London. He seemed to have forgotten the story he had told me on the verandah. I should have felt contented. Instead I felt uncomfortable and nervous. Presently I sensed the reason. The three house-boys who served us were smart, efficient and well-trained. And they seemed friendly. Certainly I could detect no hostility. Yet I was aware that I was being very closely observed. The cook who was perhaps forty and who personally served the main dish besides sliding the others through the kitchen hatch into the dining-room, never quite closed the hatch. Once when I looked up suddenly I saw his dark eyes watching me.

After dinner we went into the living-room for coffee and brandy.

'Though one can be horribly lonely in this place – lonelier perhaps than you could ever imagine – you mustn't suppose I live here all the year round,' Jack said suddenly. 'I have business to attend to in Colombo, so I stay the night occasionally. I have a flat there.'

'Are there any good nightclubs?'

'Two or three aren't bad,' Jack replied. 'And in one of them I met my only other adventure.'

'How?'

'I was at the bar and I'd just been turned down by a very pretty Ceylonese girl who had flounced off. The lighting was so discreetly dim in the place that you could hardly distinguish anyone, but I was vaguely aware of a person with a lovely face and long hair sitting on the bar-stool next to me. I thought it was a girl. Anyhow there was no mistake about the smile of sympathy. Then the person turned towards me, and with a shock, and I admit a slight thrill, I realised it was a boy. And he was very attractive. And suddenly I decided to take a chance – if I got the opportunity.

'I offered him a drink. The boy accepted. I now noticed that he was well-dressed. A Ceylonese businessman's son on a night out, I thought to myself. As we drank I gathered the bare facts of his life. His name was Nimal and he was eighteen years old. When he was fourteen, a European had picked him up on the streets of Colombo and installed him in his apartment, sent him to school, supervised his education, and left him all his money when he died.'

' "So now what do you do?" I asked.

'Nimal smiled. "Nothing," he answered. "Why should I take a job sweating over a typewriter in an office, when I can swim and lie on the Mount Lavinia beach, looking at the pretty girls around?"

' "Only girls?" I asked.

'Nimal smiled his innocent smile. "Perhaps you could say 'not *only* girls'," he replied in his pleasant educated voice. Evidently the turns of phrase and accent of his benefactor had rubbed off on him.

' "Which do you prefer?" I asked.

' "I like both. And you?"

' "I'm not sure."

'Nimal smiled at me again. I find it hard to describe his smile, but it seemed to be full of understanding and at the same time to assure one of complete devotion.

' "I think there is a question you may want to ask me," he murmured.

' "Yes?"

' "Would you think I was impertinent if I told you the question?"

' "No."

' "You want to ask me if I will go home with you tonight. And my answer is 'yes'. You need not pay me any money, because from the moment I saw you I took a liking to you."

Jack put down his glass of brandy and grinned at me.

'It seemed that Fate had given me a new chance and a most beautiful present,' he said. As he spoke, I noticed that Jack's voice was once again beginning to become slurred. 'I've always thought it was better to suffer from remorse rather than from regret. So I smiled back at Nimal,' he continued.

' "I'm glad your answer is 'yes'," I said.

' "You have a room?"

' "Quite near here."

' "And we will be alone?"

' "Most certainly," I answered.'

Jack filled up our glasses.

'Nimal and I went back to my room,' he continued. 'And I'll only say it was one of the most wonderful nights of my life. In the morning we sat in sarongs drinking coffee.

' "Where do you live?" I asked Nimal.

' "Not far from the old fort."

' "Do you have no job at all?"

' "None."

' "Do you still have money?"

'Nimal's hand dipped into the breast-pocket of his coat which had hung on a chair, and pulled out a wallet, and displayed three hundred rupees.'

' "That's all I've got left," he said.

' "Don't you want a job?"

' "Not in Colombo. I'm bored with the whole place."

' "Nimal," I said, "you told me last night that you'd taken a liking to me. Do you still feel the same this morning?"

'Nimal got up from the cushion on which he'd been sitting, came over to me, kissed my forehead and then my lips. "More so," he answered.'

Jack lit a cigarette.

'It was then I told Nimal the plan I'd made while his arms were still holding me. It was quite simple for Nimal was already educated. My clerk could teach Nimal to type. Nimal would become my secretary and my companion. He would have his own office and bedroom. In the morning he would work in the office. In the afternoon he would go out riding or swim in the pool. After dinner we could play cards or billiards. Meanwhile I would give him driving lessons, so that eventually, if he saved from the salary I would pay him, he could buy himself a second-hand car.

'To all this Nimal listened enthusiastically.

' "I have only two things to ask you," he said. "First, may I stay a week in Colombo to clear up things. Secondly, please can I go with you this morning to buy the kind of clothes I shall need up-country."

'That morning we went round the stores of Colombo and bought Nimal a complete "wardrobe" of clothes. While a jacket was being packed up for us, Nimal gave me a wink.

' "What if I keep all the clothes and don't come up-country next week?" he asked.

' "Then I shall have lost what little faith in human nature remains to me," I replied.

'Nimal laughed. "Don't worry," he said. "I'll be on that train, I can promise you." '

Jack paused and stubbed out his cigarette.

'And Nimal was indeed on the train, looking extremely elegant in his new coat,' Jack continued. 'I'd arranged a bedroom and office for him, close to mine. And from the very start he loved the place. It was a joy to me to see his happiness – and to be able to share it with him. Each night he'd creep into my bedroom, though there was no need for discretion because the house-servants guessed almost immediately. From that point of view his position could have been awkward, for in a way he was in Lalitha's situation. But Nimal had an instinctive tact which made it possible for him to dine with me and yet remain friendly and unselfconscious with the servants. He also understood from the years he had spent with his benefactor that when stodgy planters or their even stodgier wives arrived for a meal he must vanish. And he did. But by then – from the network, you might say – I'd found a few friends who secretly were "sympathetic". And we'd have gay evenings in our own discreet way.'

Jack lit a cigarette.

'That year with Nimal was one of the happiest I've ever known,' he said. 'But I knew it couldn't last for ever, so I tried to live for each day that we had. And it was all so marvellous that only gradually did I notice the faint shadow sliding across the lawn of our happiness.

'Nimal began to become restless. The first misfortune was that he failed his driving-test, so he couldn't drive my own car or the estate car into the nearest town – or beyond – to have an evening out on his own. His nervous irritation made him begin to drink more than normal. Soon he was drunk almost every night.

'The row came when I'd invited two "gay" bachelors to dine. At first, the evening went well. Nimal had put on light twill trousers, a blue shirt, and his jacket. He looked splendid. Then as he moved across the verandah soon after my guests had arrived, I saw he was drunk. Both my guests noticed it, but pretended all was well. Then, when dinner was finished and we had gone into the living-room and were drinking liqueurs, suddenly Nimal began talking about the businessman who had picked him up when he was fourteen. It would have been less unpleasant if he had told the story with his usual charm. But he chose to tell his story with a grim realism which grew increasingly nauseating as he proceeded. Every detail of seduction and fornication was described in vivid detail. "But do you know what I get out of all that hideous discomfort, night after night?" Nimal asked with a dramatic wave of his arm. "Enough to keep me in perfect *comfort* for two whole years." Nimal paused.

' "And I'm doing it yet again," he said.

'Then Nimal stumbled away to his room.

'The following day I had to attend a court case. I got back in time for dinner. Nimal was already drunk. We made casual conversation during the meal. But when we were in the living-room and the servants had brought coffee and brandy, I went over to Nimal and put a hand on his shoulder.

' "Why do you drink so much?" I asked.

'He wriggled away from me with a gesture of impatience.

' "Leave me alone," he said.

' "Just tell me *why*," I insisted.

'Nimal sprang up, went to the drinks-tray and poured himself a large brandy.

' "Why?" he repeated. "Because I feel I'm in a prison up here. What can I do in the evenings? Can I go to a cinema or a dance? No. Too far away. Is there even one single nightclub for a hundred miles around? No. Not one. And if there *were* I couldn't get to it because that wretched driving-instructor failed me – because you wouldn't give me the money to bribe him. And when you invite guests, and I'm graciously allowed to attend dinner, do you think it's much fun for me, hearing the same old stories over and over again? And when, as usual, we're alone together do you think I enjoy seeing your face staring at me across the table night after night?"

'I tried to keep my temper. "Should we go down to Colombo for a week?" I asked. "I think I could get a week's leave."

' "What difference would that make?" Nimal asked. "You'd still expect me to go with you to parties where I'd only meet people of your own age. Can't you understand? I want freedom. I want to go round the bars with my friends and have a good time."

' "But when we first met, you told me you were fed up with Colombo."

' "One gets fed up with everything after a time."

'Nimal took a gulp of his drink and smiled at me. But the smile was no longer innocent; it was sly and almost triumphant.

' "Besides," Nimal said, "I only told you I was fed up with Colombo because I knew it would please you."

' "And has it been in order to please me that you told me you liked this estate?" I asked.

' "Yes."

'Nimal was now glaring at me drunkenly.

'I made one more effort, but I promised myself it *would* be the last.

' "I can see that you must get bored and lonely at times up here," I said. "Why don't you go down to Colombo and find a friend of your own age and bring him back here so he'd be a companion to you?"

'Nimal threw his glass against the mantelpiece. For an instant he stood looking down at the smashed pieces. He was panting for breath. Then he spoke.

' "There's only one person I'd bring back to this estate," he said. "And that's my legally wedded wife." '

I left Jack a few drinks later.

'Excuse me for not driving you home,' Jack said. 'But I always ask my driver to take over at nights – when I've had a bit to drink.'

As the car drove away Jack was standing on the verandah. The moon had risen, and across the valley one could see the crests of the black mountains.

Jack waved his hand in farewell.

I find it strange that the tea-planters up-country who live surrounded by Buddhists should take so little interest in the Buddhist religion and should know so little about it. So far as I know, in the entire history of British influence over Ceylon only a handful of Englishmen have ever adopted Buddhism. Their conversion has never caused any scandal. The converts seem to be regarded as harmless freaks.

Several years ago I heard about an Englishman who had been converted to Buddhism and lived as a hermit in the jungle. I was fascinated by the story, and obtained a commission from *The People* to find out where he lived and to interview him. I found him and we made friends. I used a fictionalised version of the encounter with him in my novel *The Second Window*.* It may interest those who care to compare the facts I used in the newspaper with the story in my novel.

But the main reason why I want to record my meeting with Harold Musson is because I think it gives insight into the attitude of the Western mind towards Buddhism. I have changed little in the style of the story as I first wrote it because I do not want it to lose such rawness and vitality as it originally possessed.

I had left the car on the rutted track. My guide pointed to a small path that disappeared into the thick jungle.

'Along there,' he said.

I asked him to stay by the car. I began to walk along the path, keeping a sharp look out for snakes and leopard. It was steaming hot in the jungle of Southern Ceylon, and I could feel the sweat pouring down me. A mongoose with a long tail scuttled away into the undergrowth. As I turned a bend I passed a heap of elephant dung. Grey monkeys were chattering in the trees. It was a day of bright sunshine, but the path was in darkness because the vegetation all around was so dense.

Presently, in a small clearing a hundred yards ahead of me I saw a hut. In that hut lived the man I had travelled a long way to find.

The Ceylonese villagers knew him as a hermit Buddhist priest. They called him by the name with which he had been ordained – the Venerable Nanavira Thera. But I knew of him by the name with which he had been christened – Harold Edward Musson, born in 1920 in Aldershot.

I had first heard about Harold Musson in London – and in a curious way. After the opening of the film of a novel of mine I had left the first-night party feeling curiously depressed. The film had been a success. But for some reason I was dejected. I decided to

*Robin Maugham: *The Second Window*: William Heinemann, London: 1968.

175

go to a nightclub for a last drink. I sat down at the bar and stared gloomily at the crowded dance-floor.

'You're very deep in thought,' a voice beside me said.

I turned and saw a bluff middle-aged man with the sort of friendly creased face one takes to immediately. He looked as if he had been drinking.

'What about a whisky?' he asked. 'Another one won't harm you.'

'Thanks,' I said.

'And what were you thinking about so deeply?' he asked when the drinks arrived.

I smiled. 'If you want to know, I was wondering if this kind of life is worthwhile,' I confessed.

The man nodded his head as if in agreement.

'Strange you should say that,' he said. 'I knew a fellow in the war. He was an officer in Field Security in Algiers. Fairly ordinary kind of bloke – tall, quite well-built and healthy-looking. And quite bright – he'd been at Cambridge, I believe. Drank as much as the rest of us. Came from a good family – his father had been the Colonel of a regiment in Burma before the war. And I got the impression there was plenty of money about.'

The bluff-faced man took a swallow of his whisky.

'Well, I met my friend from Algiers once after the war at a restaurant. We recognised each other; I went up to him. I wasn't going to let on that I didn't remember his name. Probably he couldn't remember mine. Anyhow we got talking, and I asked him the stock question we were all asking each other in those days.

' "Have you got a job?" I enquired.

' "No," he answered. "I'm just drifting round having a good time."

'He was very well-dressed. I could see that he didn't have to worry about cash. That was in 1946. Now the point of my story is this. Three years later I ran into another man who had been in the same outfit in Algiers.

' "Do you remember that tall bloke in Field Security?" the man asked me, and he gave the name. Harold something-or-other it was.

' "I remember the chap," I said.

' "Well, do you know what he's gone and done?"

' "What?" I asked.

'All kinds of things came to mind – such as holding up a bank, murder, rape, arson. But none of them seemed to fit in with the gentle face of this man I'd once known.

' "What?" I repeated.

' "He's given it all up."

' "Given *what* up?"

176

' "The world, the flesh and the devil," he said. "The whole wretched rat-race."

' "How's he done it?" I asked.

' "He's escaped from it all. He's given up his worldly goods – and he was pretty well-off. He's gone off to Ceylon and become a Buddhist monk. The latest rumour is that he's living as a hermit on an island contemplating his navel." '

My friend took another sip of whisky.

'And was it true?' I asked him. '*Had* this ex-officer become a Buddhist monk?'

'Yes,' he replied. 'That's what's so perfect. He has – or so it seems. Just think of it! He's broken free. He's not tied to the old humdrum wheel like we are. He's escaped from all the worries of civilisation. He's got away from all the noise and turmoil. He's freed of all the hurry and strain we live in. He doesn't have a care in the world. He's reached his own kind of nirvana.'

I ordered another round of drinks.

'I wonder,' I said.

'Wonder what?'

'I wonder if it's as easy to find nirvana as all that. We may think it's quite easy *now* – when we've got a few drinks inside us. But when we wake up tomorrow morning with a slight hangover, won't we be grateful for the comforts of civilisation? And I wonder if you're right in thinking he's free from all cares?' I continued. 'Can we escape from our worries just by moving to an island in the tropics?'

'But he's gone Buddhist, so he believes that this life is a snare and a delusion anyhow. So why *should* he have any worries?'

'Do you suppose that he's not tortured by regret when he thinks of the life he's left behind?'

'When he thinks of London with its smog and traffic and stink, I expect he's jolly glad.'

'I'm still not sure,' I said obstinately.

'Well, why don't you go and find out?' my companion suggested with a smile.

I smiled back at him and lifted my glass.

'Perhaps I will – one day,' I replied.

I landed at the busy port of Colombo. I wanted to be central, so I resisted the attractions of the Mount Lavinia Hotel, six miles out on the beach; I put up at the Galleface Hotel, which has been described as looking like a mammoth eighteenth-century railway station. I had several letters of introduction. The Ceylonese are a pleasantly hospitable people. I soon made friends. And whenever I could, I tried to find out discreetly about the English hermit.

But no one seemed to have heard of him, and as the days passed by I began to despair of getting even a faint clue of his whereabouts.

One evening I met a Ceylonese journalist called Nalin Fernando. He was twenty-eight years old, alert and eager, with the look of a fox-terrier about him. For a short while he had been London correspondent for his newspaper; he was obviously reliable. I felt I could trust him; I told him of my quest.

'I don't know of any English hermit,' he said. 'But I'll try to find out. What you've told me should be enough to go on.'

A week later he came back. He had managed to unearth some important facts.

In November 1948, two Englishmen arrived in Ceylon and announced their intention of becoming Buddhist priests. Their names were Harold Edward Musson, then aged twenty-eight and O. J. S. Moore, aged thirty-six. They found their way to the secluded island hermitage of Polgasduwa in the south of Ceylon, sixty-five miles from Colombo.

There they went through three months of rigid discipline and work, studying the manuscripts of the writings of Buddha that are treasured on the island. These are inscribed on ola leaves in Pali and Sanskrit. The two Englishmen had already studied both these languages at Cambridge. Their teacher and guide at the hermitage was the Venerable Nyantiloka whose lay-name was Gueth. He was not only the first German to become a Buddhist monk, but the first European. He was a brilliant scholar; his works are considered one of the finest contributions to the religion. This old scholar instructed the two Englishmen, his two new acolytes. Then they took the final decision to renounce their connections with the lay world. They determined to live the rest of their lives as bhikkus and to follow in the steps of Buddha in quest of nirvana – the final state of blessedness.

Six months after arriving in Ceylon, on 24 April 1949, Harold Musson and O. J. S. Moore were ordained as Buddhist monks according to the simple traditional rites of the Sangha Sasana – the Brotherhood of Monks. The ceremony was performed by the Venerable Nyantiloka himself in the presence of nine other bhikkus. In an open glade in the island hermitage under the canopy of a spreading madan tree, he ordained them, giving Musson the name of Nanavira Thera and Moore the name of Nyanamoli.

My journalist friend had discovered that Moore was no longer alive. He had died seven years previously in the jungle. Harold Musson was evidently the man I was seeking. But was he still living? And if he was, *where* was he living? Nalin did not know. We decided to move south to the Island Hermitage to find out.

178

We drove south along the palm-fringed coast of Ceylon, past coconut plantations, past the calm waters of Hikkaduwa bay with its beautiful gardens of coral ten feet below the sea, until we reached the poor fishing village of Dodanduwa.

Twelve Buddhist monks live on the Island Hermitage, we were told by the local fishermen. They have no money and no food. Each day, at about eleven o'clock, when the sun is nearing its full height, two or three devoted Buddhists from the village-folk will climb into an outrigger canoe, balancing on their heads little baskets of food and bottles of tea. These they offer as alms to the monks.

'Sadhu! Sadhu! Blessings upon you! Blessings upon you!' they cry as the catamaran canoe glides across the mixed salt and fresh water on its journey across the inland lagoon.

This offering of food takes place almost every day of the year. These alms are the only food for the twelve monks living in meditation on the island. But on some days when the south-west monsoon is raging and the rain is pouring down in torrents, the little outrigger cannot cross the turbulent stretch of water. On some days the catch of fish is bad, and the village is nearly starving. So the villagers cannot afford to give alms. There are days when somebody forgets, and nobody else remembers. On these days the great gong that hangs from a tall tree on the island near the alms-hall does not ring. There is no meal that day. The monks have to go hungry. For they exist only on the alms daily offered to them. Their religion forbids them to sow or reap or to provide for their sustenance in any way. They may eat only what is freely given to them.

The canoe we had hoped to hire had been destroyed in a fight with a rival village. But at last we found a canoe afloat that looked sound. We arranged for the two wiry young fishermen who appeared to own it to ferry us across. The outrigger was made of the trunk of a mango tree, hollowed out. It was too narrow to sit down in, so we balanced precariously on the top of it. The two fishermen paddled us along a dark creek flanked by thick vege-tation. Gliding beneath the mangrove branches at the water's edge were long grey-black creatures that looked like young crocodiles.

'Kabragoya,' said one of the fishermen.

'Monitor lizards,' said Nalin. 'And harmless.'

But the creek led into a vast lagoon where there were crocodiles. I noticed that the canoe was taking in water.

A mile away, we could see our destination, the hermitage of Polgasduwa – the island of coconut palms – rising steeply from the flat sheet of water.

We tied up at a jetty. No one was about. The island was very silent. The two fishermen told us that the monks were at their midday meal – the last of the day – which must be finished by noon. We stepped ashore. The terrain of the island is hilly; the ground is overrun by a jungle of scrub and thorn-bushes with creepers growing luxuriantly on the palm-trees at the water's edge. The few paths that are cut through the island are arched with wild creepers. The island is infested with mosquitoes and snakes. We trod carefully.

Twelve little one-roomed cottages made of brick and mortar are dotted around in secluded places. These are the 'nivasa' or houses of the various monks. Here they sit throughout the day meditating and studying the Pali and Sanskrit texts. The only noise that can possibly disturb them is the sound of the water lapping round the island. But it is a hard life they lead. Sanitation is primitive. Outdoor pit-latrines are shared by three or four monks. There is a common bathing-well with a large wooden dug-out tub in which they dye their robes. The saffron dye is made from the boiled juice of wild creepers and the bark of trees.

Towards noon we approached the alms-hall, a plain single-storeyed building like a shed, where the monks were finishing their meal. We waited patiently. Presently they filed out past us, saying not a word. Their shaven heads were bowed over their empty alms-bowls which they carried in both hands. Some of them were German. The bullet-heads, thick necks and blue arrogant eyes were unmistakable. Their skins were very white – far whiter than ours, for the sun cannot penetrate the thick jungle foliage that covers most of the island.

But I could see no serenity in the faces of the monks. They seemed as subdued as convicts. And like convicts, they seldom glimpsed that 'little tent of blue that prisoners call the sky' – to use Oscar Wilde's words.

A young Ceylonese novice beckoned me forward. I left my sandals on the verandah and walked barefooted into the building to meet the Chief Bhikku, the Venerable Nyanaloka.

At one end of the room, I noticed a little statue of the Lord Buddha. It was surrounded by fragrant white frangipani and yellow almond blossoms – the daily, age-old tribute that is made at countless shrines in the East. Then I saw a wall-clock. It was a very English clock – with the hands just pointing at noon. Perhaps it was there to remind the monks of the discipline they must still observe in the nuclear twentieth century – two and a half thousand years after the Lord Buddha 'attained enlightenment'.

The Chief Monk rose to greet me. He was over six foot tall, very thin, and aged seventy. He looked benign and wise; there was a twinkle of good humour behind his spectacles. He acknowledged my attempt at making an Oriental bow with a little shake of his head.

I introduced myself. I explained that I was interested in Buddhism. The Venerable Nyanaloka began to talk. He spoke slowly in precise English. He sounded like an Oxford Don, but he had the Welsh intonation which is typical of most educated Ceylonese. At the first opportunity I put the question I had come to ask.

'I believe you have an English monk here,' I said. 'May I meet him?'

The Chief Monk looked at me placidly from behind his spectacles.

'I am sorry,' he said. 'You are unfortunate. There *was* an English bhikku who stayed here at one time. But he is not here now.'   Harold Musson.

I tried to conceal my disappointment.

'But there is an *American* bhikku staying here,' the Chief monk continued. 'You might learn interesting information from him.

Perhaps you would like to talk with the American?'

'Thank you,' I said. 'I would.'

I bowed again and left the alms-hall. I put on my sandals and was led along a dark path through thick foliage to a tiny little one-roomed bungalow.

As I approached, the door of the bungalow opened, and a bleak-faced man in saffron robes looked out. The novice spoke to him hurriedly, and the monk addressed me.

'Come in quickly,' he said in a strong, American accent. 'Close the door quickly behind you because of the mosquitoes.'

I entered a small cheerless room. To my left was a hard bed of planks. Opposite me was a mattress on the floor; the American motioned me to sit down on it. To my right was a rough bookcase filled with volumes on Buddhism in several languages. Next to it was a writing-table made of slats of wood. I noticed some exercise books such as Ceylonese children use at school with the head of Queen Elizabeth printed on the cover. Beside them was a small brass oil-lamp. In the centre of the room was a bench-chair like a low platform with a low back rail on which the American squatted with his legs folded in the lotus-position. His saffron robes were wound round him so that only his head and his right shoulder were bare. A short beard fringed his long, dour face. His hands and fingernails were immaculately clean. He looked about thirty.

However, I found it was difficult to draw the American monk into conversation. He tended to sidetrack each question by lecturing me on some aspect of Buddhism. He had all the zeal of a young convert. I listened as he told me of the need for mankind to find freedom from desire and greed – to achieve liberation from the illusions of life and finally to achieve Nirvana.

'Ever since I was a child,' he said, 'I kept asking myself "Why am I? Who am I? What am I?" and Christianity – the religion of my parents and schoolteachers – didn't give me the answer. I grew up still wanting an answer to my problems. I became a successful businessman. I had a real-estate business in Sacramento in California.'

For an instant I fancied I could see a look of regret in his eyes as he thought of what he had left behind him.

'I'd bought myself a yacht,' he said. 'I'd planned to sail across the Pacific and then round the world. I was all ready to go. I'd got all the provisions on board. All the tanks were full. Then on the very eve of sailing I happened to meet an elderly American woman. She told me about our Lord Buddha. Immediately my whole life was changed.'

The American glanced down at his saffron robe.

'I sold my boat. I sold up my business, and I flew to Ceylon. And here I am.'

'Will you ever go back to America?' I asked.

'If the Red tide of Communism sweeps over Ceylon,' he replied, 'then I would leave. Otherwise I shall stay here until I attain enlightenment.'

'I gather you've been here six months,' I said. 'Have you met the English Buddhist who has been a hermit for sixteen years?'

'Yes, I have,' he replied.

'Do you know where he's living?'

'Yes,' the American answered. 'He's living in a hut way out in the jungle south of here.'

'Do you know the nearest village?'

'No. But it's beyond Matara. I can tell you that.'

Matara is a small town on the seaboard on the extreme south of the island of Ceylon.

'Thanks,' I said.

I had got the information I wanted.

'Has Matara got a bank?' I asked Nalin that evening.

'It has,' he replied. 'But why do you ask?'

'Because if Musson has kept any connection with his former life, if he gets letters from his family in England or if he sometimes draws money from his former wealth, the bank in the area might know about it. And they might know whereabouts in the jungle his hut is.'

'Isn't it lucky that the manager of the bank in Matara is a friend of mine?' Nalin said. 'I'll drive over to see him tomorrow morning.'

The following evening Nalin burst into my bedroom in the hotel where I was staying in Galle on the south coast. His eyes were gleaming.

'Robin,' he said, 'we've got the best lead we've had yet. We've as good as found your hermit. But first wait.'

'What for?' I asked.

'Wait while I press the bell and get us a drink,' Nalin said. 'I'm thirsty.'

Nalin ordered a bottle of arrack, the local spirit which is distilled from the fermented juice of the coconut palm-flower. Then he told me the information he had found out from his friend the bank manager.

In April 1964 the Overseas Department of Lloyds Bank in Eastcheap in London sent a letter to the London branch of the Bank of Ceylon in Ludgate Hill. The letter said that Lloyds Bank would be grateful if a Life Certificate could be sent to them in respect of Harold Edward Musson who was living as a Buddhist priest in Ceylon. In the letter was enclosed a faded photograph for identification purposes.

After making enquiries in Ceylon, the London branch of the bank forwarded a copy of this letter to the furthest-flung branch of their bank in their home country – the Bank of Ceylon in Matara one hundred miles south of Colombo. They requested the bank manager to try to find Mr Harold Musson who was living in the jungle and was known to the natives as the Venerable Nanavira. The manager was asked to visit the Buddhist priest, if he could find him, and to confirm that he was alive. This formality was necessary before Lloyds Bank in London could release a sum of money to H. E. Musson in the form of a Life Annuity.

The manager had only recently been appointed to Matara. He made enquiries in the bank and discovered that his secretary who had lived there for eight years had met the English Buddhist priest and knew where his hut was to be found in the jungle.

At dawn on 1 May, the manager and his secretary travelled a hundred miles in a jeep into the dense jungle of southern Ceylon. That day they met the priest in his shack. They explained to him the reason for their visit.

'So you've come to see if I'm alive,' Harold Musson said calmly. 'Well, I am – as you can see.'

The bank manager then told him that once he had confirmed to Lloyds Bank in London that Musson was alive Lloyds could release to him a sum due on a life annuity.

'So if there's any money I could advance you,' the manager added, 'I'd be delighted to do so. Is there anything you want?'

'Nothing,' Harold Musson replied firmly. 'I want no money. I want nothing – except to be left alone.'

A few minutes later the two visitors left.

'We did not want to intrude on the priest's privacy any more than we could help,' the manager explained to Nalin. 'We left him some alms of food we had brought with us. We made our obeisance to him and left.'

The next day the following Life Certificate, signed by the manager, was posted to London:

> 'I hereby certify that Mr Musson,
> who is a Buddhist priest living
> under the name of the Venerable
> Nanavira, was alive on May 1, 1964.'

The manager's secretary had worked in the Matara branch since 1956. He told Nalin a sad story. In 1960 Harold Musson's mother travelled out from England to Ceylon. The purpose of her journey was to persuade her son to abandon his existence as a hermit and to return with her to a comfortable life in London. Harold Musson refused. His mother went back to England broken-hearted. She died shortly afterwards.

Before she died, Mrs Musson sent the Bank of Ceylon the photograph of a large and beautiful house that she had bought in London. She wanted the manager of the local bank to take the photograph and show it to her son. For the house was to be given him only if he would leave his lonely shack. But the photograph was of no avail. It was of no more avail than all the promises of wealth that the rich King Suddhodana made to his son Siddhartha if he would return from the wilderness and succeed to his throne. The promises were futile. For the young prince had renounced the world for the life of a monk. And to many millions the young prince is known today as the Lord Buddha.

The secretary had to go to see Harold Musson to break the news to him of his mother's death. The hermit took the news calmly and without the slightest hint of emotion.

'Death,' he explained, 'should not cause sorrow since everybody succumbs to the Law of Impermanence.'

Evidently the man who was the object of my quest was extremely remarkable and unusually strong-minded.

'Have you found out where in the jungle his shack is?' I asked Nalin.

'Yes,' Nalin replied. 'I have. We can drive there tomorrow – with any luck. But once we've reached the place, you're on your own.'

Nalin took a swallow of his arrack.

'I've come along with you so far,' Nalin said. 'But this last stage of the journey you must make without me.'

'Why?' I asked.

'Because I know from my friends in the bank that Musson is difficult to meet. He avoids strangers. He's a recluse. He won't see visitors. He leads the life of a complete hermit. If, when we arrive, he sees a dark Ceylonese face, he may withdraw into his hut and refuse to speak to us. But if he sees an English face – well, at least there's a chance he may be disposed to be friendly.'

'I wonder if you're right,' I said.

'I'm sure I'm right,' Nalin replied, draining down his arrack.

We drove south-east – away from the turquoise palm-fringed bays and the lush green paddy-fields, away from the highly-cultivated regions and into wild jungle country. Herds of buffalo and wild elephant roamed through the thorn-bushes, and presently the vegetation on either side of the sandy track grew thicker; the screech of birds and the chatter of monkeys seemed to sound louder. We stopped in a clearing. In this small patch of earth, reclaimed from the jungle, a few families managed to keep alive by planting millet and rice during the single rainy season. Nalin and the driver of our hired car asked one of the men if he knew where the Venerable Nanavira lived. And they were given directions. But to make sure, they took the villager along with us in the car. We drove three miles along a narrow bumpy track and stopped. The villager pointed to a small, barely distinguishable path that disappeared into the thick undergrowth of the jungle and said something to the driver.

'It's along there,' the driver told us.

Nalin stretched out his hand to me.

'Good luck,' he said. 'I'll send the car back for you.'

I shook his hand warmly.

'Thanks for all your help,' I said. 'See you in Colombo.'

Then, without looking back, I walked along the path. It was very hot. I could feel the sweat dripping down me. The path became narrower and darker as it led further into the dense jungle.

I turned a bend. There was a small clearing ahead of me. In the clearing was a hut. The roof projected beyond the hut's single room to form a little verandah three or four yards long.

I knew that one must advance barefooted to greet a Buddhist priest so I took off my shoes and socks. I scanned the path carefully for the snakes I had been worried about. I could feel my heart pounding against my sweat-soaked shirt.

As I approached the hut a tall figure in a saffron robe glided out on to the verandah. I made my ritual act of obeisance to a Buddhist priest.

I took a deep breath before I spoke. 'Good afternoon,' I said – and my voice sounded odd in the denseness of the jungle. 'I hope I'm not disturbing you. But I'd heard you were living here, and so I've come to meet you.'

The gaunt man stared at me in silence. He was tall and lean with a short beard and sunken blue eyes. His face was very pale. He stood there, motionless, gazing at me.

'Would you care to come in?' he asked.

His voice was clear with a pleasantly cultured intonation about it; it was calm and cool yet full of authority. He might have been inviting me in for a glass of sherry in his rooms at Cambridge.

He walked off the little verandah into a small room. I followed him. The room was bleak. There was a hard bed of planks, a wooden bookshelf and a table made from a packing-case. He lowered himself on to the bed.

'You'll find a mat in the corner,' he said to me. 'I suggest you unroll it and sit on it.'

I unrolled the straw mat and squatted down uncomfortably

A Hindu temple.

with my feet tucked beneath me. Nalin had told me that it was an affront to sit in the presence of a Buddhist priest with the soles of your feet pointing towards him.

'How did you find I was here?' Musson asked me.

'I heard of your whereabouts at the Island Hermitage,' I said.

'So you've been there. What did you think of it?'

'I found it very peaceful and fascinating.'

'Where do you come from?' he asked suddenly.

'London,' I replied.

'You're interested in Buddhism?' he asked.

'Yes,' I said. 'I am. I've read several books about it. But I can't say that I've understood them. I still feel rather lost and be-wildered.'

'What aspect worries you?'

I decided I must not hesitate.

'I can understand the idea that if one is good in this life and leads a virtuous existence, then if one is reborn one is born into a good life,' I told him. 'I can understand that if one is bad and evil in this life, then one will be reborn into a lower and worse form of life. But what I can't understand is this. What is the point of reaching nirvana – the enlightened stage? In nirvana one is said to understand the whole riddle of the universe and then the chain of rebirth ends. What is the point of ending this existence?'

Musson gave a short, dry laugh.

'The whole point,' he said, 'is to put an end to the pointless farce of living.'

He looked at me with his kind, sad eyes.

'Aren't you tired of living without any apparent reason for so doing?' he asked. 'Aren't you tired of dying only to be reborn? Aren't you tired of the pain and misery one has to suffer in this life?'

I was silent. I was wondering if I agreed. And I felt that I didn't.

'But Buddhism gives no *reason* for the farce of living – as you call it,' I said. 'Buddhism offers no explanation for our existence.'

'That is true,' Musson said. 'The Lord Buddha saw that this was beyond our powers of comprehension. And the intelligent man prefers no explanation to a false one.'

'What made you decide to become a Buddhist?' I asked.

Musson gave me a gentle smile.

'It's a long story,' he said.

'I've come a long way to hear it,' I replied.

He sat back against the wooden bedstead and stared at me pensively. I felt that he had not spoken with anyone for some time and found it difficult to order his thoughts. He was shy and reticent, yet at the same time he had the urge that all of us do to communicate.

188

'I was born in 1920 in Aldershot barracks – which was a good military start,' he began. 'I was an only child. I suppose that my first recollection of Buddhism was when I joined my father in Burma. He was commanding a battalion out there. I'd seen statues of Buddha, and I'd heard people talking about him. I remember asking someone "who was the Buddha?" And I was told: the Buddha was a man who sat under a tree and was enlightened.'

Musson smiled, almost apologetically.

'Then and there,' he said, 'I decided: "this is what I want to do."'

'At my preparatory school and later at Wellington,' he continued, 'my interest in Buddhism was dormant. At Wellington the Chaplain who had translated some books on Buddhism, gave two lectures which I attended. But I wasn't much impressed – I was too busy hating school.

'I was still pretty naïve when I left Wellington and went to Italy. I spent six months there and loosened up a little. During that period I read one or two books on Buddhism which re-awakened my interest. Then I went to Magdalene College, Cambridge, where I read mathematics my first year and modern languages my second. At the end of my first year, when I was nineteen, the war broke out. I volunteered and was given a deferment of a year to complete a two-year course.

'During my time at Cambridge I slowly began to realise that – though I might not take the decision immediately – I would certainly end my days as a Buddhist monk.'

Suddenly Musson's face was contorted by a spasm of pain; I saw his hand move, unconsciously, to his stomach. For an instant he was silent. Then with an effort he controlled himself and continued:

'I started off the war in Field Security in Wales. At the end of the year I got a commission and was sent out to security in Algiers. My job was interrogating prisoners. In the evenings there was nothing to do except drink. That was one thing I learned from the war – how to drink.

'Later I was sent to Caserta; thence to Rome, where I translated a book on Buddhism in my spare time. During that period I made a friend – Moore was his name – and we both discussed Buddhism.

'I came back to England at the end of the war; I settled in London. I had private means, so I didn't have to work. I had plenty of time and plenty of money. And I painted the town red. I tried to enjoy myself. I tried to get as much pleasure out of life as I could.'

Musson sighed as he looked back into the past.

'But somehow I found that I wasn't happy,' he continued. 'I wasn't really enjoying myself. I felt that it was all pretty futile, though I was doing a little work. In a leisurely kind of way I was translating a book on Buddhism.'

Once again Musson's face showed pain, but he made an effort to disguise it.

'Then early one evening in a bar in London I ran into my old friend Moore. He was working for the B.B.C. at the time. We began talking about our mutual interest in Buddhism. Gradually we came to the conclusion that the lives we were leading at present were utterly pointless. We shared the belief that the whole of this existence as we saw it was a farce. By the end of the evening we'd made up our minds. We decided to abandon our Western lives and go to Ceylon to become Buddhist monks.'

Musson was silent for a moment. His long slender fingers adjusted a fold of his saffron robe.

'Moore – who was about seven years older than I was – resigned from the B.B.C.'

Musson smiled at me.

'In his letter of resignation he told them he thought the B.B.C. was a waste of public money,' Musson said, his eyes narrowing with amusement. 'We settled our affairs in England as best we could and left for Ceylon. That was in November 1948. We went first to the Island Hermitage that you visited. In April 1949 we were ordained Buddhist monks.'

Musson gently brushed away a fly that had settled on his bare shoulder.

'A year later Moore died of coronary thrombosis while on a pilgrimage in the jungle. And I nearly died of typhoid – which left me with a tiresome gastric trouble – as perhaps you have noticed.'

He had seen me glancing furtively at a large bottle of Milk of Magnesia – which apart from his books was one of the only Western objects in the sparsely furnished little room.

'Did your experiences in the war have anything to do with your decision to become a monk?' I asked.

'I think the war hastened my decision,' he replied. 'Though it was inevitable, I think, in any case. But the war forced maturity on me.'

'But what first attracted you to the idea of Buddhism?' I asked.

'I was always disposed towards it, as I've told you,' he said. 'But one book did very definitely influence me. It was Aldous Huxley's *Ends and Means*. He uses this sentence: "Buddhism is the doctrine of non-attachment." And that was very important to me. Not so much *my* non-attachment – but the attachment of others to me.'

He must have seen my look of bewilderment as I sat crouched on the straw mat on the hard floor, for he added: 'You see, my parents were very fond of me – particularly my mother. And I knew I had to get away from this.'

Outside the sun was beginning to set. Monkeys were chattering in the trees and the jungle birds were screeching and calling to each other in the darkening wilderness. And when I left that hut – as I would do shortly – Musson would be left alone in that great solitude. He had certainly travelled a long distance to 'get away'.

I shifted uncomfortably on my mat and continued to take notes of what he was saying.

'Whatever action you do,' he said, 'whatever deliberate action – good or bad – brings its result in a future life. Not necessarily in the next life. It may have its results several lives later. Thus if you kill – or cause to be killed – an animal, that will have its results. This is why a Buddhist will not kill any living creature.'

I felt that by now I knew him well enough to argue with him.

'How do you reconcile that belief with eating meat?' I asked.

'Provided that one has no part in the killing of it one can eat meat,' he replied. 'So a monk can accept meat that is brought to him in alms if he doesn't either see it being killed, or if he doesn't *hear* it being killed or if he doesn't suspect that it has been killed for him. Therefore if you want to give a meal to a bhikku – that's a Buddhist monk – you go to a butcher's shop and buy a pound of beef. That's all right. Because the animal has already become meat. It has passed into the state of meat.'

I thought this argument was false and specious. It was the first thing the hermit had said that made me wonder if he was completely sincere. His argument seemed to me as bogus as that of the man who disapproves of trapping animals to make furs but who buys a fur coat for his wife and excuses himself by saying that if he hadn't bought the coat someone else would have done.

I thought that Musson's argument was dishonest, and I would have said so. But I could see that he was tired. And I knew from personal experience that if you haven't spoken with anyone for a long time, conversation is an exhausting effort. So I got up stiffly from my mat to take my leave.

'Would you find it a bore if I came back to see you tomorrow?' I asked.

The hermit smiled at me.

'Not at all,' he said in his polite Cambridge Don's voice.

'What time would suit you?' I enquired.

'About two o'clock,' he said. 'I usually meditate until then.'

'Is it correct to salute you as I did when I arrived?' I asked.

He had risen from his plank bed. Suddenly the Cambridge Don vanished; in his place was an austere Buddhist priest.

'Perfectly correct,' he said. 'It is the normal greeting in the East. You greet a layman by putting your hands together on your chest as if in prayer. And you greet a monk with the same gesture. But you bow with your hands *above* your head as a mark of respect.'

I bowed to him in the approved manner, and I bade him farewell. At the edge of the verandah I put on my shoes and socks

As I wandered back along the winding track through the dark jungle I wondered about the hermit. I liked him. I liked his mixture of gentleness and authority. I liked his diffident smile and I admired his courage. But I still wondered if he was completely sincere.

I went back the following day as arranged.

A decorated temple in Katmandu.

I turned round a bend in the path and saw his little hut in the clearing ahead of me. I took off my shoes and socks. As I drew

closer Musson appeared on the tiny verandah in his saffron robe.
I joined my hands together and bowed to him in the ritual act of
obeisance.

'Good afternoon,' he said in his precise gentle voice. 'Would
you care to come in?'

I followed him into his bare little room.

'I've got something to show you,' he said.

He stooped down to the old wooden packing-case that served
as a table and picked up a glass jam-jar with a screw top. Inside
was a large tarantula. The bite of this poisonous species of spiders
can kill a man.

'Where did you find it?' I asked.

The hermit priest smiled gently.

'I found him crawling up my leg – a few hours after you'd
left last night.'

'But why didn't you kill him?'

'Because a Buddhist does not believe in taking the life of any
living creature,' he said. 'I told you that yesterday afternoon –
though I could see that you didn't really believe me.'

'So now what will you do with him?'

Musson smiled at me. 'If you care to take a short walk we'll
release him in some place where – with any luck – he won't be
able to harm anyone.'

So we walked away from his little hut and strolled in the
opposite direction away from the village. The hermit looked very
pale in the sunlight.

'Here will do,' Musson said.

Carefully he unscrewed the top of the jam-jar and bent down
and gently shook the tarantula on to the dried-up earth.

'That tarantula must have been very bad in a previous life,'
Musson said, as we walked back to his remote hermitage in the
dense jungle. 'If you're bad, we Buddhists believe, you're likely
to have a bad rebirth lower down the scale.'

'But how can a tarantula have a *good* rebirth?' I asked.

'It's very difficult for an animal,' Musson explained. 'For
instance, a carnivore – like the leopards we have around here –
is constantly doing bad actions. But a good action in your past
existence might bump you up to a human – though not a very
good one.'

'If one is born as a cow,' I said, 'do you believe it would be
possible to be reborn as a human being?'

'Yes,' the hermit replied. 'But it will take a long time. And it's
not easy. The Lord Buddha says this: "If there is a one-eyed turtle
and a yoke floating in the sea, and the turtle puts its head out of
the water once every hundred years, it will take the same length
of time for a spirit born as a cow to be reborn as a human being
as it will for that turtle to put its head through the yoke." '

We reached Musson's hut. The surrounding tropical vegetation grew so thickly that one felt that in time the little hermitage would be entirely overgrown. The hermit sat on his bed of planks, and I unrolled the straw mat and laid it on the bare floor.

'Careful,' he said, suddenly pointing to my ankle.

I looked down. I was wearing shorts. A large caterpillar was crawling along my leg. I supposed that his curt warning was because the insect was poisonous so I brushed it off violently. Then I saw him wince. And I realised he had said 'careful' because he did not wish me to hurt a living creature.

Musson got up from his bed and gently picked up the caterpillar and carried it outside the hut and put it down in the jungle foliage. I now realised that the man most definitely lived according to the precepts he believed in.

'Aren't you lonely?' I asked him when we had settled down again. 'Don't you feel very much alone – living in this jungle with no other living person for miles around?'

'When I first came here,' the hermit replied, 'it took me some time to get used to the sounds of the jungle – especially to the trumpeting of elephants and the sound of them foraging in the undergrowth close by. But I never suffer any pangs of loneliness. Though I confess that at first I *had* wondered whether I would feel lonely.'

Musson gazed at me with his blue eyes in their sunken sockets.

'After a bit,' he said, 'you find you simply don't *want* other people. You've got your centre of gravity within yourself, as it were. You become self-contained.'

He gave me his wonderfully gentle smile.

'If people arrive and disturb you,' he said, 'then you speak only words of dismissal to them.'

'How do you eat?' I asked him. 'How do you keep going?'

'It's not really a problem,' the hermit said. 'Someone from the local village generally brings me tea – either very early in the morning or late in the afternoon. And before noon they bring me alms in the form of a gruel of rice and a little fruit. They bring that to me *before* noon because a bhikku isn't allowed to eat anything after midday.'

Musson carefully brushed away a mosquito that had settled on his arm.

'The villagers are very good about it,' he explained. 'That's partly because I'm European. You see, the villagers feel that a European must have great piety to renounce all that the West has to offer and to lead an existence where he has no possessions and nothing he calls his own. They feel that he must be a man of virtue, and therefore they believe that giving to him will bring them more merit. A Ceylonese family will give their whole sustenance for a day to a bhikku – and go hungry – for the spiritual reward this will bring them. In a sophisticated and logical way it's a matter of give and take – the giving on the materialistic level, the taking on the abstract level.

'If a villager gives food to a monk he gets more merit than if he gives food to a dog – merit for a future life, that is. Buddhists believe that there is more merit to be obtained from giving to a moral man than from giving to a rogue. And in giving, you lay up a bank balance of merit for the future.'

For an instant a look of pain came into Musson's face, and once again I saw his hand move, unconsciously, to his stomach. He was silent for a moment. Then the spasm passed and he seemed to relax.

'But sometimes the villagers forget,' he said. 'And they don't bring me any food before noon. So then I don't have anything to eat all day. But the following morning I'll take my begging-bowl into the village, and I'll be given food. You see, I have no money,' the hermit continued. 'If I ever have to go to Colombo – to see a doctor, for instance – I take my begging-bowl and stand by a bus-stop. People will come up to me and will try to put food into my bowl. But I will cover up the bowl with my hands. Then in their language they will ask me:

' "What is it you require, Venerable Sir?"

'And I will reply, "A bus-ticket." I won't say, "the money for a bus-ticket" because a bhikku must not handle money. The reason for this is that with money you can buy women. And this rule of the Lord Buddha is intended to put temptation out of a monk's way.'

The hermit stroked the side of his face with his bony hand.

'A Buddhist monk's bank balance is his bowl,' he said. 'Even his clothes are given to him. If no one gives him his robe, then he must go and scavenge on dust-heaps to find rags. And then he must dye it a saffron colour. The monk will be given the bark of a tree, and he must boil it down to make the dye. He cannot get the bark for himself because we Buddhist monks are not allowed to damage any form of plant life. So the monk will be given the bark. If it is bark of the banyan tree the dye will be dark brown. If it is bark of the jack tree the dye will be light brown.'

Musson fingered a fold of his robe.

'The robe I'm wearing now was given to me by my mother about fifteen years ago,' he said. 'And the few objects you see around this room were given me by friends.'

I looked round the room with its faded blue walls. There was a table made from a packing-case with an oil-lamp on it, a chair, a

The 'floating'
Buddha in
Katmandu.

chest and a bookcase. There were two straw brooms and two umbrellas – and his plank bed and the straw mat I was sitting on.

Musson saw me looking at the books in the plain bookcase. There were no novels or travel-books. But there were works on theology and philosophy ranging from Jean-Paul Sartre to Professor A. C. Bradley.

'If I were in a good state of health,' the hermit said, 'there would be no books in this hut. I wouldn't need them because I'd spend most of the day in meditation. But I've not been in good health for thirteen years now. Before then I was making progress on concentration. The easiest part of the day was to meditate. To all Buddhist monks, meditation becomes a delight once they have learned the technique. But to meditate, the body must be in good condition. The body mustn't be tired or in pain.'

Musson gave me an apologetic smile.

'I've got this chronic indigestion,' he said. 'When it comes on badly I roll about on my bed with the pain. So my hours of meditation are limited.'

'Living alone day after day,' I said, 'don't you ever suffer from plain simple boredom?'

'No,' the hermit replied. 'I find there's always something to do. I concentrate on some aspect of the teachings of the Lord Buddha or I meditate. Then there's this book I've been working on. It's called *Notes on Dhamma*. It's an attempt to point out certain misinterpretations of the Lord Buddha's teachings. I'm hoping to find an English publisher for it.

'Then there's work to be done in the hut,' Musson continued. 'I sweep out the room or I clean my lamp and polish its glass. I've never been bored.'

I decided to ask the question I had been longing to ask since I first met him. I took a deep breath.

'When you look back on the life you led in England,' I said. 'When you think of the wealth and comfort you enjoyed, when you remember your friends – don't you have any regrets?'

The hermit gazed at me for a while in silence.

'No,' he said after a while. 'I can't say I have any regrets at all. I was by nature a solitary person. And out here in the jungle I found after a while that I didn't want other people around me. And now, even when a villager comes only to bring me food, I find it an interruption. Then there's the question of sensuality. One advantage of these surroundings is that you don't put yourself in the way of temptation. Sensuality is like electric light. You can switch it on and off. If you are in a state of desire, concentration is impossible. But you can switch off desire by considering your flesh and dwelling on its essential foulness and its inevitable decay. I now find the thought of sex is abhorrent. I can find

pleasure in living here because I enjoy the process of concentration.'

He stroked the side of his face with his long fingers.

'All right,' I said. 'So you have no regrets. But what about your family?'

'My family,' he repeated.

He stared thoughtfully at the wire gauze that covered the window to stop the mosquitoes entering.

'My father died during the Second World War,' he said. 'So he didn't live to see what his son had done. But I'm afraid that my mother was desperately upset when I became ordained as a Buddhist priest. You see, she had been the wife of a Colonel in the Army in Burma. She had been the Memsahib – the *white* European married lady. To *her*, Buddhism was a religion for coloured servants. Almost all her servants when she had lived out East had been Buddhists. But it wasn't a religion for the Masters and Memsahibs. So she was terribly distraught. She thought I was going native. And she made no attempt to try to understand what I felt.'

There was no bitterness or resentment in his voice. And this, I reckoned, showed his humility. Because obviously he had never *expected* his mother to understand his religion.

'My mother gave me the robe I'm now wearing – as I told you,' Musson said. 'And after I'd been ordained, she came out to Ceylon to see me. And out here she became so upset because I refused to go back to England with her that she had a bad heart-attack. But I couldn't change my mind. I wouldn't leave my little hermitage. So as soon as my mother was fit to travel she left Ceylon. She went home to England and died.'

His voice was quite impassive as he spoke. I find it hard to describe the tone of his voice. Yet if I don't I shall miss the whole point of the man I'd travelled so far to see. There was no harshness in his tone. There was no coldness. There was understanding and gentleness. And it was only these two qualities that made his next remark bearable.

'My mother's death didn't worry me,' he said. 'Even now, during this life, every moment we are born and die. But we continue. We take some other shape or form in another life.'

He was silent. I could sense that talking tired him, and yet – for some reason – he felt he must speak. Perhaps it was because of the desire to communicate the truth that he had found in his solitude.

'The whole point of Buddhism,' he said, 'is to bring to an end this farcical existence. The whole point of our present existence is to reach Nirvana – complete understanding of natural phenomena – thereby ending the chain of re-birth.'

The hermit saw the look of doubt on my face.

'There is no purpose in life,' he said, 'such as going upwards and onwards. Any aim you set yourself is impermanent.'

He leaned forward on his bed and fixed me with his sunken eyes.

'Are you content to spend your life building?' he asked. 'Are you content to build knowing that *inevitably* your edifice will be hurled to the ground? *Nothing* is permanent. So the wise man, when he sees that there is nothing he can hold forever, chooses to opt out. He decides to get out of the race. But to get out of the race needs complete unselfishness and goodness and understanding.'

It was growing dark. I noticed that with the approach of darkness the myriad noises of the surrounding jungle seemed louder. From my uncomfortable position on the straw mat on the hard floor with my legs tucked beneath me I glanced up at the hermit. The lines in the sallow skin that ran from his nostrils to the corners of his mouth seemed deeper. His face was creased with fatigue. I had only one more question to put to him.

'Will you ever go back to England?' I asked.

I saw his eyes flicker towards the medicine bottle on the packing-case.

'I don't want to go back,' he said. 'And I feel it's unlikely that I will return. But if my health became so bad that I couldn't continue to lead my life as I want to out here, then I'd have to go back.'

He looked tired and ill. The light was fading. It was time for me to go. My legs were stiff from crouching on the mat. I began to move, but the hermit waved his hands in a gesture to stop me.

'You'll go now,' he said. 'And we may never meet again. But I don't want you to misunderstand me.'

He paused, and his sad eyes rested on me for a while.

'You must understand that I'm no longer concerned about my past,' he said. 'When you ask me questions about my past life, I have to think quite hard before I answer them. It's as if I were filling in a form for some purpose.'

His gaze was benign and yet without sentiment. 'Cold' is the wrong word to describe it. 'Dispassionate' is better.

'If you want to write about me,' he said, 'I don't want you to let people know my precise whereabouts in the jungle. I don't want any visitors. I want to be left alone. And I don't want you to make me out a saint. I admit I suffer pain so intense I toss and turn in my bed in anguish. I admit that *in a material sense* I've made sacrifices to lead the life I do.'

His lean fingers plucked at his robe.

'But please understand this,' he said. 'It's no sacrifice to give up *everything* for the sake of doing exactly what you want to do.'

He leaned back on his bed and was silent. Politely – humbly even – he had made it clear that our meeting was at an end.

I got up stiffly from the roll of matting.

'Goodbye,' I said. 'And thank you for being so patient with my questions.'

He smiled at me gently. He rose from his plank bed, and I followed him out on to the hut's small verandah.

Suddenly he stood still and looked at me. And I felt certain that there was something more he had to say. I paused. Perhaps he had something to say of such importance that it would change my whole life. I waited. His mellow gaze was on my face.

But then, abruptly, he turned away. Either he had changed his mind about speaking or the message had left his mind.

'Goodbye,' he said.

I put on my socks and shoes. I joined my hands and raised them above my head. I bowed to him in the ritual act of obeisance. He stood watching me in silence. His face was expressionless.

In the dim light I moved away down the little path through the jungle that joined the track that led to the village – and thence back to civilisation. The air was very close. A mongoose darted across the path and vanished into the undergrowth. I turned back.

His lean gaunt figure in a saffron robe was standing motionless on the verandah. Perhaps he knew a truth that would make the existence of millions of men a happier thing. Perhaps he knew the answer. Perhaps he had found the secret of life.

But I would never know.

I walked on down the path. Swarms of monkeys were chattering in the trees, and the jungle birds were uttering their wild curious cries.

Behind me I left the hermit – the Venerable Nanavira Thera from the Island Hermitage or Harold Edward Musson from Aldershot – alone to face the long night.

A week later I flew back to London after a farewell dinner with Nalin Fernando. Within a fortnight I had received a cable from Nalin telling me that Musson had killed himself. I felt most horribly guilty, for perhaps by spending two days with him and answering his questions about the life in England he had left I had resurrected memories which he had long since buried. I should have left him to his solitude. Then I had a short letter from Nalin telling me a little more than the cable. The manner of Musson's death was described. The doctors had allowed Musson chloroform to help alleviate the terrible stomach pains he suffered which were due to a cancerous growth. Musson had killed himself by putting drops of chloroform in a cellophane bag and placing the bag over his head. The inquest which followed helped to relieve my guilt for it was discovered that Musson had tried to kill himself on three occasions before my visit.

I often wonder about Musson. Had he tried to kill himself and finally succeeded because during the long hours of some nights of despair he had realised that all the years he had spent in work and study and meditation had been completely useless? Or had he come to the conclusion that at last he had achieved Nirvana? And, as I had learned, a monk who has attained nirvana may kill himself because since he is free of the chain of birth and rebirth the continuation of his present existence is no longer necessary.

With the hermit in a jungle in Ceylon.

I must conclude with the disturbing thought that religion of any creed may certainly bring happiness and peace of mind yet can afford the irreligious man no more definite promise of contentment than can the works of Balzac. I am also disturbed by the thought that during my life I have noticed that a person can be extremely good and yet utterly miserable while another man can be extremely wicked and notoriously immoral and enjoy life enormously to the end of his days. And if I am challenged to produce an example of the latter type I need only cite Gerald Hamilton, who prided himself on being the model for the hero of Christopher Isherwood's splendid novel *Mr Norris Changes Trains*.

Gerald was born in Shanghai on 1 November 1890, All Saints Day ('Most appropriate, my dear,' he would say), of parents whose characters and social position varied according to his mood. He was at school in England, at Rugby, but he claimed antecedents in Scotland, Ireland and China. The only certain dates in his adult life are provided by the Law. In 1915 Gerald was sentenced at the Central Criminal Court to two years' imprisonment for committing an act of gross indecency with a man. He served only nine months of his sentence. From prison he moved into the world of politics; he became great friends with Roger Casement and offered his services to the Irish cause. But as soon as his friendship with Casement began to ripen, Casement came back from Germany, landed on the Irish coast, and was arrested as a traitor. Gerald's association – so Gerald would claim – led to his being interned. Gerald's biographers will have a hard time charting the erratic course of his life, for he seldom told a true word if he could produce a false one which was more amusing. However, there is no doubt that somehow during the 1930s he was appointed sales representative for *The Times* in Germany. Here it was that he met Aleister Crowley and Christopher Isherwood. I have described Gerald in a newspaper article as the wickedest man I have ever known, but in the same article I did speak of his ready wit and facile charm. 'He was such good company,' I wrote, 'that certain people were always prepared to pay to have him around.'

Seated at a well-appointed table in an expensive restaurant with a wine he had chosen himself – for he was a founder member of the Wine and Food Society – wit would flow from his mouth as certainly as the wine would pour into it.

Gerald was about seventy when I first met him in Tangier, and though I was shocked by his blatant dishonesty I could not help being fascinated by his character. His confidences were as indiscreet as they were unexpected. At our first dinner together he took a gulp of his wine and leaned across the table to me.

'I have been married twice,' he announced unexpectedly. 'And it is my proud boast that no woman has ever seen me naked.'

His eyes turned towards the kitchen.

'That waiter loitering there is extremely pretty,' he stated. 'In fact I think I could say without any exaggeration he is the prettiest boy I have seen all evening. But the night is still young. And if that deliciously curly-headed lad doesn't deliver our omelette very soon it will be totally ruined.' His huge nose quivered and his twisted mouth gave a slight twitch. 'I was quite young and an attractive lad – if I may say so –' he added, 'when I discovered the Great Truth that whereas the charms of youth, alas, fade after a certain period in one's life, the joys of food and wine – provided they are enjoyed with discretion and preferably

at another person's expense – can last for ever.'   Gerald Hamilton.

The omelette arrived. Gerald gave the Moroccan waiter a heavy wink and slid a bank note under the table into his hand. Evidently he intended to indulge in all the pleasures of life he could glean on that night. We started to eat. Suddenly the right-hand corner of Gerald's mouth lifted in a kind of snarl.

'Time and time again I have told the aged old queen who masquerades as a chef in this establishment that I like my omelette well-flavoured with garlic. Has he listened to a word I said? He has not. I might just as well have been a voice crying across a desert. And speaking of deserts and wild places – which I hasten to reassure you are, in this country, equipped with the most luxurious hotels – may I proffer a suggestion? I would like to escort you round the southern regions of this delightful land. We would hire a car, of course. And, as it so happens, I know of a Chevrolet with a most attractive driver who I'm sure would let us employ his services at a most reasonable rate. But naturally Mustapha would expect some advance – say the equivalent of a mere two hundred pounds – which I'm sure you would easily be able to afford.'

I leaned back contentedly. This was Gerald at his conning best.

When I returned to London it was to discover that Gerald lived in a ground-floor flat in the street next to mine.

'My street is one of the most unpleasant streets in' Chelsea,' Gerald announced. 'It is called Dartrey Road, but I have christened it Dirty Dartrey. I hope I shall not stay in this vile residence for more than a few weeks because I have a certain friend who is not unconnected with Spanish royalty and who has promised me a considerable sum of money in repayment for a certain service I happen to have been able to render him.'

Gerald gave a little titter.

'But I have always found that unpunctuality is the privilege of royalty. And just at the moment I am in somewhat straitened circumstances.'

Gerald simpered coyly at me.

'If only my body were in as straitened conditions as my finances, my dear boy, I can assure you I would not need any loan. But as it is, if you could see your way to lending me some trifle – say fifty pounds – which, of course, I shall be able to repay within five days – perhaps even sooner, my gratitude towards you would be eternal.'

At that moment the extremely pleasant woman from across the road who looked after Gerald and whom I will call Elsie came in and demanded her wages.

With the precision of a performing poodle, Gerald spoke to her most earnestly of his connections with Spanish royalty. But Elsie, though devoted to Gerald, had heard the same story before. She made a pounce at his jacket, seized his wallet, took out her wages, counted the notes carefully and returned the wallet to Gerald with one pound note remaining in it. Then she left.

Gerald sighed.

'And now,' he exclaimed, 'what am I to do? You know how expensive it is to lunch at the Ritz, and alas, for some reason which escapes me, they no longer allow me any credit there. So perhaps, my dear boy, you could oblige me with a mere thirty pounds?'

'No,' I replied.

'Ah, well,' Gerald said, not in the least abashed or disappointed, 'I shall have to go elsewhere.'

'You mean you won't go to the Ritz?'

'Of course I shall go to the Ritz,' Gerald replied. 'I only meant that I shall have to go elsewhere to try my luck. Fortunately I have quite a list of friends who are good for a touch. So, my dear Robin, you needn't worry about my lunch. I could see it in your eyes that you were about to invite me to accompany you for bread and cheese in that filthy pub around the corner. But the colour of the walls gives me indigestion.'

Suddenly he leant forward.

'Is it true you're going abroad again?' he asked.

'Yes,' I answered.

'For long?' he enquired.

'I think so,' I said. 'I'm going to Timbuktu.'

Gerald tapped my knee. 'That might be a most dangerous journey,' he said. 'I do trust you have taken the precaution of making a will.'

'I haven't,' I answered.

'Then you must,' Gerald said in a stern voice. 'This very afternoon you must make a will and get it signed by two witnesses in the presence of each other. The procedure is perfectly simple.'

Gerald gazed at me for a moment and put a finger coyly to his lips.

'Would you think it bad taste on my part if I made one small request?'

'What request?' I asked.

Gerald's voice became even more coy. 'Just in case of an accident occurring to you in those dangerous climes, do you think you could see your way to including your old friend in the list of your legatees – if only for a nominal sum like fifty pounds?'

'All right,' I said. 'I will.'

'You are too kind,' Gerald murmured as I left his flat.

I was away from England for a year. Gerald welcomed me back with rapture.

'I've thought of you every day,' he said. 'And once a week your kind housekeeper has lent me the key to your delicious house in Seaton Street so that I could make sure that everything was in proper order.'

I thanked him. The house had indeed been beautifully kept.

After I had been back in England for a few months I happened to be searching for a photograph and I opened the bottom drawer of my desk in my search for it. I could find no photograph, but there – in its sealed envelope – was my will. From curiosity I opened it and began to read it through. I have never had much money, and I had disposed of my estate as best I could, leaving personal paintings and mementos to my friends. Suddenly I came upon the following:

Item 23: To Gerald Hamilton of Dartrey Road I leave the sum of £5000.

I stared at the line in amazement. I read it and I reread it. But there it was in my own handwriting. *Item 23: To Gerald Hamilton of Dartrey Road I leave the sum of £5000.* I found a magnifying-glass. I looked closer. The forgery had been expert. My executors, however surprised they might have been, would never have queried it. I put the will back in the envelope, tucked it under my arm, and walked round to Dartrey Road. I knocked at Gerald's door. He answered it and beamed with pleasure.

'My dear boy,' he said. 'I had just completed the most complex prayers to the gods of every religion I could think of that someone would appear to take me to lunch. And there you stand on my very doorstep like a good fairy in a pantomime.' Gerald simpered. 'But perhaps "fairy" is a tactless word to use in Dartrey Road,' he added.

'Gerald,' I said, 'may I have a short talk with you in your sitting-room?'

'By all means,' Gerald replied. 'Unfortunately I finished the very last drops of a positively sublime Amontillado a few minutes ago, but if you'd like to go to the wine merchants I can give you the very name and *provenance*.'

I said nothing. We entered the sitting-room and sat down. I took the brown paper envelope from under my arm.

'Do you know what this is?' I asked.

'Well,' said Gerald, 'I confess that my eyesight is unimpaired by age, so I can assure you that it is a brown paper envelope, once sealed, but with the seals now broken.'

I took out my will.

'Have you seen this before?' I asked.

'No,' Gerald replied. 'It looks like a contract of some kind. Would you like me to witness it?'

'It's not a contract,' I said. 'It's my will which I left in my desk when I went abroad. I've just read it through and I have found a curious alteration.'

Gerald settled himself comfortably in his armchair.

'Have you indeed,' he remarked complacently.

I handed him the will. 'With your brilliant eyesight,' I said, 'you will be able to read Item 23.'

Gerald turned over the pages to the item; read it, rose with surprising speed from his armchair and flung his arms around me.

'I always said you were my dearest friend in the world,' he cried. 'And now I know it for certain.'

'Gerald,' I said. 'I only left you fifty pounds in my will. That line was forged.'

Gerald threw his arms into the air and gaped at me in astonishment. I had always been warned by his victims that he was an extremely good actor.

'Impossible!' Gerald cried. 'Who ever could have forged it?'

'That's what I'm here to find out,' I said.

Gerald stared at me in amazement. 'But you couldn't possibly for an instant suspect that I who am one of your dearest friends could conceivably have perpetrated such an abominable act of deceit.'

'That's just what I do suspect.'

Gerald fell back in his armchair. 'You mustn't say these things, my dear. They are so bad for my poor heart.'

He fanned himself with a bandana handkerchief.

'And speaking of my heart – I've suddenly remembered there does happen to remain one bottle of that Amontillado of which I told you. In order to save a dying man could you possibly produce it? The bottle is standing behind my edition of Gibbon on the bookcase. You'll find the corkscrew behind Proust. If you could pour me a glass, my dear boy, it would restore my heart and improve my shattered nerves. Pour a glass for yourself, of course,' he added.

I found the bottle and the corkscrew. I poured out a glass for Gerald and a glass for myself. After all, apart from writing out my will once again – what could I do? Denounce Gerald to the police? They knew he was an old fraud anyhow and, in fact, since I was alive, his forgery had harmed no one.

We finished the bottle of sherry, and I then took Gerald to a new restaurant he had discovered round the corner where he proclaimed the food was excellent and there was a waiter who reminded him of Nijinsky.

I am writing about Gerald because though he was consciously and consistently wicked, he was one of the happiest men I have ever known. Each day seemed to bring him a fresh pleasure. One morning, for instance, he telephoned me, evidently in the grip of some new excitement. 'I have a most important piece of information to convey to you immediately,' he said.

I glanced at my watch and was not surprised to see that it was noon. Gerald always drank a glass of sherry at twelve fifteen and with any luck he would get a free lunch as well.

I watched his huge bulk ascending the stairs with a nimbleness of movement which always surprised me. Once he had selected and sunk into the most comfortable armchair in the room the bandana handkerchief was produced and he complained of severe heart trouble which could only be alleviated by a glass of sherry.

'And if you don't mind my saying so, dear boy, I would prefer the Amontillado. I advise you to give the brand you last served me to your cook.'

'What is your news?' I asked as I handed him his drink.

'Well,' Gerald answered, 'it is most impressive.' He took a large gulp of sherry. Evidently he felt the importance of his tidings deserved at least half a bottle. I waited patiently. A large wasp flew in through the window from the tiny garden. I took up a newspaper to knock it back through the window.

'Oh my dear boy, please do be careful,' Gerald exclaimed. 'Please don't kill the poor creature.'

The wasp flew out of the window.

'Why shouldn't I kill it?' I asked.

Gerald's lower lip quivered with solemnity. 'Because it is wrong to kill any living creature – as all we Buddhists know,' he announced.

'I thought you were a Roman Catholic,' I said.

Gerald put a finger to his lips and gave a little simper. 'There were excellent reasons at the time for what I might describe as my temporary conversion – besides, in my youth I was subject to violent aberrations.'

I poured Gerald another glass of sherry. 'What is the important news?' I asked again.

'How keen you are to learn the realities of life,' Gerald said. 'You must learn to be less materialistic.'

'I would have thought it was quite materialistic to drink a whole bottle of sherry before lunch,' I replied tartly.

'Not at all,' Gerald replied unruffled. 'Each man is entitled to attain his own nirvana in his own way. And you know how upset you would be if I arrived with a little Chinese boy and a pipe of opium to attain my nirvana by that method. Besides which I've made enquiries and both commodities – quite apart from being illegal, and you know how greatly I respect the Law – are exorbitantly expensive. So it is far less trouble for me to attain my noonday nirvana by drinking a glass or two of your excellent Amontillado.'

'What is the news?'

Gerald sighed. 'Well,' he said, 'since you insist on being so importunate I will tell you. Helana and Faustini – perhaps the most famous wine importers in the country – have asked both of us to a private wine-tasting lunch tomorrow week.'

'But why should they invite me?' I asked. 'We've never even met.'

Gerald looked coy. 'To be accurate,' he said, 'they didn't actually invite you in person. It was I who mentioned what distinction your presence would lend to their lunch table.'

'Ah!' I said. I was beginning to perceive the truth.

'The lunch is to take place in their vaults which are some way out of London,' Gerald continued smoothly. 'So I fear we shall be obliged to take a hire car from that firm which is always so obliging to you.'

I now saw the plot in its entirety. Gerald wanted to reach the wine vaults in a hire car without paying for it. He had arranged for me to be invited so that *I* would pay for the car. To let him know that I had seen through his subterfuge would be to spoil his fun. I accepted the invitation gladly.

'Your enchanting housekeeper answered the door to me this morning. What a charming person she is – even if she was born in Dirty Dartrey. And I asked her if there would be enough food should you be kind enough to ask me to stay to lunch. She told me there would be plenty. Besides – as you know – my appetite is extremely small. In fact you could say that I eat like a bird.' Gerald gave a titter. 'Except that I once read in a scientific journal that a bird consumes eight times its own weight in food each day.'

The day of the wine-tasting came. Gerald who had been so afraid we might be late arrived in the chauffeur-driven hire car an hour early. The time was only eleven-thirty in the morning but I offered him a glass of sherry. Gerald threw up his arms in shocked dismay.

'Drink before a wine-tasting!' he exclaimed. 'It would be sacrilege. And I shan't allow you to have a drop to drink either. You're drinking far too much as it is.'

We drove westwards out of London and stopped outside the wine vaults of Messrs Helana and Faustini. I had made it clear we would go home by taxi and therefore I sent the chauffeur-driven car away.

We were escorted down a slightly inclined ramp which led to the vaults themselves. We walked through the vaults flanked by vast casks of wine until our escort opened a panelled door with a flourish and led us into a splendidly furnished eighteenth-century boardroom. Both Helana and Faustini in their good manners disguised their surprise at our arrival over half an hour early. We were offered a rare Amontillado. I sipped the wine and truthfully told our kind hosts that it was delicious. I turned to Gerald. Now, I had always noticed that Gerald never sipped his wine; he drank it hastily in great gulps as if he feared some demon might snatch the glass away from him. On this occasion he consumed his drink with a speed that amazed his three onlookers and which was accompanied by a noise like dish-water being poured down an ill-adjusted kitchen sink.

'You may say what you like about Spain,' Gerald announced as he held out his glass to be refilled, 'but I shall always maintain that sherry is one of the finest wines ever produced from the grape.'

Once again there was a rapid gurgle. Gerald's glass was refilled, and I was led away to be introduced to some guests who had arrived.

At lunch Gerald was placed on Mr Faustini's right, and I was placed on his left, opposite Gerald. The food had been very carefully chosen to match the wines which were superb. Each different wine or course reminded Gerald of some anecdote which he told with a superb dignity only slightly marred by quick glugs as the contents of his glass disappeared in a gulp down his throat. He was almost as impressed by the food as by the wine. Indeed, he had three helpings of lobster mousse. Over the first few courses his stories were mainly concerned with deposed and exiled royalty. Over the roast beef and an exquisite Pommard he lowered the class of his subjects to writers who worked for a living. Over the vintage port he told a story about a sailor he had known in Toulon, and I began to get nervous – first, because Gerald's face had grown scarlet, next because the gurgles were becoming more frequent and, it seemed to me, more frantic, and lastly because now that his tales had reached specimens from the gallant fighting services he had met throughout the world his decorum had left him. His stories became more bawdy and more detailed, and I could see that Mr Faustini was extremely disturbed as were the other guests within earshot. But it was with the arrival of seemingly limitless quantities of Napoleon Brandy that Gerald reached his peak of indiscretion. He began a series of interlocking tales whose length might well be likened to some pornographic saga which was concerned with his life and adventures in the various prisons throughout the world in which he had been incarcerated.

It was at this stage that Mr Faustini rose to announce that a board-meeting of the firm was due to be held in half an hour's time, and therefore the table must be cleared and with the deepest regret he must bid his guests farewell. With a proliferation of hanks we all rose to our feet – with one exception. Gerald remained motionless, as if glued to his chair. Mr Faustini gave him a friendly tap on the shoulder. There was no result.

'Gerald,' I said in a loud voice across the table, 'I'm afraid it's time for us to go.'

There was no reply. Gerald stared at me with glazed eyes. Mr Faustini, whose good manners and self-control until that moment had been perfect, now gave Gerald a thump on the back. The effect was disastrous. Gerald's bulk slumped on to the table; his huge head was cradled in his arms and he remained inert.

'I'm afraid that your friend may have had a glass too much to drink,' said Mr Faustini.

'Indeed, I fear you are correct,' I answered.

'But you must remove him,' Mr Faustini insisted. 'This is the only room in which we can hold our board meeting.'

I walked round to Gerald and with Mr Faustini's assistance tried to get him to his feet, but he was wholly inert and seemed of limitless weight. It was then that I thought of the porters' trolley I had seen as we passed through the vaults.

'Could I borrow one of your porters and his trolley for a few minutes?' I asked Mr Faustini.

'Most certainly,' he answered. 'If you think it will help.'

'I think so,' I replied.

Three minutes later I returned with a hefty porter and a large trolley on the bottom of which I had affixed slats of wood to prevent Gerald's feet from slipping through. Mr Faustini, the porter and I managed to heave Gerald on to the trolley and together we wheeled him out of the room, through the vaults and up the ramp which led into a main street. There we stopped a taxi and managed to persuade the driver to accept Gerald in his unconscious state. I got into the cab beside Gerald, thanked Mr Faustini yet again, and we drove to Dartrey Road.

On our arrival, together with the taxi-driver and some kind neighbours, we managed to lift Gerald up the steps to his ground-floor flat and lay him on his bed. I took off his shoes and loosened his collar. I laid his head on one side because I remembered having been told that if you leave a drunk person with his head facing the ceiling he is liable to drown in his own vomit. I next went to call on Elsie, his housekeeper, to ask her to keep an eye on him. I then went back to Seaton Street where I took off my own shoes and lay down on my bed. I was exhausted and fell into a deep sleep.

An hour or so later the telephone rang. 'It's Elsie,' a hysterical voice announced. 'Poor Gerry's fallen out of bed and broken his hooter.'

'Broken his what?' I asked drowsily.

'Broken his hooter,' Elsie screamed. 'He's lying on the floor, and I think he's dying.'

'Now, Elsie,' I said in a deliberately calm voice, 'will you be very kind and listen to me carefully. You must dial 999 and must give Gerald's name, address, and telephone number and ask for an ambulance to be sent round immediately. I'll be with you in five minutes.'

By the time I reached Dartrey Road the ambulance had arrived and two strenuous ambulance men were lifting Gerald into the back of it. All the children of the neighbourhood had turned out to watch the scene. As Gerald's body disappeared within the ambulance they took out grubby pocket handkerchiefs and waved them cheerfully.

'Say 'ello to Jesus,' they cried. 'Say 'ello to Jesus.'

For some reason which I cannot explain it was considered proper that I should accompany Gerald to the hospital. So I was more or less pushed into the back of the ambulance beside him. Never before had I travelled in an ambulance in London. The windows were darkened so I could not see where we were going, but I could hear the loud clang of the ambulance's alarm bells and I could feel the swerves and jolts as we sped through the traffic.

I thought Gerald was unconscious, but presently he stirred and gazed at me with bleary eyes.

'There is something I feel obliged to tell you in the event of my death,' he mumbled.

'You're not going to die, Gerald,' I said. 'But by all means tell what it is.'

'It's this,' Gerald announced with surprising clarity. 'I haven't left you a penny in my will.'

After which words he fell unconscious.

We stopped at a bleak-looking hospital. I got out quickly and went to the reception desk. 'I would like a private room for my friend,' I said.

'There aren't any,' was the reply.

At that moment an intern approached me. 'Are you with the old drunk?' he enquired.

I must confess that I was still not altogether sober. 'I'm with the distinguished author Mr Gerald Hamilton, and I hope he will be treated with the greatest consideration,' I replied.

'We've put in the stomach pumps, and that's all the consideration he's going to get for the time being,' was the answer.

When I visited Gerald a few days later on his return to Dartrey Road, though his nose was almost completely covered with bandages and plaster, he had regained his usual good spirits.

'How pleasant to see you, my dear boy,' he exclaimed. 'I trust

you enjoyed our splendid expedition to the wine-tasting. And I hope that my trifling indisposition put you to no inconvenience.'

I was silent. Gerald put his finger to his lips and gave a little simper.

'I should have paid more heed to my aunt's warning,' he announced. 'She always told me to beware of lobster mousse.'

Towards the end of his days Gerald lived in a tiny room above a Chinese restaurant in the Kings Road. The restaurant was called The Good Earth. 'Better above The Good Earth,' he would say, 'than below it.' He was seldom lonely and he was seldom uncomfortable. Friends would come to see him. Some would make his bed or tidy his room; others would bring a bottle of wine or take him out to lunch.

On 9 June 1970 my old friend Brian Desmond Hurst, the film producer and director, rang me in Brighton to tell me that Gerald had died that day in St Stephen's hospital, Chelsea. The funeral was on the following day. Gerald had left instructions that he wished to be cremated. As there was a newspaper strike few of Gerald's friends knew of his death and few people attended his funeral. I can remember with clarity that it was a bright sunny morning. The rest of my memories are slightly clouded by a form of retrogressive amnesia from which I suffer. This is partly due to the shrapnel in my head and partly due to the fact that I drink too much. However, I can remember driving in a musty-smelling Daimler together with Brian Desmond Hurst whose right-hand inner-breast pocket seemed to bulge and crackle as he moved. I presumed it contained his notes for a funeral oration. With us was my friend Peter Burton who has assisted me in the writing of this book and who was a close friend of Gerald's. As we approached the crematorium we noticed several black Daimlers ahead of us and two or three behind us. We all came to a halt in front of the gloomy building at the same time. From each of the other Daimlers alighted elderly gentlemen in black suits and with a look of high intent which gave them the hallmark of literary executors. In his generosity, aided perhaps by a bottle of wine and a small loan, Gerald, I suspect, had appointed several exclusive literary executors at one moment or the other during the last twenty years of his life. But only one of them was to prove genuine – a man I had never met.

I wandered round to the side of the crematorium where the coffins were laid out with the wreaths tastefully disposed upon them. Each coffin was numbered. I passed by a large sized coffin which might have belonged to an over-weight giant from a circus and was numbered 1701. Next to it was a small coffin which might have been appropriate to a child or a dwarf or a pygmy. On it was written the number, 1702, and the name Gerald Hamilton, and above were our wreaths addressed with affectionate words for dear Gerald. Since Gerald was an enormous hulk of a man it was evident to me that some error had been made. However, what was the use of trying to do anything about it now? Both giant and pygmy were about to be consumed by the furnace.

'Party for 1702, forward,' a stentorian voice bellowed.

Obediently we trooped into a small chapel. The paper in Brian's pocket seemed to crackle still louder. Two or three crypto-literary executors hurried towards the front pew. Brian and Peter and I sat behind them. The pygmy's coffin was on a ramp which would evidently eventually slide into the furnace. A man who might well have been another literary executor but was probably a verger went to the lectern, opened the Bible – in my confused memory it now seems at random – and began to read from the Old Testament. I cannot find the precise text at the moment, but it was one of the bloodiest accounts of the Israelite wars against the Philistines. Gerald, whose real name was Souter and who, like most Jews posing as Christians, held violently anti-Semitic views and who, in any case, had consistently through the last years of his life claimed to be a Buddhist, would have disapproved of the whole performance.

'We will smite the Philistines,' read the verger (or crypto-literary agent). 'We will cut off their foreskins and hang them from our girdles. Their loins shall be pierced by our spears.'

Meanwhile I could see that Brian was surreptitiously fingering the notes for his funeral oration.* But proceedings were brisk. No sooner had the last Amalekite been circumcised than a button was pressed and the pygmy's coffin slid smoothly into the fiery furnace.

'Party 1703,' the stentorian voice bellowed from outside.

Gerald's funeral was over.

On the way home we sat in the sunshine outside a pub and got drunk. In a way it was Gerald's last party.

In view of his sympathy for the Buddhist faith it is sad that Gerald never visited Ceylon. But in as much as the country offers almost unrivalled opportunities for corruption both financial and moral perhaps it is as well. Gerald might have found the varied temptations too hard to resist. Moreover, he would have been irritated by many of the regulations imposed by the Communist-inspired government† which disturbed William and myself.

*I learned later it was a bible.
†Many of these laws have recently been rescinded.

There were two regulations which most concerned us. The first was that we had only been able to get visas for a three-month stay. The second was that if we decided to reside in Ceylon we would be subject to income tax on earnings anywhere in the world and at a very high level should we stay in Ceylon for more than six months in any year. We now realised that our visas were soon due to expire. We had decided to visit Kashmir. However, we wanted to see more of the coast of Ceylon before we left in the hope that we might find a perfect dwelling and be granted some exemption from the tax laws as another Englishman had already received.

We drove down to the coast south of Colombo and put up at one of the large hotels which are now being built along the shore to attract tourists. We shared a large room on the top floor of a new hotel, and for at least a week we were convinced we had discovered nirvana. The room was surrounded by a large balcony facing the sea on one side and the estuary of a river on the other. It was cooled by electric fans and furnished with pleasant antique cane chairs, blue carpets and fawn curtains. Outside lay one of the loveliest beaches in the world. Slender palm trees, formed in an infinite variety of shapes, bent gracefully over the white sand, their branches seeming to incline yearningly towards the sea. The beach seemed to extend forever, while the slow breakers advanced in a line of shimmering white froth to pound and crash with a resounding thud – sometimes as loud as the crack of a cannon – upon the crisp sand. Beyond the breakers, a vast expanse of turquoise-blue sea glittered in the sunshine. And it was quite easy to avert our eyes from the bulbous tourists and gaze at the lithe Ceylonese frolicking in the sunshine. Beauty seemed to lie all around us.

Only gradually did the flaws in our nirvana creep into our consciousness. The slow roll of the heavy breakers, for instance, was deceptive. For beneath the white froth of the breakers runs a vicious current. The undertow can be fatal. One afternoon, William went for a walk along the beach and found a group of people clustered around the naked bodies of two young Ceylonese boys. They had been drowned. They were students from Colombo on holiday; the undertow had caught them and swirled them round in a treacherous turbulence. There is only one doctor to look after the whole village. By the time he could be found the two boys were dead. Water dribbled from their delicate nostrils.

Perhaps it was the death of the two students which made us begin to be critical of our nirvana. Swarms of insects of infinite variety invaded our room at night unless we kept the windows tightly shut. Above the balcony there was a large nest of hornets which invaded the room by day. ('Ten stings from a hornet can kill you stone dead,' said a friend happily.) Moreover, neither

Buhardy

closing doors nor sealing windows nor blocking cracks could prevent the invasion of very large dark brown rats. These rats were so ferocious that after they had eaten all the glucose tablets which I keep by my bed because I am a diabetic and all my indigestion tablets, they would wake me by nibbling at my toes through the mosquito net. Furthermore, despite the fans which blew pages of typescript down into the foul-smelling, over-chlorinated swimming pool, the heat was intense and enveloped one like a damp rug. Each movement became an effort and every object was moist – particularly in the bathroom with its slimy floor and dripping walls, where toothbrushes, towels, razors and combs were all clammy. The ice would melt in your glass before you had finished half your drink, and the glass would form pools of moisture on the table beneath it.

One learns from experience that it seems impossible to enjoy the beauty of unspoilt nature without the disadvantages of cock-roaches and hornets. But there must be some balance between undesecrated scenery and rat-infested rooms. Each person must make his own choice between natural beauty and nature in its most unpleasant forms. This choice also applies to one's selection of a permanent companion. Will you choose wit, sympathy, intelligence and tenderness enclosed within sixteen stone of flab – or will you fall for that selfish, stupid, unread fool whose grace and loveliness are so superb that your heart leaps like a trout each time your companion gives a smile that appears on that divinely attractive face only too rarely? Perhaps the most satis-factory solution, if one can so organise it, is to spend half the year with one, and the next six months with the other. But I do appreciate that this is by no means an appropriate method of searching for nirvana.

The problem of having to choose between the benefits of civilisation on the one hand and the glories of unimpaired nature on the other confront one almost daily in Ceylon. In my own mind, there is no doubt about the solution. One should train oneself to put up with the grossest forms of physical discomfort and the most irritating manifestations of ignorance with complete equanimity by retiring into the depths of one's own soul as one might into the shade of a cool glade. But for most people, alas, this requires a particular cast of character and many years of training.

I have an uneasy feeling that I personally have begun too late.

We were sad to say goodbye to our friends in Ceylon but we had already determined to return as soon as our explorations had taken us further afield. We flew to Bombay on our way to Kashmir. A friend had engaged for us two bedrooms communicating through a bathroom. It was now late April; the heat was intense.

One afternoon William went out shopping to find a present for his mother. I lay on my bed taking notes, but my inside was upset and presently I went into the bathroom which had neither window nor air-conditioning.

The heat was almost tangible. Suddenly I felt a sense of danger, as if an assailant were about to spring on me. Even now I have a recollection – obviously the result of hallucination – of two men springing out of a corner of the narrow airless little room to attack me. Then I was conscious of a violent blow on my forehead, and as I reeled back I felt my head hit against something hard. I remember no more. When William returned he found me lying on my bed bleeding from a gash on the top of my forehead. He rang our friend Tony van Brabant who in his kindness promptly rushed round with his own doctor, for he too suffered from heart-attacks. The doctor staunched the blood, injected me, and put in stitches to close the wound on the upper left-hand side of my forehead. I still felt dazed. I was sweating heavily, so they moved my bed and put it beside the air-conditioner on the other side of the room. The doctor told me that I had had a heart-attack and that the heat of Bombay and even of Kashmir might well be fatal to me. I must return to Europe.

Since the doctor had said that I might suffer another heart-attack if I remained in the heat of India, I decided for various reasons to fly to Beirut. The town held happy memories for me, and I had known the British Ambassador, Paul Wright, since I was seventeen years old. The journey seemed interminable because the plane alighted at various 'oil' capitals where we were not allowed off for security reasons. Each airport was large and modern – a speck of technology in the vast desert of sand. At one airport a long red carpet ran across the tarmac to a completely empty grandstand which was protected from the sun by a roof of straw matting. As the aircraft rose once again into the air we could see Cadillacs streaming along the newly made roads across the flat desert, and then a jumble of derricks that had made the Emirs the richest men in the world.

Shortly after noon the plane landed at Beirut airport. We were the only passengers disembarking. And the plane left very quickly. As we walked to the airport building, it seemed to me that I could hear the noise of machine-gun fire and then of bombs falling, but I attributed this to hallucination caused by my weak health. But when we entered the building, we discovered that it was completely empty. There were no customs officers, no passengers, not a soul. Our luggage had been dumped at the entrance. We walked out of the airport to try and find a taxi. At that moment a bomb fell quite close to us, and it now became only too clear that we had landed in the middle of a battle. Later that afternoon we discovered that the battle was between the Fedayeen (the Palestinian refugees) and the Lebanese Army, supported by the Lebanese Air Force. Now and then a bomb would land on the airstrip, and a spiral of smoke and dust would rise into the clear blue sky. There was still no taxi and no car in sight. There was not a plane in the aerodrome. At that moment a battered Ford stopped close to us. It was driven by a Lebanese of about thirty with a heavy moustache and large, mad-looking eyes.

'What you want?' he shouted in English. His voice was high pitched and trembling; he was obviously shell-shocked. 'What you want?' Artillery had now gone into action close by. The noise was deafening.

'We want to go to the Hotel St Georges,' I shouted.

'Then get into the car quick!' the man shrieked out. 'And I will drive you there. But it will cost you one hundred Lebanese pounds.'

For an instant I hesitated: it seemed a lot of money. But after all, the man was offering to drive us across a battlefield. 'Right,' I said.

He opened the boot of the car and we threw in our luggage. The man was very close to complete panic. 'Be quick!' he shrieked.

The shelling sounded louder.

'Be quick,' the man said, 'get into the back.' The Lebanese was now driving as fast as the car would go. Suddenly, as we turned a bend, we saw a tank ahead of us blocking the road. I have fought in tanks: from the slow movement of this tank's turret and of its tracks, I could tell that it was manned by an inexperienced crew. The turret turned slowly until the two-pounder gun was aimed at us. Our driver gave a yelp of terror. He twisted the wheel violently, and the car lurched into a side road. Our driver was now so frantic that I was more frightened of our car driving into a brick wall than I was of the tank which had now disappeared.

'No possible to go to St Georges,' the driver gasped out. 'They will try to blow up the St Georges. I take you another hotel.' The man was so overwrought that I did not dare make any protest.

By now we had entered the centre of the town. At every window there were people watching the street, and a few Arabs mingled with the soldiers along the boulevards. Our driver still drove at high speed and disregarded all traffic lights. Then the accident happened. An Arab riding a bicycle, his burnouse drawn tight around his head as if to protect him from the machine-gun bullets, rode out from a side street. Our driver swerved. But it was too late. Our car struck the bicycle. The man fell. For an instant he lay sprawled out on the road. At that moment I thought he was dead. But suddenly he disentangled himself from the wreck of his bicycle, leapt to his feet and started shrieking at our driver, screaming in a frenzy, and shaking his fists. Appearing, it seemed from nowhere, a menacing crowd gathered round us.

'Close your windows,' the driver whispered to us. 'Quick, close them.'

Hastily we wound up the windows. Suddenly the driver revved up his engine, put the car into gear and let out the clutch with a jerk. The closest onlookers sprang aside – and we escaped. Presently, we saw a tank ahead of us. It looked like an old Crusader. The tank commander had his head out of the turret. He was peering around him in terror. He looked very young. I reckoned that we had more to fear from the Lebanese Army than from the Fedayeen. At last we reached a small hotel where the driver stopped.

Hastily, our luggage was put into the hotel. We booked two rooms. The porters brought up our luggage. I saw William into his room and then went back to my own. I undressed and tried to sleep.

I lay in bed thanking Providence – if indeed there is one – for our deliverance to date. I fell into an uneasy doze. Presently I became aware of some odd process taking place in my mind but I could not understand its nature; I only knew that it was something frightening and obscene. Then I remembered that I had injected myself with my usual morning dose of insulin in the lavatory of the plane, but I had eaten little and I was now beginning to experience the familiar symptoms of hypoglycaemia – which is a result of there being too little sugar in the blood. I felt sick and faint. I knew I must have glucose, but the glucose tablets were in my medicine case which was locked, and the keys were in my trousers which were hanging in the wardrobe. I did not have the strength to get out of bed. My mind was giddy with a terrible emptiness. I knew I must eat something sweet very quickly. Then I remembered that there was a banana lying on a tray on my dressing-table. I had only to eat it and I would feel better. I tried to move, but I could not: I was too weak. And with each movement I tried to make, my sensation of dizziness was increasing. There was no bell in the room. I cried for help but my voice was weak. No one came. Once more I tried to move from my bed. I raised my head a little but it fell back on to the pillow.

I now began to wonder if I was dreaming. But the swelling giddiness in my head – worse than any sea-sickness I had ever known – was real enough. And I now became convinced that if I lost consciousness and fell asleep, I would never awake. With a frantic effort I managed to slide out of bed and roll on to the floor. Very slowly, with awkward trembling movements, I crawled along the stained thread-bare carpet towards the dressing-table. I was very much aware of the faded fawn colour of the carpet and its rough texture. As I crawled, sometimes I would lurch over and fall on my side and lie inert for a while.

At last I reached the dressing-table. The plate with the banana on it was on the edge of the wooden top of the table. I lay still, summoning up the energy to raise myself so that I could reach it. For a moment I almost lost consciousness; hideous visions slid across my mind. Then I remembered I was still lying on the carpet beneath the dressing-table. With a sudden jerk I lifted my body. My right hand groped over the table and grasped hold of the banana. I clutched it frantically. I let my head fall back to the carpet. Then my quivering hands pulled apart the peel. Greedily, I stuffed the fruit into my mouth and munched quickly and avidly. And at that moment it happened. It was an experience both horrible and terrifying; it was intensely vivid but made vague by my dazed and exhausted condition, so that I now find it difficult to describe. But as I swallowed the fruit in eager gulps, I changed. . . . I was no longer a weak, sensitive man; I was no longer an unbalanced diabetic, lying on a dirty carpet. I was no longer human. I was a strong and hirsute creature, wide mouthed and gibbering. I was a large and heavy animal; I was simian, with a hairy paunch and fur-covered loins, obscenely endowed. And what I was swallowing so fiercely was not fruit. It was human flesh.

As the full horror of that instant surged into my mind, I lost consciousness. I could remember nothing more until I found myself lying face-down on the carpet. I was still clutching the banana skin in my right hand. I had been grasping it so tightly that my hands were sticky with its pulp.

The sugar in the fruit had given me enough energy to move. I went to the wardrobe. With trembling hands I took the keys from the pocket of my trousers. I unlocked my medicine case and ate all the remaining glucose tablets. I now had enough sugar in my bloodstream to prevent any further attack. I went into the bathroom, and I washed myself all over. Then I went back to bed and slept, without any dreams, until dawn.

That morning I telephoned the British Embassy. Paul Wright was at an important conference, for the minor civil war was still continuing, and a curfew had been imposed on the whole town. However, his kind secretary sent round an Embassy doctor who could move because doctors were exempt from the curfew. He examined me, prescribed valium, and took the stitches out of my head. In the late afternoon I felt better but could not move a foot out of the hotel because of the curfew. However, the following day Paul Wright sent round a large black Embassy car, complete with an armed detective, to bring us to lunch with him and his charming wife. Inside the old Arab house in which they lived and which I had last visited in the days of General Spears, all was quiet. As soon as I had telephoned, Paul had asked us to stay, but I had refused with many thanks because I still felt so weak that I felt I would be a nuisance to them, and for all I knew I would have another heart-attack. However, we were moved into the St Georges Hotel where we reflected that if you had to be trapped in a hotel for an indefinite period, you were lucky to be confined to one of the best hotels in the whole Mediterranean. There was rifle fire and the sound of shelling all night. By now I knew that I would soon have to enter hospital for some while and, although the *Daily Star* of Beirut proclaimed 'BEIRUT IN COMPLETE STATE OF SIEGE', we managed to escape on an Egyptian boat heading for Alexandria and thence to Venice.

When we reached Alexandria, William found a car from the tourist agency to take him to see the pyramids, but I wanted to revisit Alexandria – a town in which I had spent many of the happiest years of my life, and had certainly found my own form of nirvana. As the ship moved towards the harbour, I had stood on deck watching the beautiful sweep of the town's seafront, and as I saw the crescent of the tall buildings around the blue sea, I decided that all I had heard about Alexandria as it was nowadays must be false. Nothing important could have changed. As soon as the ship docked I longed to go ashore, but I was no longer twenty-five years old; I was fifty-seven, so I knew I must conserve my energies for the late afternoon and evening. After lunch I lay down for a siesta in my cabin. But I felt restless. My favourite town was there waiting for me. I could remain in bed no longer. I sprang up and dressed, putting a tie in my coat pocket in order to be correctly dressed for some Egyptian friends whom I hoped to visit that evening.

The ship was by now empty; the afternoon was very hot. By the time I reached the gangway I was sweating. All passengers had been told they must change dollars into Egyptian currency. I found a bank in the harbour. Five spotty youths stood behind a dusty counter. I handed them my passport and shore-pass, together with ten dollars. I was given six Egyptian pound notes, faded and greasy, and some coins. I found a taxi. 'Hotel Cecil, *min fadlak*,' I said. The taxi drove through the outskirts of the city. Surely the inhabitants looked scruffier than I had recollected and the buildings shabbier? Perhaps when we reached the centre of the town it would alter. But, alas, the shabbiness continued. The buildings looked as if they had not been touched for twenty years. Their windows were cracked and grimy – or boarded up. Three blocks away from the Cecil Hotel, where I had spent my first leave from the Western Desert, I stopped the taxi and paid the driver. I was standing beside the tall apartment block on top of which Eric Dukes had had his beautiful penthouse in which I had written *The Servant*. Memories came rushing back to me. I walked down the side street to the entrance. The doorway was unpainted. There was no *suffragi* in the hall. The stairs were cracked and the cement of the walls was crumbling. Inside was filth and darkness and a reek of sewage. All the lovely furniture had gone from the hallway. It was now unbelievably shoddy. There was no carpet. But there were a few shabby wooden chairs with red 'leatherette' backs. There were a few yellow faded cards in the slots above the mail boxes, but many were empty. I turned away sadly. I walked towards the Cecil Hotel. No smartly-turbanned porter stood outside and not a single car. Once again the Empire furniture had disappeared, and there were the same litter and hideous wooden chairs with different coloured 'leatherette' backs. I walked inland into the town. All was litter and dust and filth. Emaciated *gharry* horses clopped by, their ribs standing out as if they were skeletons.

I walked back to the front and sat down at a café which had once been the most brilliant in Egypt. Since I had last been there twenty years ago nothing had been cleaned or repaired. The chairs on the pavement outside were broken; the tables were rusty. Inside, the beautiful looking-glasses and sconces had gone. A decrepit Egyptian waiter sat asleep wearing a stained robe. I sat at a table outside. Buses and lorries roared along the front belching diesel smoke. Starved horses staggered forward, pulling heavy crates. A shrivelled donkey was harnessed to a load of bricks. A small boy walked beside it. He held a slat of wood from which projected a long nail. Rhythmically he struck at the donkey's testicles so that little spurts of blood splashed down on to the dusty road, and the donkey lurched forward. Only the cruelty of the town seemed to have remained unchanged.

I took another taxi and drove out towards Sidi Bishr through the tawdry streets. The taxi stopped outside an apartment block. The hall was in darkness, and the lift was out of action. A pleasant-faced young man carrying a baby told me my friends had left the town.

I took a taxi back to the harbour – back to the ship, and back to my memories.

As I read more books which contained dissertations on Nirvana and met more people who told me their views of Nirvana, I began to marvel at the many interpretations of the word. A strict Buddhist would tell me that the attainment of Nirvana implied the end of the chain of birth and rebirth. But others held a wider interpretation. Thus in the *Encyclopaedia Britannica** we are told that this same Nirvana literally means 'waning away (as of a flame with the fuel exhausted)'.

'What is here implied is the waning away of deluded ego-centricity, with its attendant passionate, sensual and selfish desires. According to the Buddha's analysis of the human situation, these deluded desires fetter man, together with all sentient beings, to the round of rebirth and consequent ill or suffering (dukkha), one afflicted existence succeeding another. When these desires are transcended by those who follow the Path which he announced, there is the experience of spiritual freedom and enlightenment that is Nirvana. The corresponding term, Nibbana, in the Pali Buddhist scriptures, is held by some expositors to refer explicitly to the negation (ni) of the 'jungle of lust, ill-will and delusion' (vana). In a sense, therefore, Nirvana means extinction. But most Buddhists emphasise that this does not mean annihilation; Nirvana is not the end of life, but rather the end of all that confuses life and hinders well-being; it is 'the extinction of afflictions'.

'As such, it is poetically described in Buddhist scriptures as the harbour of refuge, the further shore, the cool cave, the matchless island amid the floods, the home of ease, the holy city. It is also said to be changeless, deathless and without limitation. It is the "not born, the not-become", it is "neither origination nor annihilation". The reality beyond all change and suffering, it is peace, security, supreme joy, unspeakable bliss.

'While interpretations vary in different contexts of Buddhist thought there is general agreement that Nirvana is an exalted spiritual state that may be realised here and now.'

In this sense, it is obviously, as I have tried to explain in this book, a particular place or a particular person who can indeed provide nirvana here and now. But in my experience of life, the sadness is that this form of nirvana is transitory. Not only friends change or die. But places decay – in the way that Alexandria has – or are destroyed by the encroachment of the concrete jungle – as London has been.

One of the places that had given me the longest period of nirvana in my life had been Tangier. For this reason William and I decided to revisit it on our journey. But though I was overjoyed to meet friends I had known for over twenty years, and in whom any signs of decay had been most carefully disguised, I found the

Encyclopaedia Britannica Inc.: USA: 1970.

atmosphere of the town had been as much affected by xenophobia as other parts of the Middle East.

As Paul Bowles said to me, 'Morocco will soon shut the door completely against Europeans and Americans whom in their mind they lump together. The Moroccans will shut the door against us all. But nothing is permanent in life, so let us enjoy our existence here while we can.'

Alert, with twinkling eyes and his face only a little withered by the fifteen years since I had first met him, with short-cut curly grey hair, almost white in colour, wearing a polo-neck sweater and smart trousers, he sat crouched on the floor of his flat. And he seemed to me far less shy and far happier than when I had first met him.

'I loved the island of Taprobane,' he said. 'But when Madame Bandaranaike took power, it was no longer possible for me to stay in Ceylon since every American was her enemy.'

Paul took a sip of tea. 'But I like Buddhism,' he continued. 'Buddhists believe there is no god. But after all, each man is free to create his own god. And what pleases me about Buddhism is that it recognises that in life we are in a state of flux. Indeed, all life is flux.'

Though no longer a young man, Paul seemed lively and spry.

'We must enjoy our existence while we can,' he repeated.

However, I noticed in Tangier an uneasiness among the Europeans which had not existed before. The Moroccans listened to the voice of Radio Cairo, and Egyptian propaganda has been very successful – especially among the young.

On one of our walks, William had been pestered for nearly a mile by a shoe-shine boy.

'Please go home,' William said to the boy, 'and leave us in peace.'

'You go home,' the boy answered. 'This is our country. We own it. You go home and leave *us* in peace.'

In the years after the war one could lead a life of complete seclusion in Tangier in some wing of a villa up on the Marshan, which would cost only two pounds a week. Or one could mix for a while in the outrageous café society of the town, where splendid eccentrics such as George Kinnaird* and Peter Churchill† were

*The Honourable George Kinnaird.
†Victor Alexander Spencer Second Viscount Churchill.

to be found drifting round the bars until the small hours of the morning – though George was well over fifty and Peter was over seventy at the time. They enjoyed each other's company so much that they decided to share a villa. I viewed this move with misgivings because each considered himself more aristocratic than the other, and each of them had devoted servants who were likely to quarrel. George's servant was a splendid English bricklayer whom he had discovered at the age of forty laying a brick on the outskirts of Brighton, and who was generally known as Brighton Bob. Peter's servants were all Moroccans and all aged about fourteen.

However, the two friends rented a large villa together with their retinue. Despite George's lavish generosity, the ménage was not a happy one. Peter's horde of servants objected to Bob's somewhat simple habits – particularly his custom of stubbing out his cigarettes on Peter's exquisite Moorish carpets.

When he went out of an evening Bob would return home at three or four in the morning and would lie reading a pornographic book in bed, and smoking heavily. As he finished each cigarette he would fling it with a careless gesture on to the carpet of his bedroom where it would smoulder until it went out. The Moroccan boys put up with this outrage for several weeks, but finally they made a plot. They waited until Brighton Bob had gone out on one of his nightly excursions and they then doused the whole of the carpet in his bedroom with a mixture of petrol and paraffin.

At about four in the morning Brighton Bob returned, drunker even than usual, threw himself on his bed, picked up one of his least improving books, lit a cigarette, and when he had finished it, flung away the stub on to the carpet. At that moment the whole carpet went up in flames. Brighton Bob, badly singed and suffering from extreme shock, escaped through the window and burst into George Kinnaird's room next door to complain. George had just returned and was mixing himself a nightcap to calm his nerves because he had had a row with a taxi-driver. His temper, already inflamed by his quarrel and a large quantity of alcohol, now broke into full strength. He strode into Peter Churchill's room and woke him up by stamping his foot on the floor.

'Your horrible little servants have tried to burn my servant,' he shouted. 'And I won't have it.'

'Well you needn't have it,' Peter Churchill replied angrily. 'I am fed up with Brighton Bob.'

'Right.' George replied. 'We shall both leave immediately.'

George and Brighton Bob packed and left, hired a taxi, visited a few bars which were still open and drove to the airport. George had reached such a pitch of alcoholic fury that he wouldn't even speak to Bob. He passed through customs and strode to the aircraft which was waiting on the tarmac.

Brighton Bob's behaviour at the best was slightly erratic, but he was annoyed at being left behind by George and in order to soothe his nerves which had been shaken by the recent conflagration, he had purchased a bottle of Spanish brandy at the last bar they had visited. He now drank half the bottle of brandy which so elated him that he performed a wild jig in the middle of the airport. When a Moroccan policeman approached him, Bob hit him smartly over the head with the half-finished bottle. He was promptly arrested. Meanwhile, safely on board the plane, George had fastened his seat-belt and passed out. The plane took off.

George's friends felt they must do something to release Bob, who had been thrown into prison. A fund was formed. Bribery released Bob promptly. However, one thing was certain. It would be impossible for Bob to leave the country through the airport, so they decided to put him on the ferry and accompany him to Gibraltar, whence he could fly to England. They also decided that the only way to keep him quiet was to mix Luminal with his brandy. So each time Bob would ask for brandy, they would pop a Luminal tablet into it. Bob became more and more docile but as they approached Gibraltar airport, he did show faint signs of unwillingness to return to England. He demanded a large brandy. It was immediately produced for him. Into it they popped the rest of the bottle of Luminal tablets.

Bob walked unsteadily to the plane which fortunately was quite close to the exit. He fastened his safety-belt. The plane took off. It was a calm journey. The plane landed at Heathrow. The passengers left the plane – with one exception: Bob remained in his seat. He was snoring loudly, and bubbles of saliva had covered his lips. Immediately the airport health authorities were summoned. The first thing they did in their wisdom was to examine his passport which was in his breast pocket. From it they saw he had come from a semi-tropical country, and immediately they realised that he was suffering from some rare form of tropical disease. An ambulance was called; Bob was laid in it tenderly, and driven swiftly to the Hospital for Tropical Diseases – where he had delirium tremens for a fortnight.

After the departure of George Kinnaird and Brighton Bob from Tangier, Peter Churchill moved to Asilah with his Moroccan servants – who really should have been considered more as his friends than his servants for they adored him and were seldom paid. Peter had the wonderful quality of empathy: he could understand the problems and worries and amusement and jokes of his young Moroccan friends in a way which made them love him. Asilah is a beautiful old port forty-five kilometres south of Tangier on the Atlantic coast, with a crumbling Portuguese fortress and a lovely waterfront. Here it was, running a pleasant but almost incredibly inefficient restaurant, surrounded by hordes of unpaid cooks and waiters, that Peter Churchill at last found his nirvana. Apart from a few money worries, which he never allowed to offend his soul, he was wonderfully happy, and his happiness infected all those who visited him. Ill health drove him back to England. He died in Brighton two years ago.

When I consider how many of my friends have shortened their lives either by drinking too much or by taking drugs, I sometimes wonder if in some way – as yet undiscovered by scientists – an addiction – say to alcoholism – is 'catching' rather like an attack of measles. Was I, for instance, at around the age of twenty-five infected with this unfortunate disease by some unwittingly contagious friend of mine? Worse, has my alcoholism infected people I have met in every walk of life? But I can dispel this thought quite simply by reading the statistics of alcoholism which show that its prevalence is widespread in countries neither I nor my friends have ever visited. Alcoholism, in fact, has spread throughout most of the world – and so to a lesser extent has drug addiction.

In a fascinating essay called *Drugs That Shape Men's Minds*, Aldous Huxley has provided a reason for the growth of these two diseases. 'We love ourselves to the point of idolatry; but we also dislike ourselves,' he says. 'We find ourselves unutterably boring. Correlated with this distaste for the idolatrously worshipped self, there is in all of us a desire, sometimes latent, sometimes conscious and passionately expressed, to escape from the prison of our individuality – an urge to self-transcendence. It is to this urge that we owe mystical theology, spiritual exercises and yoga – to this, too, we owe alcoholism and drug addiction.'

It would seem that most of us yearn for some form of escape into nirvana, however transitory it may be. We can obtain our nirvana in a variety of ways – by drinking half a bottle of whisky in a bedsitter in Fulham, by listening to Beethoven, by an orgiastic night of love-making, by finding a hut by a lake – the methods are numerous. Their only disadvantage is that for most people they are transitory.

I have tried to describe the journeys I have made in search for nirvana in this book. If they have taught me anything it is that any form of nirvana dependent upon the physical senses is almost inevitably bound to be transitory. Your hut by the lake will be flooded or will rot; the city in which your apartment has brought you a waft of nirvana each morning that you awake will be taken over by Fascists or raided by the starving people that surround it, or will decay with neglect. Moreover, no physical pleasure will last forever. Obviously it is easier to seek for nirvana in a palace in Nepal overlooking the Himalayas than in one of the hovels which abound in England and are still excused and tolerated by society by being called houses. But this does not affect the essential truth.

The truth which has been proclaimed by holy men throughout the centuries is so simple and so obvious that it has been generally disregarded. It is this. Nirvana – as the word has been used in this book, with a capital N, denoting its true Buddhist meaning –

can only be obtained through the spirit and by the spirit and in the spirit. Nirvana is a process of increasingly good behaviour in all matters and an increasing disregard for physical advantages or pleasures, which will culminate in a release of the spirit from all desires either in this world or in the next. As Aubrey Menen* has said, the process is like 'learning a foreign language, and like that, it must be done by going over the same lesson again and again'. I have Aubrey's permission to quote yet another passage from his book:

'A king, a film star and a bum look very much alike to the surgeon who lays them open on an operating table,' he says. 'It is well known that the best way to stop thinking about yourself is to talk about yourself, and that is why so many people do it. The converse is also true. When you know yourself for what you are – or what the world has made of you – you prefer to shut up about it.'

I would like to have ended this book with an exhilarating description of some simple dwelling which I had at last discovered at the end of all my journeys, where I had discovered the inspiration and tranquillity I seek. Or – what would make me still happier – I would like to have been able to reveal in plain terms how at the end of some fifty years of a life which has often had to be violent because of circumstances and a sense of duty, I had at last discovered the peace of mind and liberation from all desire which true Nirvana offers to the world. But the fact is that were I to attempt to conclude this book on a note of triumph I would be dishonest.

An article about me by Peter Burton has suggested 'Robin will never find Nirvana. It is a hopeless quest like the Arthurian knights' quest for the Holy Grail. Possibly there *is* a nirvana for Robin Maugham. But where he least expects it. For it sometimes seems to me that Nirvana for Robin Maugham lies in the questing for it.'

But so far as I am concerned, I think that for me the state of nirvana – on the rare occasions I have been able to attain it – is as yet merely a temporary condition. I can only hope that one day it will become a permanent one.

*Aubrey Menen: *The Space Within The Heart*: Hamish Hamilton, London: 1970.

Index